Absolute

Love

NOT THE GOD YOU ARE IMAGINING

By

ROGER I. WILLROTH

PROISLE PUBLISHING

Proisle Publishing Services LLC
1177 6th Ave 5th Floor
New York, NY 10036, USA
Phone: (+1 347-922-3779)
info@proislepublishing.com

ISBN: 979-8-9863274-0-2

Table of Contents

Addendum "An Unpublish Essay on the Trinity"

by

Jonathan Edwards Public Domain

Foreword

Exodus 3:14 God said to Moses, "I AM WHO I AM."

Exodus 34:6,7 The LORD passed before him and proclaimed, "The LORD, the LORD, a God merciful and gracious, slow to anger, and abounding in steadfast love and faithfulness, keeping steadfast love for thousands, forgiving iniquity and transgression and sin

Ps. 33:5 He loves righteousness and justice; the earth is full of the steadfast love of the LORD

Galatians 5:22 But the fruit of the Spirit is love, joy, peace, patience, kindness, goodness, faithfulness, gentleness, self-control: against such things there is no law.

I John 4:8,16 God is Love

There is a single unified message throughout the Bible.[1]

I believe that there is one connecting absolute that we can agree upon. The absolute is that love is universal; love is an absolute among human beings.

We all want to be loved; we all feel the need for love and we all yearn to have another person that we can share love with.

This book is about what, or to be more exact who Love IS.

Love exists and the topic of this book is, where does Love come from?

Why is Love an Absolute?

Who, is this Absolute Love?

What does this Absolute Love look like?

Love exists. Yet not everyone will agree on how to define love or where love comes from.

In this study I come to the conclusion that Love is an entity, one entity, a unity of substance, purpose and power. Love is a personal being that is ultimate power and absolute personhood.

All else is relative to Love, created by Love, sustained by Love, defined by Love and ultimately judge by Love.

God is Love, and we become like the person we love. This is the purpose for everyone to become like God.

Love is not sentimentality, not weak capitulation to others, not passive acceptance of all things, and certainly it is not sexual intercourse.

Love flows into us by producing humility, humility produces belief or faith in the One who is Absolute Love. Belief in Absolute Love produces trust, acceptance, confidence, gratitude, compassion, freedom, stewardship, servanthood, loyalty, purity, justice, rest and determination.

Love is the overflowing character of the only absolute in the universe it flows throughout the One who is Love and establishes everything.

The God who is Absolute Love does not want us to Worship (Love) Him

because He is power hungry. He wants to give us life, an abundant life.

When Moses spoke he told the people God was setting His commands to Love Him alone, he said it was for their good. God's Glory and our good are inseparable.

Deuteronomy 30:19-29 states "I call heaven and earth to witness against you today, that I have set before you, life and death, blessing and curse.

Therefore choose life, that you and your offspring may live, loving the LORD your God, obeying his voice and holding fast to him, for he is your life and length of days,…"

Jesus exclaimed his purpose by saying; John 10:9-10 "I am the door. If anyone enters by me, he will be saved and will go in and out and find pasture. The thief comes only to steal and kill and destroy. I came that they may have life and have it abundantly."

More than covering our sins and providing a way back to God through forgiveness of sin, Jesus came to change our lives. To fill us with His Spirit and make us different people.

Life change is a product of Loving God. Peter encourages us to strive toward this changed life.

2Pe 1:3-8 says; "His divine power has granted to us all things that pertain to life and godliness, through the knowledge of him who called us to his own glory and excellence, by which he has granted to us his precious and very great promises, so that through them you may become partakers of the divine nature, having escaped from the corruption that is in the world because of sinful desire.

For this very reason, make every effort to supplement your faith with virtue, and virtue with knowledge, and knowledge with self-control, and self-control with steadfastness, and steadfastness with godliness, and godliness with brotherly affection, and brotherly affection with love. For if these qualities are yours and are increasing, they keep you from being ineffective or unfruitful in the knowledge of our Lord Jesus Christ."

This book is about what the characteristics of loving looks like in God through His Word and what God builds into our lives through loving Him.

All of these characteristics of love relate to a positive affect, that impact individual and corporate life, psychological, physiological and relational/sociological transformation.

Humility is the characteristic of love that gives us the ability to admit our needs, weaknesses and limitations so that we can submit to the power of God in our life and receive our strength from Him and through others.

Humility is not powerlessness; it is knowing where the power comes from. Humility is the beginning of Faith, that LOVE works in us as we look outside of ourselves to God. Humility involves being able to give to others but also to receive from others as we keep our eyes fixed on God and thereby become more like Him in love.

When Love enters our lives, we do not think less of ourselves. We do not think of ourselves chiefly, our focus remains on the one who Loves us. This focus produces a belief or faith in the other person.

The opposite affect of humility is narcissism leading ultimately to rebellion and anarchy.

Belief is an overwhelming sense of hope based on understanding of past actions and in the fulfillment of future promises that gives encouragement, so that we can be enthusiastic, in order that we might grow through developing, God gifted potential.

Belief then begins to transform all of our life and characteristics, we trust. The opposite affect of belief or faith in God's Love is a sense of being lost or despairing.

Belief produces hopefulness and the ability to be encouraging.

Trust is the characteristic outgrowth of believing that gives us the ability to be open and share who we are and what we have been given, so that we can be catalysts in the development of openness and candor in others. We can become accepting.

The opposite affect of trust is suspiciousness and stinginess.

Acceptance is the characteristic outgrowth of believing that gives us the ability to forgive ourselves and others so that healing and understanding can take place. We become confident, accepting that we are loved.

The opposite affect of acceptance is judgementalism and selfishness.

Confidence is the characteristic outgrowth of believing that gives us assurance of our being accepted, and gives us the ability to look past self-promotion to the promotion of others, so that their confidence is built up. Confidence is not a lack of humility.

The opposite affect of confidence is inconsistency and uncertainty.

Gratitude is the characteristic outgrowth of believing that gives us the ability to look at all good things as gifts from God. Gratitude causes us give in return, so the gifts can be shared by all.

The opposite affect of gratitude is demanding, expecting and ungratefulness.

Compassion is the characteristic outgrowth of believing that gives us the ability to be gracious "giving undeserved favor" and merciful "not demanding retribution" so that we might live in a way that will be most beneficial to ourselves and others, and glorifying to God.

The opposite affect of compassion is being degrading of self and others, to use others.

Freedom is the characteristic outgrowth of believing that gives us the ability to set aside personal desires and postpone pleasure; i.e. physical, emotional gratification, in order that we be liberated to find complete satisfaction in God, freed from enslaving entanglements.

The opposite affect freedom is being controlled by lustful desires to have an insatiable appetite for things because only God's love satisfies our desires.

Stewardship is the characteristic of believing that gives us the ability to be inter-connected with each other in a truly loving manner. We do not lose any integral parts of ourselves or disintegrate into another person, yet we value and need each other's gifts and uniqueness, for the full use and completion of our own giftedness.

The opposite affect of stewardship is being unhelpful, hoarding and codependent.

Servanthood is the characteristic of believing that gives us the ability to worship in everything that we do by looking to God to fill us and overflow through us into the lives of others, for thoughtful attentiveness to God's desires for them.

The opposite affect of servanthood is neediness, being uncaring and inattentive.

Loyalty is the characteristic outgrowth of believing that gives us the ability to remain true or faithful to God, ourselves and others so that we are not pushed or led along by demands other than God's.

The opposite affect of loyalty being unreliable.

Purity is the characteristic outgrowth of believing that gives us the ability to be unmixed in our allegiance toward God, so that we won't be driven by any other purpose than to love, glorify and enjoy God, to the ultimate benefit, enjoyment and fulfillment of ourselves and others.

The opposite affect of purity incongruence and confusion.

Justice is the characteristic outgrowth of believing that gives us the ability to act rightly on behalf of God, so that despots (those who want to control, oppress and use others for personal gain) are not allowed to triumph, and the defenseless are defended.

The opposite affect of justice is bullying, becoming overbearing and apathetic.

Determination is the characteristic of believing that gives us the ability to persist until that which has been started is completed.

The opposite affect of determination is inability to follow through, indecisiveness.

Rest is the characteristic of believing that gives us the ability see past obstacles to our own wellbeing, and the wellbeing of others, so that we can peacefully work to overcome those obstacles.

The opposite affect of rest is anxiety, restlessness leading to panic.

These aforementioned characteristics are not exhaustive of Absolute Love or how God's love transforms our lives, but they are a beginning point. Absolute Love is inexhaustible, God's Love is an unfailing love and a sacrificial love.

Someone may ask, "why do many religious people seem to display the opposite qualities of the characteristics outlined above?" So many religious people are prideful and judgmental.

One answer is, Love is not finished working in any of us yet.

None of us measures up to Absolute Love.

Another answer may be that most of us resist Love in one way or another.

However, the best answer is we want our own way and we are lost and prideful. We are not able to humble ourselves and ask for direction.

Religious activity and association is shielding us from Love, instead of opening us up to Love.

We look to our own selves instead humbling ourselves before God.

Religion sometimes blinds us.

Religion can take on a relativistic orientation leading to a view of God as having no sense of justice, anything goes and God's love is unconditional. In this vein we see no demands from love to love in return. Love is a one-way street not a pulsating conduit of power.

Religion can take a view of self-righteousness and legalistically claim; we must earn our way into God's Love. Though God's love cannot be earned, it is only through the impossible and costly act of loving God, through the change in our lives graciously gifted to us by God's love.

God's Love comes to us moment by moment, we can only choose, each moment, to embrace God's Love or suppress God's Love.

Jesus Christ, Yeshua Messiah, Isa Al Masih says it well; Mat 22:37-40 "And he said to him, "You shall love the Lord your God with all your heart and with all your soul and with all your mind. This is the great and first commandment. And a second is like it: You shall love your neighbor as yourself. On these two commandments depend all the Law and the Prophets."

We know a God, but not the God who is Absolute Love. He is not the God you are imagining.

1 Daniel P. Fuller; THE UNITY OF THE BIBLE Unfolding God's Plan For Humanity; Zondervan Publishing House 1992. Pp 23,24 "Since Paul summarized his message as the whole purpose of God, it is clearly that he regarded it as unity. The word for "purpose" ... in this phrase implies the deliberate choice to pursue a certain goal step-by-step, in a methodical way.

x

CHAPTER ONE

Absolutes

Exodus 3:14 God said to Moses, I AM WHO I AM.

Exodus 33:18 Moses said, "Please show me your glory." …

Exodus 34:5-7 The LORD descended in the cloud and stood with him there, and proclaimed the name of the LORD. The LORD passed before him and proclaimed, "The LORD, the LORD, a God merciful and gracious, slow to anger, and abounding in steadfast love and faithfulness, keeping steadfast love for thousands, forgiving iniquity and transgression and sin, but who will by no means clear the guilty, visiting the iniquity of the fathers on the children and the children's children, to the third and the fourth generation."

John 1:14 "And the Word became flesh and dwelt among us, and we have seen

his glory, glory as of the only Son from the Father, full of grace and truth. "

Absolutes, is there a possibility that something or someone absolute exists? That one person, or a collective group of persons, could proclaim their idea as absolute is a scary thing. The thought of someone else placing their idea of an absolute upon me, as an individual, brings up all kinds of thoughts of rebellion and rejection. We are all rebels at heart.

My daughters' elementary school and the school administrators must believe that there are absolutes, at least, for being good elementary students. Without question of religious or personal preference all of the children in her elementary school were impressed upon the "absolute truths" of the "six pillars of character".

On my computer I found this about the Character Counts program; "The CHARACTER COUNTS! approach to character education doesn't exclude anyone. That's why we base our programs and materials on six ethical values that everyone can agree on — values that are not political, religious, or culturally biased. ..."

The universally desired, "absolute" character traits are as follows: *"Trustworthiness Be honest • Don't deceive, cheat, or steal • Be reliable — do what you say you'll do • Have the courage to do the right thing • Build a good reputation • Be loyal — stand by your family, friends, and country*

Respect Treat others with respect; follow the Golden Rule • Be tolerant and accepting of differences • Use good manners, not bad language • Be considerate of the feelings of others • Don't threaten, hit or hurt anyone • Deal peacefully with anger, insults, and disagreements

Responsibility Do what you are supposed to do • Plan ahead • Persevere: keep on trying! • Always do your best • Use self-control • Be self-disciplined • Think before you act — consider the consequences • Be accountable for your words, actions, and attitudes • Set a good example for others

Fairness Play by the rules • Take turns and share • Be open-minded; listen to others • Don't take advantage of others • Don't blame others carelessly • Treat all people fairly

Caring Be kind • Be compassionate and show you care • Express gratitude • Forgive others • Help people in need

Citizenship Do your share to make your school and community better • Cooperate • Get involved in community affairs • Stay informed; vote • Be a good neighbor • Obey laws and rules • Respect authority • Protect the environment • Volunteer"

These seem, to me, to be very good character traits and according to the persons who wrote these traits, they are absolute, "they are values that everyone can agree on." The originators claim; "These values are not politically, religious or culturally biased".[1]

Is this what we should codify as loving character?

To be clear about what I am talking about, here is a dictionary definition of absolute. [2]

Noun 1. absolute – something that is conceived or that exists independently and not in relation to other things; something that does not depend on anything else and is beyond human control; something that is not relative;

What do religions codify as loving character?

Religious concepts of who God is are not often like these definitions, that is, they are often full of social and political baggage by region or country.

Formalized religious organizations, in order to cohesively unite, set up doctrines and rules that are not seen as absolute, even within the greater body of

In the history of Christianity for instance there is the early split between Constantinople and Rome, then later the split between Rome and the Protestant Reformation.

I grew up in a small protestant church group that was started, in the United States, by immigrants to the U.S. who were escaping from persecution of the State-run Lutheran Church over the doctrine of Christian baptism.

In Sweden after the establishment of Lutheranism as the State Church, people who later submitted to adult baptism by immersion under water, as a public testament to their faith, were sought out and drowned.

It is not my aim in writing this to establish some religious doctrine or rule of action.

I do intend to hold up two truths about God that are, I believe, to be held in as absolute by the Bible. That is that God is Absolute and that all truth is relative if not established by the God who is absolute. The major religions grounded in the roots of Abraham in the Tanahk would agree that God is the one absolute.

By this, it is my hope that dialog and openness can characterize discussions about absolutes. Where in fact I believe everyone can affirm, that if there is an absolute, it is in what all people would call God.

God existing, if believed, must mean that God is the absolute and everyone and every thought is only given absolute truth in relationship to God.

Likewise, apart from direct confirmation from God (Revelation), all things are relative to partiality, incomplete, possibly flawed or perverted belief.

I know what you're thinking. Where is this going? Are you crazy Roger, these religions do nothing but fight with each other! Do you remember or have you even heard of all the history of fighting and killing for religion? If you will walk through this study with me, whether you are a Jew, a Muslim, an Agnostic, Atheist, Christian or of some other religious or worldview, an inner revolution may take place.

You may find that you don't know all the answers. You may find that more talking about things would be beneficial. You may find that repentance in some form may be in order.

How does perception or viewpoint change belief?

Could a change of viewpoint be helpful? A word from Dr. John White might be helpful at this point; "I do not believe, however, that all inner revolutions are equally positive or healthy. My experience has shown me that repentance is positive only to the extent that it involves aligning oneself, with the way the universe is made. Reality is not subjective; there is a moral structure to the universe. The essence of positive and lasting change is aligning ourselves with that structure." [3]

I ask you to walk with me on a journey away from political, social or religious rhetoric, towards a search for absolutes and ultimately toward a search for what it means to walk with the Absolute Love of God.

Dietrich Bonhoeffer writes about the ethical dilemma of deciding what good is, and this has helped me, in thinking through the idea of Absolute Love. He says we must turn from asking "how can I be good" to asking "what is God's will".

"Whoever wishes to take up the problem of a Christian ethic must be confronted at once with a demand which is quite without parallel. He must from the outset discard as irrelevant the two questions which alone impel him to concern himself with the problem of ethics, "How can I be good?" and "How can I do good?," and instead of these he must ask the utterly and totally different question "What is the will of God?" This requirement is so immensely far-reaching because it presupposes a decision with regard to the ultimate reality; it presupposes a decision of faith. If the ethical problem presents itself essentially in the form of inquiries about one's own being good and doing good, this means that it has already been decided that it is the self and the world which are ultimate reality. The aim of all ethical reflection is, then, that I myself shall be good and that the world shall become good through my action. But the problem of ethics at once assumes a new aspect if it becomes apparent that these realities, myself and the world, themselves lie embedded in a quite different ultimate reality, namely, the reality of God, the Creator, Reconciler and Redeemer. What is of ultimate importance is now no longer that I should become good, or that the condition of the world should be made better by my action, but

that the reality of God should show itself everywhere to be the ultimate reality. Where there is faith in God as the ultimate reality, all concern with ethics will have as its starting-point that God shows Himself to be good, even if this involves the risk that I myself and the world are not good but thoroughly bad. All things appear distorted if they are not seen and recognized in God. All so-called data, all laws and standards are mere abstractions so long as there is no belief in God as the ultimate reality. But when we say that God is ultimate reality, this is not an idea, through which the world as we have it is to be sublimated. It is not the religious rounding-off of a profane conception of the universe. It is the acceptance in faith of God's showing forth of Himself, the acceptance of His revelation. If God were merely a religious idea there would be nothing to prevent us from discerning, behind this allegedly "ultimate" reality, a still more final reality, the twilight of the gods and the death of the gods. The claim of this ultimate reality is satisfied only in so far as it is revelation, that is to say, the self-witness of the living God. When this is so, the relation to this reality is not merely a gradual advance towards the discovery of ever more profound realities; it is the crucial turning-point in the apprehension of reality as a whole. The ultimate reality now shows itself to be at the same time the initial reality, the first and the last, alpha and omega. Any perception or apprehension of things or laws without Him is now abstraction, detachment from the origin and goal. Any inquiry about one's own goodness, or the goodness of the world, is now impossible unless inquiry has first been made about the goodness of God. For without God what meaning could there be in a goodness of man and a goodness of the world"…

"Good is now no longer a valuation of what is, a valuation, for example, of my own being, my outlook or my actions, or of some condition or state in the world. It is no longer a predicate that is assigned to something which is in itself in being. Good is the real itself. It is not the real in the abstract, the real which is detached from the reality of God, but the real which possesses reality only in God. There is no good without the real, for the good is not a general formula, and the real is impossible without the good. The wish to be good consists solely in the longing for what is real in God. A desire to be good for its own sake, as an end in itself, so to speak, or as a vocation in life, falls victim to the irony of unreality. The genuine striving for good now becomes the self-assertiveness of the prig. Good is not

in itself an independent theme for life; if it were so it would be the craziest kind of quixotry. Only if we share in reality can we share in good."[4]

I thought these words from Bonhoeffer may help others see my thought process regarding two often quoted but misguided maxims concerning truth. Each of these thoughts, I believe, convey some degree of reality, but not ultimate or absolute reality.

First, often we hear academics saying "All truth is relative" especially secular academics.

Second, more frequently, of late, we hear evangelical Christian academics saying "All truth is God's truth".

At first my reaction is to stand with the latter statement and reject the former.

Yet, having contemplated the ramifications of each statement, I am more inclined to slightly change the first statement and reject the second out of hand.   Instead, I think we should say, "Some truth is relative" and "Only absolute revealed truth is God's truth".

One thing that brings me to think, this is the way we should think about truth, is Jesus confrontation with a man who asked: "Good teacher, what shall I do to inherit eternal life?" and Jesus replied, "Why do you call me good? No one is good except God alone."

A second trigger has been a paper written by John Piper. In it Dr Piper writes, *"God never had a beginning! "I am" has sent me to you. And one who never had a beginning, but always was and is and will be, defines all things. Whether we want him to be there or not, he is there. We do not negotiate what we want for reality. God defines reality. When we come into existence we stand before a God who made us and owns us. We have absolutely no choice in this matter. We do not choose to be. And when we are, we do not choose that God be. No ranting and raving, no sophisticated doubt or skepticism, has any effect on the existence of God. He simply and absolutely is. "Tell them 'I am' has sent you".*

If we don't like it, we can change our mind, for our joy, or we can suppress this truth, to our destruction. But one thing remains absolutely unassailed. God is. He was there before we came. He will be there when we are gone. And therefore, what matters above all things is this God. I cannot escape the simple and obvious truth that God must be the main thing. Life has to do with God because every atom and every emotion and every soul of every angelic, demonic and human being belongs to God, who absolutely is. He created all that is, he sustains everything in being, he directs the course of all events, because "from him and through him and to him are all things, to him be glory (in our ministries!) forever" (Romans 11:36).[5]

M. Scott Peck has written about this ethical dilemma by saying; "To be ethical is, at the very least, to be 'humanistic,' which by definition means having the attitude that people are precious... The problem with secular humanism is that it says nothing about why human beings are precious, nor why they should be treated accordingly. Consequently, secular humanism, being unrooted in any kind of theology, is often a fair-weather phenomenon. That is why I define civil behavior not simply as 'ethical' but specifically as 'ethical in submission to a higher power.' For if, as I said light, truth, and love are all synonyms of a sort for God, and if we are truly submitted to these things, our behavior will be godly even though we may not think of ourselves as religious."[6]

A third contemplation is Einstein's' THEORY OF RELATIVITY, where at least part of this theory sorts out for us how matter distorts the space/time continuum. So that, we have been able to discover how the earths gravitational pull alters the use of energy, allowing us to discover, among many other important applications, how to travel outside our earth's atmosphere.

Science tells us that empirical data is altered by both the limitations, constraints that we put upon experimentation and the presuppositions that guide the processes of experimentation. We must therefore, if we are honest, conclude that through empirical sciences, we know relative truth. That is, truth that is only true, to the limitations that we have placed upon that truth in our finite understanding.

What has been said should not lead us to believe that nature (or truth revealed by nature) is unreal. $E=MC^2$ is a verifiable formula or equation. Nature is governed by laws that are unbreakable, because they are derived from ultimate reality, Absolute Love. That is to say from God.

Now, what has been said, does mean, unless we see these realities as pointing back to the ultimate reality, the meaning of these verifiable truths will be subject to relativism. As Romans 1: 20 tells us; "For since the creation of the world His invisible attributes, His eternal power and divine nature, have been clearly seen, being understood through what has been made, so that they are without excuse."

According to Einstein's theory, there is no observable absolute motion, only relative motion. There must be something ultimate to which our understanding of truth is relative, or measured against. This is a probable explanation to why, educational institutions from the Judeo-Christian world have developed scientific theories of practical impact and economical value, to a much greater degree than the rest of the world.

Humility must be the starting point

So, if we accept that we are finite, limited beings, we will acknowledge that what we do know from experience, is not absolutely true or absolute reality. Absolute reality must be revealed by the absolute, or else it is distorted, this is why it is absolute folly for man to try to gain understanding apart from a living relationship with God. Distortion, perversion and absolute error are the ramifications of saying "all truth is God's truth".

On the other hand, the importance of humility in handling revealed truth and "speaking the truth in love" is a great caution for us to hold on to, if we feel we know what God has revealed as truth.

In our finitude and limited understanding the truth is as given in I Corinthians 13:12, 13 "For now we see in a mirror dimly, but then face to face.

Now I know in part; then I shall know fully, even as I have been fully known.

So now faith, hope, and love abide, these three; but the greatest of these is love."

We can be far from the mark of the application God wants us to convey. Our understanding of situations is always limited, relative to not knowing all of the circumstance.

All of our understanding also of God, though it is reality revealed in His Word (The Bible), our understanding is limited in perspective. An example is the caution of James 1:19 to be careful, "being quick to hear, slow to speak and slow to anger; for the anger of man does not achieve the righteousness of God."

Our anger, even if justified, is limited to our perspective. Therefore anger in us produces, more often than not, immoral or unrighteous results.

Yet, God can be angry and bring about righteousness. 2 Corinthians 5:21 tells us: "He made Him who knew no sin, to be made sin on our behalf, so that in Him we might become the righteousness of God".

This is why judgment is so heinous to Jesus and why blaming and shaming of others is often improper and unhelpful in changing behavior in others.

So, let us be compassionate toward one another and acknowledge that, in so far as it goes, some truth is relative. If we are open and honest and unafraid to face this fact then perhaps, we can dialogue with them about truth in a way that does not alienate. On the other hand, let us be careful about what truth we assign to God and, in all humility, let Him define what that truth is.

What I am saying is probably better said by J. I Packer in his book <u>TRUTH & POWER,</u> A book written as a powerful defense of the authority of the Bible Packer says, *"we are children, and therefore victims, of reaction- negative stances of recoil blinding us to the value in the things we reject. Human reaction never results in God's righteousness; it is not discerning enough. . . .*

I am talking about what sociologists call cultural prejudice. I am saying we all suffer from it, most of all those of us who think we don't, and that as a result we are constantly missing things that are there for us in the Bible. We are ourselves part of the problem of understanding because of the way that tradition and reaction have conditioned us. When, therefore, we ask God to give us understanding we should be asking him to keep us not only from mistakes about meaning of texts but also from culturally determined blind spots. We cannot hope in this world to lose our blinkers entirely; we shall always be men and women of our time, nurtured by our cultural milieu and also narrowed by it. That is the inescapable human condition. But we can at least be aware of the problem, and try to surmount it as far as possible."[7]   *"As Albert Einstein cautioned, 'we should take care not to make the intellect our god. It has, of course, powerful muscles, but no personality. It cannot lead, it can only serve.*"[8]

This was a powerful event in a Junior High classroom.

A lesson learned early

When I was in Junior High School, our teacher had two boys in our class stage a fight at the beginning of class. This, though a very realistic conflict, was all planned ahead of time, though none of us knew that.

The fight was broken up by the teacher and the two boys sent out of the room, supposedly to the principles' office and the teacher came back in asking for any viewpoints as to how the fight might have started.

Of course, you can already guess that there were several different versions and differences of opinion as to who was at fault. The same thing happens in regard to reporting of accidents, mediating disputes, getting differing opinions from physicians and from educators who argue dogmatically on either side of the nature/nurture debate.

Those who trust in empirical sciences as absolutes should take a look at the variances between separate dating of fossilized material using carbon 14 methodology.

Likewise, students of psychology need to weigh the differences between successes of behavioral theorists and psycho-dynamic theorists.

This is not to say that, truth, absolute truth, is incompatible with natural truth, but truth learned naturally, truth revealed by nature, must come under investigation by revealed truth.

Also, truth learned naturally, can at times, merely be relative truth.

As M. Scott Peck explains: *"Science, therefore, is an activity submitted to a higher power (except of course, in those instances when the ego of scientists get in the way of their search for truth). Since God is the epitome of our higher power- God is light, God is love, God is truth — anything that seeks these values is holy. Thus, while it cannot answer all questions, science, in its proper place, is a very holy activity."* [9]

Something can seem good yet have a bad affect

Returning to Bonhoeffer's point, the question of what is good is not a question that can be answered, very well, from a finite perspective.

For instance, we know that it is not good to, out of love for a family member who is alcoholic (or any addictive behavior we might name), compensate for the inabilities that are brought on by that addiction.

On the other hand, compensation for others inabilities is the essence of spirit giftedness in the Body of Christ, this type of dependency is very good.   Therefore, when we are told to do good and bless those who hate and persecute us for being devoted to Jesus, does not mean we become helpful to them in doing so.

We must balance the good of blessing with the call to provide justice to the defenseless and the truth that love provides for discipline. "Those whom the LORD loves He reproves and disciplines." So, to ask what is good in a relative sense can be very unhelpful. As Bonhoeffer says, we need to ask "What is the will of God?"[10]

In the final analysis, there are several cautions we need to give to ourselves. First, we must find and always return to the ground of truth, which, if there is such a ground, is in revealed truth by the ultimate reality, the God of Abraham.

Second, we must be careful to handle this truth with the sense that we need to be accountable to others, both to protect ourselves and others, from error and disgrace.

Yet, a final caution is that we must be open to learn from nature, and the finest thinkers in science of all kinds, so that we can delve deeper into truth with the least amount of cultural blindness.

My main comfort level is with the Christian Bible so, if you are Jewish or Muslim please hang in with me and give some latitude to my bias.

Religion can be perverted by it's followers

For those who are agnostic or atheistic, I can agree that religion can be dangerous and lots of bad things have been done in the name of various religions. Isn't that just to say that human beings do terrible things to one another and to their environment? In other words, we have lost much of our ability to love.

In turn wouldn't you agree that if we could find a common ground, an absolute, which would lend itself to better love one another, it would be a better world in which to live?

After all, lots of warlords and political despots were also people who had no belief in God or absolutes. Please take a brief walk toward contemplating Absolute LOVE and see if you agree.

Whether you are Muslim, Jewish, Christian, Agnostic, or Atheistic I think all would agree Love is needed.

To rephrase a well-known axiom; "Love IS, therefore Love exists".

End Notes

1. Josephson Institute Center for Youth Ethics. http://charactercounts.org
2. Dictionary.com. http://dictionary.reference.com
3. White, Dr. John, *CHANGING ON THE INSIDE;* Ann Arbor, Mi. Servant Publications: 1991, page 40.
4. Bonhoeffer, Dietrich. *ETHICS;* New York, NY, Touchstone Publishing; Translated by Neville Horton Smith, Chr. Kaize Verlag, Munich 1949, page 186-189

5. Piper, Dr. John. *JOHN CALVIN AND HIS PASSION FOR THE MAJESTY OF GOD*. Wheaton, IL. Crossway Books, A division of Good News Publishers; 2009, page 13.
6. Peck, M. Scott M.D. *THE ROAD LESS TRAVELED AND BEYOND*. New York, NY, Touchstone Publishing; 1997, page 175
7. Packer, Dr. James I. *TRUTH & POWER*. Wheaton, IL. , Harold Shaw Publishers: 1996, pages 144-146
8. Goleman, Daniel; Boyazatis, Richard and McKee, Annie. *PRIMAL LEADRSHIP*. Boston. MA., Harvard Business School Press, 2002, page 27
9. Peck, M. Scott M.D. *THE ROAD LESS TRAVELED AND BEYOND*. New York, NY, Touchstone Publishing; 1997, page 131
10. Bonhoeffer, Dietrich. *ETHICS;* New York, NY, Touchstone Publishing; Translated by Neville Horton Smith, Chr. Kaize Verlag, Munich 1949, page 186

CHAPTER TWO

Love IS

Gen 17:1,2 When Abram was ninety-nine years old the LORD appeared to Abram and said to him, "I am God Almighty; walk before me, and be blameless, that I may make my covenant between me and you, and may multiply you greatly."

Exo 3:14 God said to Moses, "I AM WHO I AM." And he said, "Say this to the people of Israel: 'I AM has sent me to you.'"

Joh 8:58 Jesus said to them, "Truly, truly, I say to you, before Abraham was, I am."

If you call yourself a believer, or aren't sure what you believe, let's agree at the outset; loving your families, your husbands and wives, your children, your brothers and sisters and your neighbors is a much better way to live than being in turmoil and constantly fighting.

As Stephen Carter has written; "But if we have no time to listen with love and respect to those who disagree with us, then we have no time for awe in God's creation, and thus no time for lives of civility." [1]

Differences can be helpful and not divisive

I know we have differences. My two sisters and my brother, though we grew up together, are definitely different and we all four live in different areas of the United States.

We don't always agree on everything, but I know they would stand up for me and care for me in need. It really helps that we have a long history together and know what the others have been through in life. We understand where each other is coming from. How can we be more effectively involved in learning from and loving one another?

From Steven Covey we hear; "Seek first to understand then to be understood"[2]

If you're set in your mind that you don't believe faith has any benefit but to start war and strife, I think you can still agree that loving one another or at least getting along is a better way to live than ignoring or scoffing at others who have an absolute frame of reference.

At least can't you acknowledge that all the questions about our existence have not been answered yet, people are still seeking and it might not hurt to at least know why they are so passionate.

Love is a means of heathy existence

Perhaps you will welcome a doctor's advice. "Love is intimately related with health. This is not a sentimental exaggeration. One survey of ten thousand men with heart disease found a 50 percent reduction in frequency of chest pain (angina) in men who perceived their wives as supportive and loving."; quotes Larry Dossey, M.D. in his book, HEALING WORDS.[2]

Dr. Dossey also goes on to document the value of belief in God, he says; "Over two dozen studies demonstrate the health promoting effects of simply attending church or synagogue on a regular basis." The Dr. also sights work by Jeffrey S. Levin, Ph.D. where he says; …Levin has uncovered over 250 empirical studies published … in which spiritual or religious practices have been statistically associated with particular health outcomes…Positive effects for both morbidity and mortality have been found for cardiovascular disease, hypertension, stroke, nearly every type of cancer, colitis and enteritis."[3]

I am aware that there are important differences between Jews, Christians and Muslims. There are also wide gaps between people of faith and atheists. In fact, there are differences between various groups internally, within all three faiths.

However, if you have come with me this far, let's together see if we can find some common ground, maybe even some absolutes?

Common Ground

The journey toward knowing who God is, starts with God revealing His name to us. Jews, Christians and Muslims are all people of a revealed God, an Absolute Creator. In the Tanakh, the writings of Jesus followers; (all who were Jewish by birth and faith), and the Koran, I believe we can come to at least seven points of agreement among believers in God as to the nature of God.

- First God is absolutely self-existent. God was, is and forever shall be uncreated and unending.
- Second God is absolutely sovereign.
- Third God is creator and sustainer of life, beginning and end. Life exists and continues to exist because God persists in allowing life to exist.
- Fourth God is absolutely personal, in other words God is a unique personal being. There is no other being like God. God is wholly other that created beings.
- Fifth God is absolutely self-revealing. We only know God as He has revealed Himself to us. We are finite God is eternal and beyond our discovery

unless God allows us glimpses into eternity.

- Sixth God is a relational God, if God has chosen to reveal Himself than God is relational in the sense that He reaches out to relate to us.
- Seventh God is absolutely LOVE.
Ok, many people even religious people doubt that God is Love. Yet many have hope that He is loving. Many fear He is not loving.
To explain what I mean that God is absolutely LOVE is the reason for this book. LOVE is the character of God, but it is a differently defined love than we think of or exhibit ourselves. I know this is difficult to comprehend but it is what is revealed. (I probably will need to do some more convincing on this point)

The truth is there is often so much cultural or political history that mitigates against loving others from different countries, political reference points, religious contexts and intellectual points of view.

It is very difficult to let go of what we know and reach out to what is unknown. We cannot imagine things as being different than our present frame of reference and rebuild our paradigms in other directions is seemingly impossible.

However. God is absolute, we will rarely find truth about God out of what we imagine.

G.K. Chesterton says; "Nobody can imagine how nothing could turn into something. Nobody can get an inch nearer to it by explaining how something could turn into something else. It is really far more logical to start by saying "in the beginning God created heaven and earth" even if you mean "In the beginning some unthinkable power began some unthinkable process." For God is by its nature a name of mystery, and nobody ever supposed that man could imagine how a world was created any more than He could create one."[4]

Abraham the Father of Faith

All three "religions of the book", claim their God to be the God of Abraham. Our journey to finding the absolute begins in the Tanakh (the Jewish Holy Book) consisting of three parts, The Law, the Prophets and the Writings). Christians have also claimed the Tanakh as part of their Bible usually called the Old Testament. This shouldn't be very surprising Jesus of Nazareth was Jewish and followed Jewish customs, such as going to the Jewish Temple to celebrate Passover at age twelve as was the Jewish custom at the time.

All of the writers of the Christian New Testament grew up following Jewish customs and they filled their writings with quotes from the Tanakh. (The Old Testament in the Christian Bible)

Abram, later called Abraham was a Bedouin who lived in the middle east over 5,000 years ago, there was nothing dogmatic in Abraham's believe in God only faith. Judaism, Christianity and Islam all trace their roots back to this area and the man Abraham.

In the Tanakh it is recorded. Gen 11:31 – 12:4 Terah took Abram his son and Lot the son of Haran, his grandson, and Sarai his daughter-in-law, his son Abram's wife, and they went forth together from Ur of the Chaldeans to go into the land of Canaan, but when they came to Haran, they settled there… Now **the LORD "YAHWEH"** said to Abram, "Go from your country and your kindred and your father's house to the land that I will show you. And I will make of you a great nation, and I will bless you and make your name great, so that you will be a blessing. I will bless those who bless you, and him who dishonors you I will curse, and in you all the families of the earth shall be blessed." So Abram went, as the LORD had told him, and Lot went with him. Abram was seventy-five years old when he departed from Haran.

The word LORD in this passage is in Hebrew יהוה , or YHWH

The word YHWH is never spoken out loud in strict Jewish traditions, "the LORD" is always said out loud (pronounced) when this personal name for God is encountered in the reading of the Tanakh. It is considered irreverent to say the name aloud.

YHWH in the root is a form of the personal pronoun I. YHWH is usually rendered "I AM" or "I AM that I AM" The name speaks to God's absoluteness, self-existence, eternality, sovereignty, personal existence and self-revealing character.

These characteristics are also true within the Koran. "And your god is One God; there is none who has the right to be worshipped but He, the Most Beneficent, the Most Merciful." (Quran 2:163 "God! There is no god but Him, the Living, the Self-Sufficient. He is not subject to drowsiness or sleep. Everything in the heavens and the earth belongs to Him. Who can intercede with Him except by His permission? He knows what is before them and what is behind them but they cannot grasp any of His knowledge save what He wills. His Footstool encompasses the heavens and the earth and their preservation does not tire Him. He is the Most High, the Magnificent." (Quran 2:255)

That God is absolute, a frame of reference by God and derived only from God, can be agreed upon by Christians, Muslims and Jews.

If you are presently, by which I mean temporarily, atheistic or agnostic, you surely will not agree that God is absolute, you may agree though, that persons exist and that existence seeks some permanence, some absoluteness either within or outside of oneself. According to an often-repeated philosophical axiom from philosopher Rene Descartes, "I think therefore I am."

If you will permit I will for, myself, drop the necessarily ambiguous God as the subject of this journey and call the ONE who I am referring to as "I AM" or "the ONE who IS" sometimes simply "Absolute Love" for that is my deduction. I do this out of reverence for "I AM" and to use a reference that might carry less baggage for everyone involved. IAM carries with it the connotation of absoluteness, my assertion is that; LOVE IS Therefore LOVE exists.

That love exists possibly poses a greater barrier to atheistic thinking than; the fact that horrible atrocities are committed in the name of some people's god. The atrocities committed by people often pose a barrier to the notion that "I AM "exists.

As C.S Lewis writes in, THE PROBLEM OF PAIN; "Until the evil man finds evil unmistakably present in his existence, in the form of pain, he is enclosed in the illusion. Once pain has roused him, he knows that he is in some way or other 'up against' the real universe: either he rebels (with the possibility of clearer issue and deeper repentance at some later stage) or else makes some attempt at an adjustment, which, if pursued will lead him to religion." [6]

Religion, though, is most often a way of appeasing or gaining gods favor, but LOVE or I AM is not looking for anything that could gain favor; we have nothing to give except love in return.

I AM as self-existence is in need of nothing.

I AM's relationship with us is an over flow of love because LOVE IS. We don't need to appease I AM there is no way that we could.

As Dr. John Piper writes in the book DESIRING GOD; "God has no deficiencies that I might be required to supply. He is complete in himself. He is overflowing with happiness in the fellowship of the Trinity. The upshot of this is that God is a mountain spring, not a watering trough. A mountain spring is self-replenishing. It constantly overflows and supplies others. But a watering trough needs to be filled with a pump or bucket brigade. So, if you want to glorify the worth of the watering rough you work hard to keep it full and useful. But if you want to glorify the worth of the spring you do it by getting down on your hands and knees and drinking to your heart's satisfaction, until you have the refreshment and strength to go back down in the valley and tell the people what you've found. You do not glorify a mountain spring by dutifully hauling water up the path from the river below and dumping it in the spring. What we have seen is God is like a mountain spring, not a watering trough. And since God is the way God is, we are not surprised to learn from Scripture- and our faith is strengthened to hold fast- that the way to please God is to come to him to get and not to give, to drink and not to water. He is most glorified in us when we are most satisfied in him."[7]

To believe in this God is a giant step on the way to personal growth, because it will involve a significant amount of loss, leading to gain. Loss of self and surely loss of things that we have held as dear to us, it will cost the loss of things we now love to find Absolute Love.

Robert Greenleaf in his book on leadership writes; "No one can judge, from where one now stands, how difficult the next step along the road of spiritual growth will be. Those of good works, the upright moral citizens, and the pillars in the church may find the next step of staggering proportions. Their seeming opposites-the unsuccessful, the misfit, the unlovely, and the rejected- may take the next step with ease. We cannot assume with assurance that we are relatively advantaged or disadvantaged for any stage of the inward journey."

"To be on the journey one must have an attitude toward loss and being lost, a view of oneself in which powerful symbols like burned, dissolved, broken off- however painful their impact is seen to be- do not appear as senseless or destructive. Rather the losses they suggest are seen as opening the way for new creative acts, for the receiving of priceless gifts. Loss, every loss one's mind can conceive of, creates a vacuum into which will come (if allowed) something new and fresh and beautiful, something unforeseen- and the greatest of these is love. The source of this attitude toward loss and being lost is faith: faith in the validity of one's own inward experience; faith in the wisdom of the great events of one's history, events in which one's potential for nobility has been tested and refined; faith in doubt, in inquiry, and in the rebirth of wisdom; faith in the possibility of achieving a measure of sainthood on this earth from which flow concerns and responsibility and a sense of rightness in all things. By these means mortals are raised above the possibility of hurt. They will suffer, but they will not be hurt because each loss grants them the opportunity to be greater than before. Loss, by itself, is not tragic. What is tragic is the failure to grasp the opportunity which loss presents."[8]

Look with me at the earliest of revelations of I AM with Adam and Eve. God sets up a paradise a garden that Adam and Eve have neither need nor wants but to enjoy the relationship they have with each other, the world around them and with I AM. I AM sets up one single matter of trust with them not to eat of the tree of the knowledge of good and evil. Outside of loving and trusting relationship with one another and outside of loving and trusting relationship with I AM they were breaking faith.

Can you imagine giving someone your everything; all they need or could want, being totally open and loving towards them yet in desire to keep them from harmful affects you ask them to stay away from a person you know may corrupt and harm them? I will let you imagine that person's characteristics yourself. You come home at night and the person you love is nowhere to be found. You call and call and the loved one doesn't answer.

Finally, you find them hiding in a corner, disheveled and shaken. They cannot look at you. You know that trust has been broken. Your loved one no longer wants your love and protection. They are not sorry for their breach of trust; they excuse it and hold up very good reasons for doing what they did. They are filled with defiant blame even amidst the shame of being exposed. They don't care that it showed great disrespect and ultimately a lack of love towards you. What would you do?

I AM covered them with clothes and promised to make things right. I AM showed that He cared even though they had betrayed trust. However broken trust has brought broken relationship and separation.

God reveals His loving character

Separation has caused severe consequences and because I AM is LOVE, the giver and sustainer of life, death will come and begin with a real inability to love in the same way as I AM is LOVE.

Fast forward through Genesis and part of Exodus, I AM has shown to overflow with LOVE to people though people continue to be hateful and dangerous towards each other. I AM has seen the back-breaking slavery of the descendants of Abraham. I AM seeking always to release from bondage and tyranny to replace people in a loving environment-community. The descendants of Abraham are freed from the deadly rule and religion of the Egyptians. The community of refugees is brought to a mountain where Moses their leader and the representative of I AM is to go up to the mountain to receive instructions from I AM.

On the mountain, I AM is instructs Moses and writes on two tablets of stone the summary of those instructions. There are basically two parts of the instructions given; First, Love I AM! Second, Love each other! Because of the separation from I

AM the instructions had to be more detailed, the connection to LOVE is still broken and the ability to be in the image of I AM is perverted.

<u>Deu 6:5</u> You shall love the LORD your God with all your heart and with all your soul and with all your might.

Moses in receiving the revelation from I AM is gone a long time and while he is gone the people who have just been led out of bondage and tyranny turn back to the gods and the religion of the land they have been rescued from. Instead of loving relationship they again turn to the bondage of religion.

> Moses realizes that without the very presence of God any attempt at establishing the community in love is impossible so Moses says: "Exo 33:13-19 Now therefore, if I have found favor in your sight, please show me now your ways, that I may know you in order to find favor in your sight. Consider too that this nation is your people." And he said, "My presence will go with you, and I will give you rest." And he said to him, "If your presence will not go with me, do not bring us up from here. For how shall it be known that I have found favor in your sight, I and your people? Is it not in your going with us, so that we are distinct, I and your people, from every other people on the face of the earth?" And the LORD said to Moses, "This very thing that you have spoken I will do, for you have found favor in my sight, and I know you by name." Moses said, "Please

show me your glory." and he said, "I will make all my goodness pass before you and will proclaim before you my name 'The LORD.' And I will be gracious to whom I will be gracious, and will show mercy on whom I will show mercy."

Here is the moment of I AM telling Moses what His character is, what is the absolute nature of God? Exo 34:5-7The LORD descended in the cloud and stood with him there, and proclaimed the name of the LORD. The LORD passed before him and proclaimed, "The LORD, the LORD, a God merciful and gracious, slow to anger, and abounding in steadfast love and faithfulness, keeping steadfast love for thousands, forgiving iniquity and transgression and sin, but will by no means clear the guilty…"

Do you notice the description? In my own words "I AM, I AM merciful, gracious, I don't get angry very easily, I overflow with steadfast love, and faithfulness, I continue forever to keep overflowing with love for thousands, I continually forgive your wrong doing, immorality and your just plain blowing it. Still I will make sure justice is done."

The essence of I AM being overflowing Hesed (Loving-kindness, Steadfast Love, Absolute Love), in Hebrew it is a word that is translated and used as loyalty, kindness, mercy, beauty, devotion, faithfulness and goodness. The connotation is so full of meaning it is almost indefinable to us. The sense is of an overflowing, unbounded love that spills over from the inner being of I AM.

This conclusion of who God is resonates with Hebrew followers of Jesus. John, who is the last survivor of those who were the initial followers and friends writes this; 1Jn 4:16-19 "So we have come to know and to believe the love that God has for us. God is love, and whoever abides in love abides in God, and

God abides in him. By this is love perfected with us, so that we may have confidence for the day of judgment, because as he is so also are, we in this world. There is no fear in love, but perfect love casts out fear. For fear has to do with punishment, and whoever fears has not been perfected in love. We love because he first loved us."

John says; "God is love". The word that is translated love here from the ancient Greek language is agape'. Love in the sense of agape' is unexpected love, a kind of love that stops you in amazement, a love that goes beyond understanding that flows undeserved and unbounded from the giver. It is Sacrificial, Absolute Love. This love is beyond natural, it gives from the essence of the giver and not because of anything derived from the recipient.

I AM is LOVE, love overflows from the essence of I AM. It is sometimes defined as unconditional; I believe that is a misunderstanding. This love may be said to be sacrificial love, but not selfless love, not unconditional love. It is absolute love flowing out from within the self of God. It is absolute love flowing out from God.

The conditions come from the absoluteness of I AM. It is definitely sacrificial love, but it is not unconditional. Absoluteness is unalterable and I AM must maintain absoluteness or in turn Love will be diminished. As I AM says to Moses; Exo 33:19 And he said, "I will make all my goodness pass before you and will proclaim before you my name 'The LORD.' And I will be gracious to whom I will be gracious, and will show mercy on whom I will show mercy."

Absoluteness not arbitrariness, I AM reserving the justice of overflowing love by maintaining the absoluteness of his character, "I will by no means clear the guilty." This is not unconditionality. The guilty are those who continue to deny

LOVE IS, who will not accept Love and who will not cherish Love.

This very idea was concisely stated in believers in the past by the statement, "The chief end of man is to glorify God and enjoy Him forever."

Dr. John Piper recently in his book DESIRING GOD has restated that phrase by saying; The chief end of man is to glorify God by enjoying Him forever."[9] This is what I AM intended for mankind in the beginning. Enjoying His Loving Sovereignty. Glorifying Him by Loving Him. Hesed is often translated by compound construct, lovingkindness or steadfast-love, even by abundant in mercy.

In Islam also among the 99 names of God, the most famous and most frequent of these names are "the Compassionate" (*al-rahman*) and "the Merciful" (*al-rahim*): from research on line at Wikipedia, the free encyclopedia. These have the meaning of being beneficent, gracious, caring, having tender affection for or in relationship to Allah, the most merciful in essence.

That LOVE IS or, that God is love, is the conclusion of the Tanakh, the Quran and the New Testament. All three look for a savior a redeemer. The Tanakh does not name this Messiah except with the title "The Son of Man" a title that Yeshua the carpenter's son clearly used for Himself. The Quran clearly names him, Isa- Al Masih, this same Yeshua born in Bethlehem, Judea. Yeshua (Hebrew language of the Tanakh), Isa (Aramaic language of the Quran) and Jesus (Greek language of the New Testament) name the same person who lived in Nazareth with his parents over 2000 years ago,. This conclusion is no "pie in the sky, head in the sand" declaration. I realize there are significant differences between the proponents of each faith. If you can walk a bit farther with me, laying aside the differences for now, holding on to the fact that LOVE IS.

Hesed (Loving-kindness, Steadfast Love, Fidelity, Mercy, Goodness, Compassion, Kindness)

Gen 19:19, 20:13, 21:23, 24:12, 24:14, 24:27, 24:49, 32:10, 39:21, 40:14, 47:29,**Exo** 15:13, 20:6, 34:6, 34:7,**Lev** 20:17,**Num** 14:18, 14:19,**Deu** 5:10, 7:9, 7:12,**Josh** 2:12, 2:14,**Judg** 1:24, 8:35,**Ruth** 1:8, 2:20, 3:10,**1 Sam** 15:6, 20:8, 20:14, 20:15,**2 Sam** 2:5, 2:6, 3:8, 7:15, 9:1, 9:3, 9:7, 10:2, 15:20, 16:17, 22:51,1 Ki 2:7, 3:6, 4:10, 8:23, 20:31, **1 Chr** 16:34, 16:41, 17:13, 19:2,**2 Chr** 1:8, 5:13, 6:14, 6:42, 7:3, 7:6, 20:21, 24:22, 32:32, 35:26,**Ezra** 3:11, 7:28, 9:9,**Neh** 1:5, 9:17, 9:32, 13:14, 13:22,Est 2:9, 2:17, **Job** 6:14, 10:12, 37:13,**Psa** 5:7, 6:4, 13:5, 17:7, 18:50, 21:7, 23:6, 25:6, 25:7, 25:10, 26:3, 31:7, 31:16, 31:21, 32:10, 33:5, 33:18, 33:22, 36:5, 36:7, 36:10, 40:10, 40:11, 42:8, 44:26, 48:9, 51:1, 52:1, 52:8, 57:3, 57:10, 59:10, 59:16, 59:17, 61:7, 62:12, 63:3, 66:20, 69:13, 69:16, 77:8, 85:7, 85:10, 86:5, 86:13, 86:15, 88:11, 89:1, 89:2, 89:14, 89:24, 89:28, 89:33, 89:49, 90:14, 92:2, 94:18, 98:3, 100:5, 101:1, 103:4, 103:8, 103:11, 103:17, 106:1, 106:7, 106:45, 107:1, 107:8, 107:15, 107:21, 107:31, 107:43, 108:4, 109:12, 109:16, 109:21, 109:26, 115:1, 117:2, 118:1, 118:2, 118:3, 118:4, 118:29,119:41, 119:64, 119:76, 119:88, 119:124, 119:149, 119:159, 130:7, 136:1, 136:2, 136:3, 136:4 136:5, 136:6, 136:7, 136:8, 136:9, 136:10, 136:11, 136:12, 136:13, 136:14, 136:15, 136:16, 136:17, 136:18, 136:19, 136:20, 136:21, 136:22, 136:23, 136:24, 136:25, 136:26, 138:2, 138:8, 141:5, 143:8, 143:12, 144:2, 145:8, 147:11, **Prov** 3:3, 11:17, 14:22, 14:34, 16:6, 19:22, 20:6, 20:28, 21:21, 31:26,**Isa** 16:5, 40:6, 54:8, 54:10, 55:3, 57:1, 63:7, **Jer** 2:2, 9:24, 16:5, 31:3, 32:18, 33:11,**Lam** 3:22, 3:32,**Dan** 1:9 9:4,**Hosea** 2:19, 4:1, 6:4, 6:6, 10:12, 12:6,**Joel** 2:13,**Jonah** 2:8, 4:2, **Micah** 6:8, 7:18, 7:20,**Zec** 7:9

Agape (Love)

Mat 24:12,**Luke** 11:42,**John** 5:42, 13:35, 15:9, 15:10, 15:12, 15:13, 17:26,**Rom** 5:5, 5:8, 8:35, 8:39, 12:9, 13:10, 14:15, 15:30,**1 Cor** 4:21, 8:1, 13:1, 13:2, 13:3, 13:4, 13:8, 13:13, 14:1, 16:14, 16:24,**2 Cor** 2:4, 2:8, 5:14, 6:6, 8:7, 8:8, 8:24, 13:11, 13:14,**Gal** 5:6, 5:13, 5:22,**Eph** 1:4, 1:15, 2:4, 3:17, 3:19, 4:2, 4:15, 4:16, 5:2,

6:23,**Phil** 1:9, 1:17, 2:1, 2:2,Col 1:4, 1:8, 1:13, 2:2, 3:14,**1 Th** 3:6, 5:8, 5:13,**2 Th** 1:3, 2:10, 3:5,**1 Tim** 1:5, 1:14, 2:15, 4:12, 6:11,**2 Tim** 1:7, 1:13, 2:22, 3:10,**Titus** 2:2,**Phile** 1:5, 1:7, 1:9,**Heb** 6:10, 10:24,**1 Pet** 4:8, 5:14,**2 Pet** 1:7,**1 John** 2:5, 2:15, 3:1, 3:16, 3:17, **4:7, 4:8, 4:9, 4:10**, **4:12, 4:16, 4:17, 4:18**, 5:3,**2 John** 1:3, 1:6,**3 John** 1:6,**Jude** 1:2, 1:12, 1:21,**Rev** 2:4, 2:19

Agapao Mat 5:43, 5:44, 5:46, 6:24, 19:19, 22:37, 22:39,**Mark** 10:21, 12:30, 12:31, 12:33,**Luke** 6:27, 6:32, 6:35, 7:5, 7:42, 7:47, 10:27, 11:43, 16:13,**John** 3:16, 3:19, 3:35, 8:42, 10:17, 11:5, 12:43, 13:1, 13:23, 13:34, 14:15, 14:21, 14:23, 14:24, 14:28, 14:31, 15:9, 15:12, 15:17, 17:23, 17:24, 17:26, 19:26, 21:7, 21:15, 21:16, 21:20,**Rom** 8:28, 8:37, 9:13, 9:25, 13:8 13:9,**1 Cor** 2:9, 8:3,**2 Cor** 9:7, 11:11, 12:15,**Gal** 2:20, 5:14, **Eph**1:6, 2:4, 5:25, 5:28, 5:33, 6:24,**Col** 3:12, 3:19,**1 Th** 1:3, 1:4, 3:12, 4:9,**2 Th** 2:13, 2:16, **2 Tim** 4:8, 4:10,**Heb** 1:9, 12:6,**James** 1:12, 2:5, 2:8,**1 Pet** 1:8, 1:22, 2:17, 3:10, **2 Pet** 2:15,**1 John** 2:10, 2:15, 3:10, 3:11, 3:14, 3:18, 3:23, 4:7, 4:8, 4:10, 4:11, 4:12, 4:19, 4:20, 4:21, 5:1, 5:2,**2 John** 1:1, 1:5, **3 John** 1:1,**Rev** 1:5, 3:9, 12:11, 20:9.

1. Carter, Stephen L. . *CIVILITY,* Basic Books, New York, NY. 1998, page 140
2. Covey, Steven. *THE SEVEN HABITS OF HIGHLY EFFECTIVE PEOPLE,* Fireside Books, Simon and Schuster Inc., New York, NY, Habit # 5Pages 235-260.
3. Dossey, Larry M.D. . *HEALING WORDS; The Power of Prayer and the Practice of Medicine,* Harper Collins, New York, N.Y. , 1993, Page109
4. IBID, pages 251-252
5. Chesterton, G. K. . *THE EVERLASTING MAN,* Ignatius Press, San Francisco, CA. , First Published The Royal Literature Fund, 1925, Reprinted 1993, 2008, pages 24-25
6. Lewis, C. S. . *THE PROBLEM OF PAIN,* McMillan Publishing, New York, NY. 1962, 21st printing 1978, Page 95.

7. Piper, Dr. John. *THE PLEASURES OF GOD; Meditations on God's Delight in Being God*, Multnomah Publishers, Inc., Sisters, OR., 1991, Pages 215-216

8. Greenleaf, Robert K. . *SERVANT LEADERSHIP*, Paulist Press, New York, N.Y. , 1977, page 327

9. Piper, Dr. John. *DESIRING GOD; Confessions of a Christian Hedonist*, Multnomah Publishers, Inc. Sisters, OR. , 1986, page 14.

CHAPTER THREE

Fear, Love and Faith.

Gal 5:14.15 For the whole law is fulfilled in one word: "You shall love your neighbor as yourself." But if you bite and devour one another, watch out that you are not consumed by one another. "

I AM, seems a vague and confusing name for the one who is LOVE, for God. It is a name that describes being absolute, self-existent.

I often have a difficult time with uncertainty and not knowing. It is the history of man to try to manipulate and control. As this is true it demonstrates a deep level of mistrust and a lack of love.

The very nature of man in response to questioning by the serpent was to misconstrue and go along with the implied mistrust of the questioning.

"Gen 3:1 Now the serpent was craftier than any other beast of the field that the LORD God had made. He said to the woman, "Did God actually say, 'You shall not eat of any tree in the garden'?" Gen 3:4 But the serpent said to the woman, "You will not surely die."

Fear that God is not Absolute Love takes away the ability to be in the presence of Absolute LOVE, and because I AM is beyond us, a completely other being, we separate ourselves. In fear that God is not love, we try to make I AM more manageable, we try to make I AM into our image and likeness.

Knowing God is our purpose through eternity

This is the way we want to worship a god; we want a god we can fully understand and somewhat control, not the eternal, all powerful, all knowing, creator; but a created likeness so we make images and idols. We fashion a god, or gods, that have some power, in as much as it serves our thinking and supposed needs.

Yet these little imaginings of ours are not absolutes, they cannot really help us get past our fear. So, we establish rituals and rules because they give us some sense of control. Yet, we are still afraid of unknowns and fear keeps us from Absolute LOVE.

Fear ultimately brings death.

David Viscott, M. D. says; "No one can deal with fear of the unknown, for it is fear without limitation. It contaminates your judgment and paralyzes you. …When you live in fear, you bring upon yourself the very losses you dread most"[1]

What happens when we become separated from, I AM? We start blaming, we feel shame, we want to hide, and we don't want to be exposed.

"Gen 3:10-13 And he said, 'I heard the sound of you in the garden, and I was afraid, because I was naked, and I hid myself.' The man said, 'The woman whom you gave to be with me, she gave me fruit of the tree, and I ate.' Then the LORD God said to the woman, 'What is this that you have done?' The woman said, 'The serpent deceived me, and I ate.'"

Trust is broken, the ability to walk with I AM is forfeited, LOVE requires relationship and the building blocks of a loving relationships consist in at the least fifteen qualities of faith that establish the basis for continuing in relationship.

These fifteen qualities of faith, that come from abiding in Love, are humility, belief, trust, acceptance, confidence, gratitude, compassion, freedom, stewardship, servant hood, loyalty, purity, justice, rest and determination.

These qualities flow from and through I AM; Absolute LOVE, they come from Him as a result of walking with Him and being in His presence. "**Gen 5:24** Enoch walked with God, and he was not, for God took him."

This mysterious passage gives hint to the relationship that I AM desires, a simple walking alongside is all.

This is what was happening in the first instance of I AM's relationship with mankind. They thought; (and we think), that I AM might be withholding something really desirable from us, so we look for fulfillment outside of I AM. Instead of receivers we become takers, even hoarders. Instead of satisfaction we find that our needs are insatiable and we die.

Gen 3:17-19 And to Adam he said, "Because you have listened to the voice of your wife and have eaten of the tree of which I commanded you, 'You shall not eat of it,' cursed is the ground because of you; in pain you shall eat of it all the days of your life; thorns and thistles it shall bring forth for you; and you shall eat the plants of the field. By the sweat of your face you shall eat bread, till you return to the ground, for out of it you were taken; for you are dust, and to dust you shall return."

Dr. John White says; "all of us have an insatiable craving to be loved. And we have a deep-down fear that we won't be." Love is essential to all higher life forms. The higher the life form, the more necessary love becomes to physical survival. Without love we begin, quite literally to die. For this reason, all of us harbor a terrible fear of rejection. They may be buried deep in our unconscious minds. Yet subtly and powerfully, these feelings influence our behavior and distort our view of life around us. The deep and insatiable need for love and the consequent fear of rejection lie at the root of our difficulty in changing."[2]

Not only have we become takers without ever finding a way to satisfy our desires, not only are we dying, we also kill one another.

Gen 4:3 In the course of time Cain brought to the LORD an offering of the fruit of the ground, Gen 4:4 and Abel also brought of the firstborn of his flock and of their fat portions. And the LORD had regard for Abel and his offering, Gen 4:5 but for Cain and his offering he had no regard. So Cain was very angry, and his face fell. Gen 4:6 The LORD said to Cain, "Why are you angry, and why has your face fallen? Gen 4:7 If you do well, will you not be accepted? And if you do not do well, sin is crouching at the door. Its desire is for you, but you must rule over it." Gen 4:8 Cain spoke to Abel his brother. And when they were in the field, Cain rose up against his brother Abel and killed him. Gen 4:9 Then the LORD said to Cain, "Where is Abel your brother?" He said, "I do not know; am I my brother's keeper?" Gen 4:10 And the LORD said, "What have you done? The voice of your brother's blood is crying to me from the ground. Gen 4:11 And now you are cursed from the ground, which has opened its mouth to receive your brother's blood from your hand. Gen 4:12 When you work the ground, it shall no longer yield to you its strength. You shall be a fugitive and a wanderer on the earth."

Even in the ways we try to please I AM we fail because we are not connected to the LOVE that flows from I AM. In our need, we become more fearful and that fear produces rebellion, despair, suspicion, a judgmental nature, uncertainty, insatiable desire, ungratefulness, degradation of others, codependences, uncaring attitudes, unreliability, bullying, the inability to follow through, anxiety and a sense of being confused.

We carry a deep inability within ourselves to not be able to hold out absolute love apart from the connection to I AM. So, we live in fear. We fear our weakness, we fear our frailty and we fear being rejected by others. Yes, we even fear being killed when we are all dying.

Dr. John White a psychiatrist calls all of what I have been describing an even harsher reality, he calls the result of this fear in us evil. In his book CHANGING ON THE INSIDE Dr. White says; "Beyond the philosophical debates, however, we must deal with human actions and decisions. Here on this basic level, evil is hard to deny and even harder to accept. Evil vaunts its proud hatred in religion, in politics, in every aspect of life. We have only to think of racial hatred and violence, or the abuse and abandonment of children, or the blind greed of corporations to know that evil must be fought wherever it appears. Evil on this planet typically has to do with "man's inhumanity to man" This reality reveals itself in cruelty, exploitation of the weak, racism, violence and sexual exploitation in families. It manifests itself primarily in the disruption of the relationships we have with one another as human beings. Evil cannot be tolerated. But can it be overcome? That question rests at the heart of the issue of change. …How explain it? Evil is part of the reality of who we are. It exists in us all because we-the entire human race-have chosen to run our lives our own way. If we believe we have evil under control, then we have never seriously tried to get rid of it". [3]

I, deep down, say; "I am not evil", Oh sure, at times I might callously think why should I burden myself with other people's pain or problems, but I have never really hurt anyone.

I most of the time have no trouble with my self-esteem or thinking well of myself. I feel occasionally bad that some people have not liked me. I, more seldom than I should, feel bad that I don't lose the weight that my doctor tells me to lose. I have never stolen from another person or killed anyone.

Then I remember how when a young boy some friends and I stole some cigarettes and smoked them out behind the bushes. I remember that I turned pale green and was sicker than any flu I have had. I remember my parents not making a very big issue with the episode because I was so sick.

I also remember several times becoming annoyed and angry enough to kill. When my younger brother would goad me, I would chase him around yelling "I'm going to kill you".

Then I remember the time, oh! Then there was that time, Oh My; And then that other time! As I recall those memories my failures and inconsistencies become innumerable. Yet, I continue to think of myself as not so bad.

We are weak and needy

M. Scott Peck M.D. explains; "We need moments when we realize that we do not have it all together and that we are not perfect. … So there is a difference between insisting that we always feel good about ourselves (which is narcissistic and synonymous with constantly preserving our self-esteem)" and " … the further we proceed in diminishing our narcissism, our self-centeredness and sense of self-importance, the more we discover ourselves becoming less fearful of death but also less fearful of life. And this is the basis for learning to be more loving. No longer burdened by the need to constantly protect and defend ourselves, we are able to lift our eyes off ourselves and truly recognize others. And we begin to experience a sustained, underlying sense of happiness that we have never experienced before as we become progressively more self-forgetful and hence more able to remember God…"[4]

While fear causes us to be unloving towards others, it also can have devastating physical effects, especially if the fear is incessant or prolonged. The following is an excerpt from a public blog by Dr. Anthony DeMarco on the physiological effects fear can have on a person. "The first noticeable change is an increase in perspiration, as well as heart and respiratory rates. This physical reaction is due to the activation of a small, walnut sized structure in the fore-brain, called the amygdala. This structure, in turn, then stimulates the hypothalamus to produce CRH, or corticotrophin-releasing hormone. This hormone, then, triggers the production of adrenocorticotropic hormone, known as ACTH, in the pituitary gland, a small, oval gland at the base of the brain. Finally, this signal travels to the adrenal gland, sitting just above the kidney, which produces cortisol, causing an increase in glucose production to provide additional fuel for the muscles and brain to deal with the stress. This complex series of direct communications between the hypothalamus, pituitary gland, and adrenal gland is known as the hypothalamic-pituitary-adrenal, or HPA, axis, a vital and major part of the neuroendocrine system that controls the reaction to stress, amongst other body processes. Clearly, the simple physical responses to fear are the product of a chain of biological events."[5]

Dr. Demarco goes on to explain some of the physical changes caused by a sense of fear; "When one is confronted by a perceived threat, there are many more physical responses that are less evident, such as: pupil dilation; increased muscle tone; decreased blood flow to the skin, intestine and kidneys; and bowel and bladder emptying"[6] When fear is prolonged and incessant it can become anxiety and cause anxiety attacks as Dr. DeMarco explains; "Often, manifestations called panic attacks can develop. These episodes carry many of the same symptoms as heart attacks, and are often misinterpreted as such. Anxiety can last for as long as the stressor is evident, and it has been linked, through various studies, to a myriad of health issues, such as arthritis, migraines, allergies, and thyroid disease."[7]   The prolonged effect of this fear and anxiety can have devastating effects on us physically, Dr. DeMarco explains: "Most commonly, continuous anxiety has been linked to gastrointestinal problems, such as peptic ulcers. While a mechanism tying these disorders together has yet to be discovered, studies have shown a remarkable correlation of people who have experienced both generalized anxiety disorder, or GAD, and stomach ulcers. Chronic anxiety has also been linked to cardiovascular disease." [8]

The fear we carry in us from being unloving and uncaring a difficult burden to carry, most of the time we deny and ignore the fears we have. Sometimes we turn to activities, even religious activities. Or we turn to substances, that alter our physical and emotional responses; to mask, dampen or deaden the fear.

Every recovery program that I know of begins with an acknowledgement that we have a problem and are in trouble. In most recovery programs in order to recover, we need to admit that we are powerless to overcome the problem and we must admit the need for help from a higher power, a power outside ourselves.

To remember and be reminded, to believe that I AM is LOVE is the most life changing of things to have as a gift in life. To be able to draw near in relationship with LOVE is a life altering phenomenon. The presence of I AM changes us.

In fact, we were fashioned to be like the person we are most close to in relationship. Relational connections change us.

Children take on characteristics of their parents, peers take on characteristics of their companions and married partners take on characteristics of their mates. If it is a very good partnership, a mutually giving, loving partnership will help each of them to take on the best parts of the other. The partners become a better entity together than they would be apart.

In the book PRIMAL LEADERSHIP, the authors say: "Research in intensive care units has shown that the comforting presence of another person not only lowers the patient's blood pressure, but also slows the secretion of fatty acids that block arteries. More dramatically, whereas three or more incidents of intense stress within a year (say, serious financial trouble, being fired, or divorce) triple the death rate in socially isolated idle-aged men, they have no impact whatsoever on the death rate of men who cultivate many close relationships. … one person transmits signals that can alter hormone levels, cardiovascular function, sleep rhythms and even immune function inside the body of another. That's how couples who are in love are able to trigger in one another's brains surges of oxytocin, which creates a pleasant, affectionate feeling. But in all aspects of social life, not just love relationships, our physiologies intermingle, our emotions automatically shifting into the register of the person we're with. The open-loop design of the limbic system means other people can change our very physiology- and so our emotions." [9]

We separate ourselves from Love to our detriment

No wonder I AM said, if you eat of the fruit forbidden by me you will die. To be separated from the giver of live, from LOVE mankind would no longer have access to the tree of life. To break the trust of I AM and our relationship with life and love would cause a process of fear and death to begin. "If you want to go it on your own deciding what you know as the difference between good and evil you must go apart from me", says I AM. "You are subject to your limitedness as a creature, I AM is absolute LOVE and He cannot remain loving in the midst of allowing evil."

We do not recognize how evil unbelief or the guilt of being unloving really is, it destroys our lives. Yet LOVE does not leave us in this spiral of death however,   I   AM continually comes back, time and time and time again in rescue missions. What is meant by saying God is love is not what is often thought.

C. S. Lewis talks about our misconceptions of the love of God; "Of course, what these people mean when they say that God is love is often something quite different: they really mean 'Love is God'. They really mean that our feelings of love, however and wherever they arise, and whatever they arise, and whatever results they produce, are to be treated with great respect. Perhaps they are; but that is something quite different from what Christians mean by the statement 'God is Love'. They believe that the living, dynamic activity of love has been going on in God for ever and has created everything else."[10]

Lets' look deeper into what God is Love means.

It is almost always thought, that in the declaration of the glory of I AM to Moses, the phrase "visiting the iniquity of the fathers on the children and the children's children, to the third and the fourth generation." Is a declaration of continued judgment? I do not agree.

In fact. the Hebrew word here "paqad" can mean visit either for good or bad intention. It can be translated deliver or oversee. In the time of this text it was most often used of visiting a village that had been plundered by marauders in order to see to the needs of the survivors.

Spiros Zodiates in his Lexicon of Old Testament words says of *paqad*, "it's true meaning is an action taken on the part of God which produces a beneficial result for His people.(see Ruth 1:6, I Samuel 2:21 Jeremiah 29:10)" [11] When I AM gives Moses a glimpse of His glory by declaring; Exo 34:6 The LORD passed before him and proclaimed, "The LORD, the LORD, a God merciful and gracious, slow to anger, and abounding in steadfast love and faithfulness, Exo 34:7 keeping steadfast love for thousands, forgiving iniquity and transgression and sin, but who will by no means clear the guilty, visiting the iniquity of the fathers on the children and the children's children, to the third and the fourth generation." Exo 34:8 And Moses quickly bowed his head toward the earth and worshiped. Exo 34:9 And he said, "If now I have found favor in your sight, O Lord, please let the Lord go in the midst of us, for it is a stiff-necked people, and pardon our iniquity and our sin, and take us for your inheritance." Exo 34:10 And he said, "Behold, I am making a covenant. Before all your people I will do marvels, such as have not been created in all the earth or in any nation. And all the people among whom you are shall see the work of the LORD, for it is an awesome thing that I will do with you."

It is clear that Moses believed I AM's presence in the midst of the people was the prerequisite for their survival. It was also clear that I AM was not going to give up on these people even though they had broken the integrity of the relationship. He certainly wasn't going to continue to visit them to their destruction, I AM was going to continue to visit them for their ultimate benefit.

This is the struggle all throughout the history recorded for the people of the book. To have faith in the One who is LOVE. To accept that I AM is the source, and sustainer of a life of love is our continued struggle.

To pursue a renewed relationship with LOVE is the way to life and will result in the removal of fear.

I will let one of the closest followers of Jesus say it more eloquently; 1Jn 4:16 So we have come to know and to believe the love that God has for us. God is love, and whoever abides in love abides in God, and God abides in him. 1Jn 4:17 By this is love perfected with us, so that we may have confidence for the day of judgment, because as he is so also are we in this world. 1Jn 4:18 There is no fear in love, but perfect love casts out fear. For fear has to do with punishment, and whoever fears has not been perfected in love. 1Jn 4:19 We love because he first loved us. 1Jn 4:20 If anyone says, "I love God," and hates his brother, he is a liar; for he who does not love his brother whom he has seen cannot love God whom he has not seen. 1Jn 4:21 And this commandment we have from him: whoever loves God must also love his brother.

For this reason, other writers of the Bible can write in regard to whether to eat foods that were offered to idols, Rom 14:23 "But whoever has doubts is condemned if he eats, because the eating is not from faith. For whatever does not proceed from faith is sin."

Sin, evil; is not essentially the actions of our life, ultimate evil is the rejection of faith that I AM is LOVE. To stop believing or to have a heart full of doubt about I AM breaks connection, for I AM cannot become something He is not or He ceases to be.

The great King David in the Tanakh says this; "Psa 51:4-17 Against you, you only, have I sinned and done what is evil in your sight, so that you may be justified in your words and blameless in your judgment. Behold, I was brought forth in iniquity, and in sin did my mother conceive me. Behold, you delight in truth in the inward being, and you teach me wisdom in the secret heart. Purge me with hyssop, and I shall be clean; wash me, and I shall be whiter than snow. Let me hear joy and gladness; let the bones that you have broken rejoice. Hide your face from my sins, and blot out all my iniquities. Create in me a clean heart, O God, and renew a right spirit within me. Cast me not away from your presence, and take not your Holy Spirit from me. Restore to me the joy of your salvation, and uphold me with a willing spirit. Then I will teach transgressors your ways, and sinners will return to you. Deliver me from bloodguiltiness, O God, O God of my salvation, and my tongue will sing aloud of your righteousness. O Lord, open my lips, and my mouth will declare your praise. For you will not delight in sacrifice, or I would give it; you will not be pleased with a burnt offering. The sacrifices of God are a broken spirit; a broken and contrite heart, O God, you will not despise." I AM wants us to return to relationship with Him in faith. It is this loss of connection, brokenness of relationship that causes death and the fear of death, so we live in fear.

It is my hope to see a picture of I AM in this book that will help build faith, hope and love in us. 1Co 13:13 "So now faith, hope, and love abide, these three; but the greatest of these is love."

If you are Muslim, or a follower of Judaism I pray that references from the Bible will not keep you from continuing on the journey. We all need to begin to learn more of faith and love. If you are an atheist, I ask that you continue to seek for places that might allow you to have faith.

Faith begins in the seeking heart. Jer 29:11-14 "For I know the plans I have for you, declares the LORD, plans for welfare and not for evil, to give you a future and a hope. Then you will call upon me and come and pray to me, and I will hear you. You will seek me and find me, when you seek me with all your heart. I will be found by you, declares the LORD, and I will restore your fortunes…"

Fear is a characteristic of uncertainty which is rooted in the suppression of truth and accompanied by guilt and shame. This "fear" begins with an inability to believe or not having someone to believe in, that is, not having someone who is ultimately good and loving to rely upon. In reality the uncertainty comes from disobeying love as too demanding or hard and believing the lie that you are left to yourself.

Absolute-Love is an eternally passionate commitment to the ultimate benefit of another.

Faith is the characteristic quality of a life that has surrendered to LOVES purposes for them, though unseen and unknown, it includes elements of fear but it is a certain fear that is convinced that if love is not obeyed it would result in the worst possible existence for them.

Primarily the characteristics of faith are born through humility that enables belief, belief builds trust, acceptance, confidence, gratitude, compassion, freedom, stewardship, servanthood, loyalty, purity, justice, rest, and determination.

1. Viscott, David, M. D. ., *EMOTIONAL RESILIENCE,* Harmony Books, Crown Publishers, Inc., 1996, Page 74
2. White, Dr. John, *CHANGING ON THE INSIDE;* Ann Arbor, Mi. Servant Publications: 1991, page 41.
3. Ibid., pages 58-59
4. Peck, M. Scott M.D. *THE ROAD LESS TRAVELED AND BEYOND.* New York, NY, Touchstone Publishing; 1997, page 113-117
5. DeMarco, Dr. Anthony,. *PREEMPTIVE HEALING,* www.preemptivehealing.com
6. Ibid.
7. Ibid.
8. Ibid.
9. Goleman, Daniel; Boyazatis, Richard and McKee, Annie. *PRIMAL LEADRSHIP.* Boston. MA., Harvard Business School Press, 2002, page 7
10. Lewis, C. S. , *MERE CHRISTIANITY,* MacMillan Publishing o., New York, N. Y., 1943, Page 151
11. Zodhiates, Dr. Spiros., *COMPLETE WORD STUDY DICTIONARY,* AMG Publishers, Chattanooga, TN., 1994

CHAPTER FOUR

I AM is ONE

Gen 1:26 Then God said, "Let us make man in our image, after our likeness. And let them have dominion over the fish of the sea and over the birds of the heavens and over the livestock and over all the earth and over every creeping thing that creeps on the earth."

Deu 6:4 "Hear, O Israel: The LORD our God, the LORD is one.

Col 1:15-20 He is the image of the invisible God, the firstborn of all creation. For by him all things were created, in heaven and on earth, visible and invisible, whether thrones or dominions or rulers or authorities—all things were created through him and for him. And he is before all things, and in him all things hold together. And he is the head of the body, the church. He is the beginning, the firstborn from the dead, that in everything he might be preeminent. For in him all the fullness of God was pleased to dwell, and through him to reconcile to himself all things, whether on earth or in heaven, making peace by the blood of his cross.

I AM is not a vague name or incomprehensible, it is however a name beyond fully understanding or of inexhaustible meaning. In Islam, Judaism and Christianity there are many names referring to God, yet all refer to one respective God. There is one God.

No, I am not saying that the characteristics of the one God who is worshipped by all Christians, Jews and Muslims are the same; religions have a way of becoming tied to cultures, language structures and political imperative that color the character of religious expression.

I AM transcends religion, politics and language structures, the one who is Absolute LOVE goes beyond our ability to fully comprehend.

This is why Love should be considered as absolute. We can however really know some things about I AM when it is revealed to us, and Jews, Muslims and Christians all of us are people of the book. We believe that God has revealed some of Himself to us and we agree that full understanding of God is beyond that disclosure. Let us continue our dialogue in the spirit that we agree on these things.

Those who disagree that God can be really known, who claim to be atheists, I have often found, disagree with the idea of God because religion has such a negative history in delivering love and hope to the world in their estimation.

I have found, many of the instances of religious intolerance and hatred can be traced back to when the state (government or political groups) become entwined with and inseparable from religion.

Yet when separated from religious rhetoric controlled by political agenda and moved to a relational context belief in a higher power has a powerful healing effect. In fact, the people of God have often stood against religion, especially government-controlled religion.

Larry Dossey, M. D. in HEALING WORDS relates a study done by a cardiologist, Dr. Randolph Bird who did a study on the effects of prayer on healing. Dr. Byrd studied 393 patients over a ten-month period. In a blind study a computer randomly picked 192 patients who would be prayed for by a home prayer group and 201 patients who would not be remembered in prayer. In any case the fact that people, acting on behalf of political entities for personal gain, have stood behind religion as a justification for injustice, is not a good reason to doubt in Absolute LOVE.

Dr. Dossey writes; "The study was designed according to rigid criteria, the kind usually used in clinical studies in medicine. It was a randomized, double-blind experiment in which neither the patients, nurses, nor doctors knew which group the patients were in. Byrd recruited various religious groups to pray for the designated prayed-for group." What were the results of this study? "Byrd explained. The prayed-for patients differed in several areas; 1. They were five times less likely… to require antibiotics… 2. They were three times less likely to develop pulmonary edema…3. None of the prayed-for group required endotracheal intubation… 4. Fewer patients in the prayed for group died…." Dr. Dossey also relates; "Even some hard-boiled skeptics agreed on the significance of Byrd's findings. Dr. William Nolan, who has written a book debunking faith healing acknowledged, 'It sounds like this study will stand up to scrutiny… maybe we doctors ought to be writing on our order sheets, Pray three times a day.'"[1]

It is as much an argument for Absolute LOVE to say, that when people have no absolute reference point, there is no reason to believe that we should act in a loving manner towards each other.

As   C. S. Lewis writes; "My point is that those who stand outside all judgments of value cannot have any ground for preferring one of their own impulses to another accepts the emotional strength of that impulse. We may legitimately hope that among the impulses which arise in minds thus emptied of all 'rational' or 'spiritual' motives, some will be benevolent…. I am very doubtful whether history shows us one example of a man who, have stepped outside traditional morality and attained power, has used that power benevolently."[2]

In our loss of love, our separation from LOVE we want to control others and be in control ourselves. Science is an effort to find absolute truth, and we should admit that is the nature of discovery, yet the secularization of scientific study as an effort to be objective leaves man to grope in the dark and make many subjective conclusions.

I am not saying scientific methods should be disregarded, but that scientific conclusions may be clouded by limited understanding and overstatement. In other words, scientific theory cannot normally be characterized as absolute.

"The instinct of self-preservation in fallen man seeks fulfillment not by trusting God, and thereby exalting his name, but by employing his own human genius, thereby making a name for himself."; writes Dr. John Piper[3]

In other words, to set up intellect and human discovery as our god: i.e. what we see as the ultimate place to seek for meaning is the same sin as Adam and Eve in the garden. Atheism sets up man and man's intellect as god, which really means the atheist sets themselves up as god, the ultimate arbiter of the knowledge of good and evil.

In his well-written and witty book, WHO MADE GOD, the scientist Edgar Andrews writes: "It is not unreasonable to say that the sole purpose of scientific research is to discover principles or theories that unify human experience. This is extremely valuable because it not only helps to satisfy our curiosity about the world we live in but represents knowledge that can be applied for our benefit. (It can, of course, also be applied to do us harm; science has no built-in morality.) But although scientific theories advance our understanding of the way things work in our universe, they seldom, if ever, trace our experiences and observations back to a priori concepts that need no further explanation. Indeed, in their search for unification they often lead us into profound and inexplicable mysteries-conceptual quagmires…"[4]

Dr. Andrews goes on to show quite convincingly, how science when logically applied, leads us to the same conclusions of the human authors of the Tanakh and the Jewish authors of the New Testament.

"We have no instinctive urge to keep promises or to respect individual life; that is why scruples of justice and humanity – can be properly swept away when they conflict with our real end, the preservation of the species." writes C.S. Lewis.[5]

The individual books of the Bible, a collection of writings from many authors, are truly one story. Here is where we are always brought to: mystery! I AM is mystery, but not totally unknown, I AM is the revealer of self and what is revealed is certainly knowable. Just as in science we can discover much, but there is always more to be revealed.

If, as Christians, Muslims and Jews believe God has revealed Himself to us what do the books agree on? The Koran teaches that the revelations to Moses are from God. In Sura 6:91 "No just estimate of Allah do they make when they say: "Nothing doth Allah send down to man (by way of revelation). " Say: Who then sent down the Book which Moses brought? – a light and guidance to man." The Koran agrees that the Torah ascribed to Moses is sent from God and "a light and a guidance to man. The Koran also acknowledges that Jesus was sent from God: in Sura 5:46-47 "And in their footsteps We sent Jesus the son of Mary, confirming the Law that had come before him; We sent him the Gospel: therein was guidance and light, and confirmation of the Law that had come before him: a guidance and an admonition to those who fear Allah. Let the people of the Gospel judge by what Allah hath revealed therein" Sura 10:94 goes on: If thou wert in doubt as to what We have revealed unto thee, then ask those who have been reading the BOOK from before thee: the Truth hath indeed come to thee from thy Lord, so be in no wise if those in doubt." There is much to agree on here. Muslims who acknowledge the teachings of the Koran should also seek out from the Bible the good news of what is revealed there.

The Jewish authors of the New Testament writings were all searching, and quoting to substantiate their conclusions, from the Tanakh. All three faiths conclude that God is the only God, I AM is one. There is only one self-existent entity that made all things and is in control of all things all of the books agree on this.

Yet revelations mysteriously point to a reality of I AM, being a community, a unified self in three, an organization (organism) of three co-existent and equal entities. The mystery begins in the very first words dictated by Moses. Gen 1:1 "In the beginning, God created the heavens and the earth." The Hebrew word Elohim is meant God, the one God, it is plural in syntax.

Uniquely, Elohim is not dual two, but plural more than two. This is explained by many as a fullness of the one God yet this still leaves mystery.

Even more mystery is added when the Torah relates; Gen 1:26 Then God said, "Let us make man in our image, after our likeness." Here plural God (plural Elohim), the one God says: "let us" (plural) make "in our" (plural). "Gen 1:27 So God created man in his own image, in the image of God he (singular) created him; male and female he created them."

The image of God is here reflected in community, relatedness. Persons are one in kind, essence and form (man or human) but different in role and function. Likeness meant for unity, that is, meant for loving community.

Here indeed is a mystery of how being created as community is being created in the likeness of God.

Peter Toon writes; "The decision by God to create man in his image was an interpersonal decision. Elohim (God in his plurality)... the decision of the Three. Yet the Three acted as one: 'Elohim created man in his own image; in the image of Elohim he created him (where the plural noun takes the singular verbs). If God is simply a monad then he cannot be or known personally. To be personal otherness must be present together with oneness; the one must be in relation to others."[6]

Another author says; "Love is an indefinable term, and its manifestations are both subtle and infinite. But it begins, I believe, with one absolute condition: unlimited liability! As soon as one's liability for another is qualified to any degree, love is diminished by that much.".

Personhood is only a reality where there are relations, relatedness and relationships." [7] Wow, what a mystery! The entire Tanakh reveals God in this way, in this construct. Often with (YHWH, Elohim) or (the Lord, God), (I AM, God (Plural)) followed by a singular verb.

We might ask are there other pointers to this reality? This conclusion is often a separator for religious people, especially if God and religion is tied to political or cultural fear of separation from culture and family. To be relationally attuned to I AM, though is the only way to bring cultures together, to unite.

If we want to have relationship with Absolute LOVE, we must look beyond cultural, political and religious boundaries to I AM as revealed to us.

Eugene Peterson writes; "The world, in fact, is not as it has been represented to us. Things are not all right as they are, and they are not getting any better. We have been told the lie ever since we can remember: that human beings are basically nice and good… How we can keep on believing this after so many centuries of evidence to the contrary is difficult to comprehend, but nothing we do or nothing anyone else does to us seems to disenchant us from the spell of the lie."[8]

Petersen writes further: "The lies are impeccably factual. They contain no errors. There are no distortions or falsified data. But they are lies all the same because they claim to tell us who we are and omit everything about our origin in God and our destiny in God. They talk about the world without telling us that God made it"[9] A world where God is absent is a lie and gives no absolute help to retrieve healthy relationships, to gain community.

Likewise, a religion that is tied to political or cultural tradition apart from relationship with I AM is a lie. I am not pointing fingers at anyone, I am talking about all mankind whether Christians, Muslims or Jews.

People from all religious backgrounds (and not merely the religions formerly named) have in the past, and many now, wrap up their faith in political and cultural fear instead of in the LOVE of I AM. "If you turn your life over to your own concept of God, how do you know whether that concept is powerful enough?

Not the God you are imagining

To help me God has to be more than a concept… . No if I am to turn my life over to God, it must be God as he is. Not God as I conceive him, but God as he conceives himself to be. If there is a God then He is a person, not an idea."[10;] writes Dr. John White

What happened when mankind broke relationship with I AM? We decided we could, apart from relationship with I AM, rightly decide between what was good for us relationally and what was harmful for us relationally. We distort and suppress the truth about ourselves as being unable to be absolutely loving. We have the desire to be loved but not the ability to be absolutely loving.

The Absolute Love of God is an eternally passionate commitment to the ultimate benefit of another.

This is the LOVE that the organizational entities of the ONE I AM (the three in one) demonstrate to one another. This Love overflows from within I AM to all of us though we all reject this love in many ways, this is the sickness of sin. The ability to fully accept this Love was discarded by mankind in the garden.

This is the LOVE only an eternal being could grant. This is the relationship lost through the brokenness of community granted by I AM, love now is temporal and relative, not eternal and absolute. When mankind is separated from, I AM we begin to worship things, created beings, self.

Mankind makes idols, and the exchange we have made is from I AM as an overflowing fountain of the glory of Loving-kindness, to images of ourselves. We have exchanged abounding, overflowing steadfast love with idols to our personal, political and cultural biases. God is not who you imagine.

I AM will not give His glory to another and thereby displace Absolute LOVE. "I will by no means clear the guilty" Ex. 34:7. In that exchange we idolatrous people do terrible things, "Rom1:28-32 And since they did not see fit to acknowledge God, God gave them up to a debased mind to do what ought not to be done. They were filled with all manner of unrighteousness, evil, covetousness, malice. They are full of envy, murder, strife, deceit, maliciousness. They are gossips, slanderers, haters of God, insolent, haughty, boastful, inventors of evil, disobedient to parents, foolish, faithless, heartless, ruthless. Though they know God's decree that those who practice such things deserve to die, they not only do them but give approval to those who practice them."

This sounds like the nightly news, or if you like, a television program watched for evening entertainment. This was written over 2000 years ago. Would the atheist really ask why an Absolutely Loving God would decree death and destruction upon evil people?

Should we not rather ask, "why an Absolutely Loving God continues to give us the grace of life?" This is an absolute blow to the modern cult of intellect, self-esteem and narcissism. A blow to mankind as the final arbiter of good and evil.

To human beings I AM says; You shall not eat of the tree of the knowledge of good and evil". This is I AM's only command, only prescription for life.

Someone may ask; "Well now; in most of the world, there is not a lot of idol worship. We don't have people sacrificing their children or virgins to idols like they did in ancient civilizations. We don't have temple prostitutes, men and women, who were enslaved in the service of idol worshippers like they did in the ancient empires? No, today in the modern world we have more sophisticated idolatries; they are still images of self-worship (creature worship).

In the present-day men, have found more palatable ways to idolize self. When the philosopher Rene Descartes came to his intellectual end and believed that through intellectual reasoning there was no absolute reality, his famous dictum of his own absolute reality was uttered; "I think therefore, I am." Man in his own intellectual wisdom cannot come up with a different answer.

In classes on psychology in college and in seminary the modern idea put forth by the psychologist Abraham Maslow about mankind's hierarchy of needs was put forth. Maslow's hierarchy begins with basic needs of survival i.e. food and shelter and crescendos to the top as self-actualization. How novel an idea! Webster's Dictionary describes self-actualization as "full development of one's abilities." Almost every business seminar and many church seminars I can remember presenters holding up Maslow's pyramid of man's essential needs as gospel truth about our need, and the proper response to that need, as the rebuilding of self-esteem.

The BAKER ENCYCLOPEDIA OF PSYCHOLOGY describes Maslow's claim in developing the hierarchy, that it; "fuses the functional tradition of James and Dewey with the holism of Wertheimer, Goldstein, and Gestalt psychology, as well as the dynamism of Freud, Fromm, Horney, Reich, Jung and Adler"

Further it is stated Maslow was, "convinced that human values can be found within human nature with no need to appeal to external sources." In other words, there is no need for God or absolutes outside of self. Further down it is noted, "Maslow believed that the negative criterion of self-actualization was the absence of neurosis, psychopathic personality, psychosis, or strong tendencies in those directions, and the positive criterion was the full utilization of talents, capacities, and potentialities."[11]

Again, it is said: Maslow himself envisioned a psychological utopia in which all basic human needs would be met, a Taoist, loving society, which he called Eupsychia."[12] Is it any wonder that many psychological theorists move from the area of scientific research to the realms of psychic mystery? Why are we in such a quandary?

Paul Tournier writes, "Why is it, then, that science, which has studied man minutely, for centuries has remained blind to such utterly important phenomena? The answer is that ever since Descartes it has imposed upon itself absolute prejudice: it refused any longer to take into account spiritual and moral realities."[13] I would say this goes back a lot further than Descartes; however, Dr. Tournier is talking about the failure of modern philosophies and psychologies. Dr. Tournier later says, "The modern man, like an adolescent in profound crisis, appears to us to present a strange and contradictory mixture of naïve superstition, disillusioned skepticism, and partisan spirit. For in repressing values, repressing them without having freed himself from them, without being able to free himself from them- he has repressed the very principle of his inner harmony: The Spirit."[14]

Many secular psychologies end up in the place of embracing mystical practices and the mantra of finding "the mystical OTHER" within ourselves. In the vein of inner enlightenment along with Hinduism, Buddhism and Taoism, we find business groups with yoga seminars and sports figures envisioning and thinking into being their inner desires.

The new psychology becomes the same as ancient shamanism and nature worship a new magic. God is not absolute being, but a life force in everything and everyone.

Likewise, LOVE is not absolute being revealed in relationship to I AM, love is unconditional and relative to our level of higher consciousness (Self-Actualization).

I must let J.I. Packer and Thomas Howard speak, they write: "1. Humanism is one mutation of mankind's continuing bid for independence from our Creator and for self-sufficiency in personal and community life. 2. It supposes, confusedly and unrealistically, that this is the highroad to happiness and fulfillment for every human being-even, apparently, the unborn and crippled children and the handicapped and elderly people for whom it has in mind a 'good death'.3. Its exponents, like the rest of men, take their own wisdom and adequacy for granted and do not consider that it might be beyond the power of man as he is to know what is good for him. 4. Its hostility to any thought of acknowledging and listening to and learning from God the Creator and of exchanging intellectual and moral autonomy for 'theonomy' in other words, of humbly becoming subject to God's revelation-expresses not only a recoil from unworthy expressions of religious faith, but ultimately the revolt against serving God which started in Eden and is now instinctive to us all. 5. Its refusal to be serious about personal guilt in any form reflects its ultimate unwillingness to allow that we are answerable to a transcendent and eternal Judge- that deep down we are not good but bad, so we really do have something to answer for. 6. It understands freedom in terms, not of contentment in God, but of what the Roman moralist Seneca called slavery to oneself... and the veneer of its professed concern for society conceals the same single-minded, self-deifying egoism into which Adam and Eve were originally betrayed. 7. For its manipulators and those whom it manipulates alike, humanism points away from the human fulfillment which it rightly seeks. 8. It stands revealed as one form of the broad and attractive man-made roads that leads to final destruction, above and beyond the immoralities it will commit and miseries it will cause here and now if given its head. 9. It is from every standpoint tragic folly; the confident kind of folly that has been parading itself as wisdom ever since the world began."[15]

It seems clear that scientific discovery and human intellect will not save the day, and it will certainly not provide me with ultimate meaning or peace to "go calmly into the night", this is what we must all face.

Edgar Andrews again states; "As we have seen, Einstein and other leading scientists have stressed this difference, pointing out that beneath our scientific descriptions of the universe there may well lie 'realities' that we do not (and perhaps cannot comprehend. And it is possible, even inevitable, that sometimes science's laws and models lead us away from these realities rather than towards them."[16]

I must also stop and say that; neither the belief that ultimate reality (God) is found in all religions nor the belief that my cultural and socio-political God is the actual God will suffice. Neither of these ideas can stand and both lead away from LOVE.

The first will cite the many near death experiences chronicled by the new age mystics and say "see they all report a beautiful, warm light drawing them to itself."

The second will seek to destroy their fellow man in the name of loyalty to God.

I would say history shouts loudly to us that many people claiming to be Christians, Jews and Muslims have violated this revelation of God. "… this means that the command to love is grounded in the nature of God and the way he acts toward people. The love which the Israelites are to render is a love which springs from the greater love they have already been shown by God (Dt 10:15 ff)[17]

The Koran holds a high place for Isa (Yeshua-Jesus) and uses the name "al-Masih" or the "The Messiah", meaning "the anointed one." Yeshua's Jewish followers believed him to be I AM, Mat 16:15 "He said to them, "But who do you say that I am?" Mat 16:16 Simon Peter replied, "You are the Christ (Messiah, anointed one), the Son of the living God." Mat 16:17 And Jesus answered him, "Blessed are you, Simon Bar-Jonah! For flesh and blood has not revealed this to you, but my Father who is in heaven.

Jesus claimed that this is His identity; Joh 4:21-26 Jesus said to her, "Woman, believe me, the hour is coming when neither on this mountain nor in Jerusalem will you worship the Father. You worship what you do not know; we worship what we know, for salvation is from the Jews. But the hour is coming, and is now here, when the true worshipers will worship the Father in spirit and truth, for the Father is seeking such people to worship him. God is spirit, and those who worship him must worship in spirit and truth." The woman said to him, "I know that Messiah is coming (he who is called Christ). When he comes, he will tell us all things." Jesus said to her, "I who speak to you am he."

And Jesus claimed to be the I AM of the Tanakh; Joh 8:52-58 If anyone keeps my word, he will never taste death.' Are you greater than our father Abraham, who died? And the prophets died! Who do you make yourself out to be?" Jesus answered, "If I glorify myself, my glory is nothing. It is my Father who glorifies me, of whom you say, 'He is our God.' But you have not known him. I know him. If I were to say that I do not know him, I would be a liar like you, but I do know him and I keep his word. Your father Abraham rejoiced that he would see my day. He saw it and was glad." So the Jews said to him, "You are not yet fifty years old, and have you seen Abraham?" Jesus said to them, "Truly, truly, I say to you, before Abraham was, I am."

How do we know that Jesus is this messiah? How can we be sure of the accuracy of this testimony of the Jewish man Yeshua who lived long ago? How can we understand His place in the community of three that is I AM, the one God? It is not within the scope of this book to delineate all of these proofs. There are many books written detailing the historical accuracy of the events surrounding this Jewish man Yeshua of Nazareth and there are many empirical studies that point to the historical accuracy of these testimonies, yet in the end there is mystery, and in the end, we must begin the search by faith.

LOVE works into relationship with us through faith; Gal 5:5-6 "For through the Spirit, by faith, we ourselves eagerly wait for the hope of righteousness. For in Christ Jesus neither circumcision nor uncircumcision counts for anything, but only faith working through love."

Circumcision is only outward evidence of faith in the Tanakh, but I AM desires love as an outworking of faith.

Faith is the characteristic quality of a life that has surrendered in humility, to LOVES purposes for them, though unseen and unknown, it includes elements of fear but it is a certain fear that is convinced that if love is not obeyed it would result in the worst possible existence for them. Primarily the characteristics of faith or belief, are trust, acceptance, confidence, gratitude, compassion, freedom, loyalty, justice, servant hood, rest, determination and purity.

Reality cloaked in Mystery

I know there is mystery here. Don't let mystery, be turned to uncertainty. Faith is steeped in certainty, but acknowledges mystery. Absolute LOVE is "THE ONE"; "The Three in One" They are the one and only absolute to whom all others things are relative. This is mystery; however, it is mystery revealed.

Gerald Bray explains; "The language of generation and procession used in the New Testament must be understood in relational terms, not causal ones. This means that in some mysterious way unknown to us, the three persons of the Godhead must have decided to relate to each other in the ways just described. The sonship of the second person is not an accident of birth but the result of a voluntary act—not his alone, but that of all three persons, since they have a single will that is common to them all. Similarly, the identity of the third person is the result of a free choice, made not only by him but by the three persons acting together. Finally, the fatherhood of the first person, though not described in such terms, must also be the result of a free act on the part of all three, a reminder to us of their common mind and purpose. How this can be is a mystery that goes beyond our ability to understand, because it speaks of things that subsist in the eternal being of God, which is incomprehensible to us. When we speak of a "voluntary decision" taken by the three persons acting together, we are using a human concept to explain a divine reality that is worked out in eternity. As far as we are concerned, it has always been like that and always will be—there never was a time when things were or will be otherwise, because there is no time in God. The mutual relationships of the three persons of the Trinity are perfect and all-embracing. The Father loves the Son and the Holy Spirit fully and absolutely, but in a way that is peculiarly appropriate to his identity as the Father. The Son also loves the Father and the Holy Spirit to the same degree, but in a way that is especially indicative of his identity as the Son. The Holy Spirit loves the Father and the Son likewise, but again in a way that brings out the particular nature of his relationship to each of them. This theme is deeply embedded in the Scriptures, but it has never been fully elucidated by theologians, probably because so many of them have been tied to the causation model of Trinitarian relations which makes a balanced presentation of the subject more difficult. As a result, a great deal has been written about the ways in which the Son relates to his Father, but much less about the other way around. There is also a considerable body of literature dealing with the relationship between the Holy Spirit and the Son, but much less about the Spirit's relationship to the Father and almost nothing about the Father's relationship to him."[18]

*For a thoughtful treatise on the relational nature of the One God; see the Addendum of this book; "An Unpublish Essay on the Trinity" by Jonathan Edwards.

1. Dossey, Larry M.D. . *HEALING WORDS; The Power of Prayer and the Practice of Medicine,* Harper Collins, New York, N.Y. , 1993, pages 179-180
2. Lewis, C.S., *THE ABOLITION OF MAN,* MacMillan Publishing Co., Inc., New York, NY. , 1947, page 78
3. Piper, Dr. John. *DESIRING GOD; Confessions of a Christian Hedonist,* Multnomah Publishers, Inc. Sisters, OR. , 1986, page 256

4. Andrews, Edgar., *WHO MADE GOD: Searching For a Theory of Everything,* EP Books USA, Carlisle, PA., 2009, page 31, Faverdale North, Darlington DL3 OPH, England

5. Lewis, C.S., *THE ABOLITION OF MAN: How Education Develops man's Sense of Morality,* MacMillan Publishing, New York, NY. 1947, Pages 44-45

6. Toon, Peter., *OUR TRIUNE GOD: A Biblical Portrayal of the Trinity,* A Bridgepoint Book, Victor Books, SP Publications, Inc. Wheaton, IL., 1996 , page 199.

7. Greenleaf, Robert, *SERVANT LEADERSHIP: A Journey into the nature of Legitimate Power and Greatness,* Paulist Press, San Francisco, CA. 1977   page 38.

8. Peterson, Eugene H.., *A LONG OBEDIENCE IN THE SAME DIRECECTION,* Intervarsity Press, Downers Grove, IL., 1980, page 22

9. Ibid, page 23

10. White, Dr. John, *CHANGING ON THE INSIDE;* Ann Arbor, Mi. Servant Publications: 1991, page 158.

11. Benner, David G. ed., *BAKER ENCYCLOPEDIA OF PSYCHOLOGY,* Baker Book House, Grand Rapids, MI. 1985 page 685.

12. Ibid., page 686

13. Tournier, Dr. Paul., *THE WHOLE PERSON IN A BROKEN WORLD: A Biblical Remedy For Today's World,* Harper and Row Publishers, New York, Hagerstown, San Francisco and London, 1964, pages 13-15, translation from De'sharmonie de La Vie Moderne, Delachau and Nestle' SA, Paris, 1947.

14. Ibid., pages 34-35

15. Packer,   J.   I.   and   Howard,   Thomas., *CHRISTIANITY THE TRUE HUMANISM,* Word Books, Waco, TX., 1985, pages 31-32

16. Andrews, Edgar., *WHO MADE GOD: Searching For a Theory of Everything,* EP Books USA, Carlisle, PA.,

2009, page 141, Faverdale North, Darlington DL3 OPH, England

17. Piper, Dr. John., *LOVE YOUR ENEMIES: Jesus' Love Command in the Synoptic Gospels and the Early Christian Paraenesis,* Cambridge University Press, Paper Back edition Baker Book House, Grand Rapids, MI. page 31.

18. Bray, Gerald., *GOD IS LOVE: A BIBLICAL AND SYSTEMATIC THEOLOGY,* CROSSWAY, Wheaton, IL. 2012 Kindle Edition Pages 115, 116

CHAPTER FIVE

Absolute LOVE Humility

Mic 6:8 He has told you, O man, what is good; and what does the LORD require of you but to do justice, and to love kindness, and to walk humbly with your God?

Php 2:5 -11 Have this mind among yourselves, which is yours in Christ Jesus, who, though he was in the form of God, did not count equality with God a thing to be grasped, but emptied himself, by taking the form of a servant, being born in the likeness of men. And being found in human form, he humbled himself by becoming obedient to the point of death, even death on a cross. Therefore God has highly exalted him and bestowed on him the name that is above every name, so that at the name of Jesus every knee should bow, in heaven and on earth and under the earth, and every tongue confess that Jesus Christ is Lord, to the glory of God the Father.

My own paraphrase of Micah 6:8 in the Tanakh or Old Testament of The Bible; "He has shown you, mankind, what will bring gladness and wellness, I mean the way to follow I AM, it is to do all you do focus on these things, acts of bringing about justice to others, having a passionate desire for absolute love, and to be continually, humbly conversant with the I AM YAHWEH."

When I AM the three in one (Elohim-Yahweh) finished the initial creation of the world, "it was very good". What I AM had made was an intricate, detailed design that pointed to his glory. The glory of the creator was very good for the creation.

The creation flourished under absolute LOVE. Do you remember how I AM passed by declaring the glory that belonged to Him to Moses? I AM declared, "I will have mercy, upon whom I have mercy" I will not give up my sovereignty it would be a violation of steadfast love, which is His passion.

He promised, He would not leave the guilty unpunished, it would diminish His love to sentimentality. It would be an ultimately unloving act to not pursue justice for betrayal and hatred towards Himself and His created goodness.

Leon Morris writes "In modern times we often confuse love with sentimentality, and we do not see as clearly as the prophets did that there is a stern side to real love. An easy sentimentality will decline to take stern action when the beloved does what is wrong. But this leaves the beloved secure in wrong doing, unfairly confirming the very action that makes him less of a person. Because sentimentality refuses to do what is distasteful, it ignores the long-term benefits of reproving the beloved; because it sees that he will dislike the immediate unpleasantness. Sentimentality thus takes the easy way out.

But the more one loves, the more one hates the things that prevent the beloved from enjoying the fullest and most abundant life. And if these are really hated, then every effort will be made to see that they are put away. . ..

True love will lead the you to the best possible path. We walk off the path. And that will mean that from time to time correctional measures will be taken. The Bible clearly points out that God disciplines his people to deter them from destructive sin.

The Old Testament saints did not doubt that the sufferings and trials of this life are meaningful. They evidence that God does love his people. They are his way of bringing his people out of their petty sins and leading them along the way of right into the place of blessing."[1]

The absolute revealing of His glory was, I AM, the three in one; I AM overflowing (abounding) with loving-kindness. I AM merciful and gracious; I forgive perverse acts, rebellious acts and offences. This has to be the most beautiful picture of absolute LOVE placed before our eyes.

When Abraham Maslow talked about the hierarchy of mankind's needs, the top of the hierarchy was not self-actualization as it is popularized in psychology and business. Maslow believed the top of the hierarchy was an aesthetic need, the craving to experience pure beauty.

In the Baker Encyclopedia of Psychology we read; "In contrasting healthy with unhealthy growth Maslow used the terms Being-cognition and Deficiency cognition and the correlative concepts of B-Love and D-Love." Being-Love was the healthy growth that emerged from a self-actualized individual. It is further stated; "Peak experiences, common with self-actualizing people, include aesthetic, creative, love, insight and mystical experiences."[2]

Compelling us to come follow Love

In contrast to the vision of Maslow, John Piper writes in his book, THINK; "I use the phrase 'compellingly beautiful' to shift our focus from slight pointers to solid reasons; … You cannot merely decide to love classical music-or country western music—much less God. The music must be compelling. Something must change inside you. The change makes possible the awakening of a compelling sense of its attractiveness. So, it is with God. You do not merely decide to love him. Something changes inside you, and as a result he becomes compellingly attractive. His glory-his beauty- compels your admiration and delight. He becomes your supreme treasure. You love him."[3]

Beauty is all around. Aesthetics, beauty, nature, man, creation, the world was made very good. It is marred now, but we can see beauty everywhere. Whether you look to unseen truths, evidenced in cell structure, (we humans are made up of over 75 trillion cells), studies in DNA and human genomes, (we have about 34,000 genes in our makeup); or studying the galaxies and the extent of the universe (over 100 billion stars in our galaxy and over 40 billion known galaxies).

Within our Universe and outside there are myriads of awe-inspiring discoveries that have been observed and are being observed.

We cannot see them if we are focused on ourselves.

The person with a microscope or a telescope both experience awe and unspeakable beauty, intricacy, aesthetic delights. The person who stands on a high bluff or 10,000 feet above the earth on a mountain and the person who looks upon a new born baby are often overwhelmed by the sheer and immense majesty of what they look upon.

The main common denominator between these things is they make us forget about self. What we experience at such times of awe, wonder and beauty is not something worked up within us, it is a change that comes over us.

This beauty is what I AM, the three in one experience at all times, have experienced from eternity. Isa 57:15 "For thus says the One who is high and lifted up, who inhabits eternity, whose name is Holy: "I dwell in the high and holy place, and also with him who is of a contrite and lowly spirit, to revive the spirit of the lowly, and to revive the heart of the contrite." Psa 147:6 "The LORD lifts up the humble; he casts the wicked to the ground." I AM, the three in one, gives no dwelling thought to distinction of presence, power, place or perfection of self as the individual persons of the entity that is I AM. The persons are only ever distinct in role or function. Sometimes "The word of I AM", sometimes "The messenger of I AM", sometimes "the Spirit of I AM"; or Father, Son and Holy Spirit; or YHWH Elohim (I AM the three in one). No distinction of presence, power, place or perfection only eternal existence.

The individual persons of I AM do not demean or down grade themselves, they are simply, only, eternally focused upon one another. The three look fully upon the glory of the others and eternal love overflows outside of themselves from the beauty and glory of the others, so that there is no thought of self. This is the essence of humility, healthy God like humility. 1Co 13:4-7 "Love is patient and kind; love does not envy or boast; it is not arrogant or rude. It does not insist on its own way; it is not irritable or resentful; it does not rejoice at wrongdoing, but rejoices with the truth. Love bears all things, believes all things, hopes all things, endures all things."

This is the image of God, humility displayed in LOVE, that Adam and Eve lost by the rebellion in the garden. Romans 3:23 My own paraphrase; "we all have missed the mark, falling short of displaying the glory of the image of God."

We lost the simplicity of this awe filled beauty, all of us, when we turned away from seeing the LOVE of I AM as the most glorious beauty.

The beauty of the image of God is now diminished in us, perverted and marred because we all have taken our eyes off I AM and sought to know what is best on our own. The result is sickness and death.

As Dr. Paul Tournier has written; "The reader may object, however, that everybody comes up against difficulties in life- disappointments, remorse, injustice, conflicts- but everybody does not fall ill. The truth is that we all experience functional disturbances in varying degrees of intensity and persistence. If we examine closely the psychological reactions which are interfering with the normality of behavior in a neurotic, we are compelled that they are not of a different kind of our own, but merely more intense: they are still, fear, jealousy, susceptibility, anger, dissimulation, self-pity, sentimentality, erotic desire, and depression. What characterizes the neurotic is the fact that the very intensity of his reactions sets up a vicious circle from which he is unable to escape on his own."[4]

Psychology may be somewhat helpful to restore function to being less interruptive but the answers of theories of psychology must still be presented as practice, as medicine, and all sciences must be considered as practice and theory, not absolute reality. In MODERN PSYCHO-THERAPIES the authors note; "A recent work identified 260 distinct schools of psychotherapy."[5]

There is hardly a consensus of truth in psychology. Maslow's hierarchy of needs must be turned on its head.

I am amazed at how many people who have nothing in this world, basic needs barely being met, who are contentedly happy with family, friends and God, they find the beauty of relational love.

I am equally taken back by how many learned, wealthy, "self-sufficient" people are discontent, unhappy and self-absorbed.

To view the wonders of God's nature as awesome and beautiful, full of wonder, whether viewing though microscope, telescope or standing on the crest of a hill. In viewing to see the various and resplendent pointers to the creator, I AM. Finally allowing that beauty to be contemplated in the revelations of I AM in the life of (Yeshua, Isa, Jesus of Nazareth).

The habit, the folly, the missing of the mark is hard to break away from. We are captivated by our choice to turn to ourselves. We are trapped by turning to worshiping the creation rather that the creator. Scientists rely on their intellectual prowess and devise ways to raise their standing in the scientific community. Religious followers set up outward idols and meaningless religious activity in order to build standing among other religious followers. In the midst of this is the stench of death.

How will we be freed from the curse of establishing our own knowledge of good and evil? Romans 6:23 my own paraphrase, "How you get rewarded by missing the mark is death (the ever more difficult task of establishing glory for yourself), however God's free gift, (fellowship with I AM), is perpetual abundant living which is found in Christ Jesus the I AM." Amazingly, wonderfully beautiful, this perpetual abundant happens to us by looking at, learning of, following after I AM-Yeshua, Isa, Jesus.

Paul Tournier says; "What remains of genuineness to our life is what comes from God and not from ourselves, from His grace and not from our own merits. This may be the appropriate but humiliating return to oneself to which He leads us by psychoanalysis. God has dealings with us: He speaks to us: He acts within us and lays hold of us. When this is experienced, we know there is genuineness, the sole genuine content, which alone is of vale and is sufficient for us, and that we can now abandon all those values by which we thought to gain merit before Him."[6]

Tournier later says; "Anyone who claims to love without limit does not know what love is; for one who knows it truly admits that he is incapable of it. But this, behavior of patients shows the vital need we all have of finding something absolute upon which we can count absolutely, something unfailing which gives the lie to all the relativities life teaches us through many sufferings, wherein every trust has its limits, every hope its disappointments, every friendship its eclipse. The absolute is God; and what our patients are looking for when they put us to the test…is at least some reflection of God, of a love which goes beyond mere convention; and it is roof that they all seek God, even without knowing it."[7]

The beginning of returning to LOVE, of learning from and looking to I AM is humility.

Humility, of course, it is said that as soon as you believe you have achieved it you have lost it. This is a misunderstanding of humility, the humility that I AM displays.

Humility in I AM the three in one is the overflow of love between the persons, who look upon one another and are not focused on themselves. This humility allows them to give and receive from each other. The Father gives and receives from the Son. The Son gives and receives from the Father. Both the Father and Son give and receive from the Spirit. Giving and receiving, looking only at the other and not self, overflows through love, in creation and also to sustaining the creation.

This is the special love of I AM displayed by mercy. I am says: Mat 11:28 "Come to me, all who labor and are heavy laden, and I will give you rest." And Jas 4:1"What causes quarrels and what causes fights among you? Is it not this, that your passions are at war within you? Jas 4:2-10 You desire and do not have, so you murder. You covet and cannot obtain, so you fight and quarrel. You do not have, because you do not ask. You ask and do not receive, because you ask wrongly, to spend it on your passions. You adulterous people! Do you not know that friendship with the world is enmity with God? Therefore, whoever wishes to be a friend of the world makes himself an enemy of God. Or do you suppose it is to no purpose that the Scripture says, "He yearns jealously over the spirit that he has made to dwell in us"? But he gives more grace. Therefore it says, "God opposes the proud, but gives grace to the humble." "Submit yourselves therefore to God. Resist the devil, and he will flee from you. Draw near to God, and he will draw near to you. Cleanse your hands, you sinners, and purify your hearts, you double-minded. Be wretched and mourn and weep. Let your laughter be turned to mourning and your joy to gloom. Humble yourselves before the Lord, and he will exalt you."

Humility is then not something that is a means to be less than, it is a means to be more.

Humility is not self-effacing or self-denigrating; it is looking away from self. If we draw near to I AM, I AM will draw close to us. If we take our eyes off ourselves turn our mindfulness toward I AM, I AM will exalt us.

Love always turns us to focus on the Lover and the love that is being given.

Mercifulness is Loves' evidence in humility of, I AM the three in one, that allows for the free gift of providing justices demand so that absolute LOVE can remain true. This is summarized for us in the revealing; Php 2:3-11 "Do nothing from rivalry or conceit, but in humility count others more significant than yourselves. Let each of you look not only to his own interests, but also to the interests of others. Have this mind among yourselves, which is yours in Christ Jesus, who, though he was in the form of God, did not count equality with God a thing to be grasped, but made himself nothing, taking the form of a servant, being born in the likeness of men. And being found in human form, he humbled himself by becoming obedient to the point of death, even death on a cross. Therefore, God has highly exalted him and bestowed on him the name that is above every name, so that at the name of Jesus every knee should bow, in heaven and on earth and under the earth, and every tongue confess that Jesus Christ is Lord, to the glory of God the Father."

Jesus fully relied upon The Father, not taking any of the focus on Himself. 1Pe 2:19-24 "For this is a gracious thing, when, mindful of God, one endures sorrows while suffering unjustly. For what credit is it if, when you sin and are beaten for it, you endure? But if when you do good and suffer for it you endure; this is a gracious thing in the sight of God. For to this you have been called, because Christ also suffered for you, leaving you an example, so that you might follow in his steps. He committed no sin, neither was deceit found in his mouth. When he was reviled, he did not revile in return; when he suffered, he did not threaten, but continued entrusting himself to him who judges justly. He himself bore our sins in his body on the tree, that we might die to sin and live to righteousness. By his wounds you have been healed."

Because Jesus was the fully obedient man, who always looked to The Father and The Spirit for what was good and what was evil, not focusing on self and because Jesus was. I AM, he was perfectly fitted to mesh justice and love, in humility and mercy.

Richard P. McBrien writes "If love is the soul of Christian existence, it must be at the heart of every other virtue. Thus, for example, justice without love is legalism; faith without love is ideology; hope without love is self-centeredness; forgiveness without love is self-abasement; fortitude without love is recklessness; generosity without love is extravagance; care without love is mere duty; fidelity without love is servitude. No virtue is really a virtue unless it is permeated, or informed, by love."[8]

For us then, Humility is the characteristic of believing that gives us the ability to admit our needs, weaknesses and limitations so that we can submit to the power of God in our life and receive our strength from Him and through others, it is not powerlessness, it is knowing where the power comes from. Humility enables belief.

C.S. Lewis writes of our misconceptions of humility as it relates to being loving; "All those expressions of unworthiness which Christian practice puts into the believer's mouth seem to the outer world like the degraded and insincere grovel lings of a sycophant before a tyrant, or at best a facon de parler like the self-depreciation of a Chinese gentleman when he calls himself "this coarse and illiterate person." In reality, however, they express the continually renewed, because continually necessary, attempt to negate that misconception of ourselves and of our relation to God which nature, even while we pray, is always recommending to us. No sooner do we believe that God loves us than there is an impulse to believe that He does so, not because He is LOVE, but because we are intrinsically lovable. The Pagans obeyed this impulse unabashed; a good man was "dear to the gods" because he was good. We, being better taught, resort to subterfuge. Far be it from us to think that we have virtues for which God could love us. But then, how magnificently we have repented!

As Bunyan says, describing his first illusory conversion, "I thought there was no man in England that pleased God better than I."

Beaten out of this, we next offer our own humility to God's admiration. Surely He'll like that? Or if not that, our clear-sighted and humble recognition that we still lack humility.

Thus, depth beneath depth and subtlety within subtlety, there remains some lingering idea of our own, our very own, attractiveness. It is easy to acknowledge, but almost impossible to realize for long, that we are mirrors whose brightness, if we are bright, is wholly derived from the sun that shines upon us. Surely, we must have a little-however little-native luminosity? Surely, we can't be quite creatures.

For this tangled absurdity of a Need. Even a Need-love, which never fully acknowledges its own neediness, Grace substitutes a full, childlike and delighted acceptance of our Need, a joy in total dependence. We become "jolly beggars." The good man is sorry for the sins which have increased his Need. He is not entirely sorry for the fresh Need they have produced. And he is not sorry at all for the innocent Need that is inherent in his creaturely condition. For all the time this illusion to which nature clings as her last treasure, this pretense that we have anything of our own or could for one hour retain by our own strength any goodness that God may pour into us, has kept us from being happy. We have been like bathers who want to keep their feet-or one foot-or one toe-on the bottom, when to lose that foothold would be to surrender themselves to a glorious tumble in the surf. The consequences of parting with our last claim to intrinsic freedom, power, or worth, are real freedom, power and worth, really ours just because God gives them and because we know them to be(in another sense) not "ours" . . . .

But God also transforms our Need-love for one another, and it requires equal transformation. In reality we all need at times, some of us at most times, that Charity from others which, being Love Himself in them, loves the unlovable. But this, though a sort of love we need, is not the sort we want. We want to be loved for our cleverness, beauty, generosity, fairness, usefulness. The first hint that anyone is offering us the highest love of all is a terrible shock. This is so well recognized that spiteful people will pretend to be loving us with Charity precisely because they know that it will wound us. To say to one who expects a renewal of Affection, Friendship, or Eros, "I forgive you as a Christian" is merely a way of continuing the quarrel. Those who say it are of course lying. But the thing would not be falsely said in order to wound unless, if it were true, it would be wounding.

How difficult it is to receive, and to go on receiving from others a love that does not depend on our own attraction can be seen from an extreme case. Suppose yourself a man struck down shortly after marriage by an incurable disease which may not kill you for years; useless, impotent, hideous disgusting; dependent on your wife's earnings; impoverishing where you hoped to enrich; impaired even in intellect and shaken by gusts of uncontrollable temper, full of unavoidable demands. And suppose your wife's care and pity to be inexhaustible. The man who can take this sweetly, who can receive all and give nothing without resentment, who can abstain even from those tiresome self-depreciations which are really a demand for petting and reassurance, is doing something which Need-love in its merely natural condition could not attain. . . . But what the extreme example illustrates is universal. We are all receiving Charity. There is something in each of us that cannot be naturally loved. It is no one's fault if they do not so love it. Only the lovable can be naturally loved. You might as well ask people to like the taste of rotten bread or the sound of a mechanical drill. We can be forgiven, and pitied, and loved in spite of it, with Charity; no other way. All who have good parents, wives, husbands, or children, may be sure that at times-and perhaps at all times in respect of some one particular trait or habit- they are receiving Charity, are loved not because they are lovable but because Love Himself is in those who love them."[9]

Humility is the beginning of faith that LOVE works in us as we look outside of ourselves to I AM. Humility involves being able to give to others but also to receive from others as we keep our eyes fixed on I AM and thereby become more like Him in love. The Key Element of humility is mercifulness. Isa Al-Masih, Yeshua born of the lineage of David, Jesus of Nazareth said; Mat 5:3 "Blessed are the poor in spirit, for theirs is the kingdom of heaven."

Aniy (Humble, poor, afflicted, weak, lowly) **Exo** 22:25.**Lev** 19:10,23:22,**Deu** 15:11,24:12, 24:14,24:15, 2 **Sam** 22:28, **Job** 24:9,24:14,29:12,34:28,36:6,36:15,**Psa**9:12,9:18,10:2,10:9,10:12 ,10:17,12:5,14:6,18:27,22:24,25:16,34:2,34:6,35:10,37:14,40:10, 69:29,69:32,70:5,72:2,72:4,72:12,74:19,74:21,82:3,86:1,88:5,10 2:1,109:16,109:22,140:12,**Prov**3:34,14:2,15:15,16:19,22:22,30:1 4,31:9,31:20,**Eccl**6:8,**Isa**3:14,3:15,10:2,10:30,14:32,26:6,32:7,4 1:17,49:13,51:21,54:11,58:7,66:2,**Jer**22:16,**Ezek**16:49,18:12,18: 17,22:29,

Amos 8:4,**Hab** 3:14,Zep 3:12,Zec 7:10,9:9,11:7,11:11

Anav (Humble, Meek, Needy, Poor) **Num** 12:3,**Job** 24:4,Psa 9:18, 22:26, 25:9,37:11,76:9, 147:6,149:4,**Prov** 14:21, Isa 11:4,29:19,32:7,61:1,Amos 2:7,8:4, **Zep** 2:3

Anavah (Humility) Psa 18:35,Prov 15:33, 18:12,22:4,**Zep 2**:3

Anah (Bowed down, Afflicted, Humble) **Gen**15:13,16:6,16:9,31:50,34:2,**Exo**1:11,1:12,10:3,22:22,22:23, 32:18,Lev 16:29,16:31,23:27,23:29,23:32,

Num24:24,29:7,30:13**Deu**8:2,8:3,8:16,21:14,22:24,22:29,26:6, **Judg**16:5,16:6,16:19,19:24,20:5,**2Sam**7:10,13:12,13:14,13:22,1 3:32,22:36,1 Ki 2:26,8:35,11:39,**2 Ki** 17:20, 2 **Chr** 6:26,**Ezra** 8:21,**Job**30:11,37:23,**Psa**35:13,55:19,88:7,89:22,90:15,94:5,102: 23,105:18,107:17,116:10,119:67,119:71,119:75,119:107,132:1**E ccl**1:13,3:10,**Isa**27:2,31:4,53:4,53:7,58:3,58:5,58:10,60:14,64:12

Lam 3:33,5:11,**Ezek** 22:10,22:11, **Dan 10:12**,

Nahum 1:12,Zep 3:19,**Zec** 10:2

Tapeinos (humble, low, undistiguished, pliant, bow down, modest) **Mat 11:29**,Luke 1:52, **Rom** 12:16, 2 **Cor** 7:6,10:1,**James** 1:9,4:6,1 **Pet** 5:5

Tapeinophrosune Acts 20:19, **Eph** 4:2,**Phil 2:3**,Col 2:18,2:23,3:12,1 **Pet** 5:5

Tapeinoo Mat 18:4,23:12,**Luke** 3:5, 14:11,18:14, **2 Cor** 11:7,12:21,**Phil 2:7,2:8**,4:12,**James 4:10,1 Pet 5:6**

Tapeinosis Luke 1:48,**Acts** 8:33,**Phil** 3:21,**James** 1:10

1. Morris, Leon., *TESTAMENTS OF LOVE; A Study of Love in the Bible,* Wm. B. Eerdmans Publishing Co., Grand Rapids, MI., 1981 , Page 25

2. Benner, David G. ed., *BAKER ENCYCLOPEDIA OF PSYCHOLOGY,* Baker Book House, Grand Rapids, MI. 1985 page 685.

3. Piper, Dr. John., *THINK; The Life of the Mind and the Love of God,* Desiring God Foundation; Crossway Publishers, Wheaton, IL. 2010, Pages 86,87.

4. Tournier, Dr. Paul., *THE HEALING OF PERSONS,* Harper and Row Publishers, New York, NY. 1965, page 46

5. Jones, Stanton L. and Butman, Richard E.., *MODERN PSYCHOTHERAPIES,* Intervarsity Press, Downers Grove, IL. , 1991, Page 11

6. Tournier, Dr. Paul., *GUILT AND GRACE; A Psychological Study,* Harper and Row Publishers, New York, Evanston and London, 1969, page 131, English Translation by Arthur W. Hethcote, Asst. by J.J. Henry and P.J. Allcock, Originally Published Switzerland, 1958, Delachaux and Nestle'

7. Ibid., page 193

8. McBrien, Richard P.., *Catholicism,* CHRISTIANITY TODAY, www.ctlibrary.com, January 8th, 1996.

9. Lewis, C.S.., *THE FOUR LOVES; in The Inspirational Writings Of C. S. Lewis,* Inspirational Press, New York, NY. 1960 by Helen Joy Lewis, pages 283-284

Chapter 6

Belief and Trust

Heb 11:1 Now faith is the assurance of things hoped for, the conviction of things not seen.

Heb 11:6 And without faith it is impossible to please him, for whoever would draw near to God must believe that he exists and that he rewards those who seek him.

1Jn 4:7 - 8 Beloved, let us love one another, for love is from God, and whoever loves has been born of God and knows God. Anyone who does not love does not know God, because God is love.

When mankind denies there is a God, or replaces I AM the three in one with a created or imagined substitute, truth is suppressed psychologically and emotions are repressed.

The outcome of suppressing the truth is living a lie, being ashamed and hiding from truth.

Gen 3:7-10 "Then the eyes of both were opened, and they knew that they were naked. And they sewed fig leaves together and made themselves loincloths. And they heard the sound of the LORD God walking in the garden in the cool of the day, and the man and his wife hid themselves from the presence of the LORD God among the trees of the garden. But the LORD God called to the man and said to him, "Where are you?" And he said, "I heard the sound of you in the garden, and I was afraid, because I was naked, and I hid myself."

David Wells writes, "It is no coincidence, then that this generation knows a lot about failed relationships and has experienced the moral ambiguity that modern culture inflicts upon those who feast at its table. For this generation, in particular, codependency groups and twelve step programs have offered the way out. They provide relationships, a community, and people who will listen- and a safe environment....

In these groups, it is assumed, and often explicitly stated, that our innate drives tend not toward destruction, but toward growth, health and happiness; and that society is burdensome and oppressive to the self. ... The inevitable outcome of treating the self as the locus of meaning and of all moral values, however, is that both meaning and values become relative to each self. If self-consciousness is private, unique and individualized, then moral values, if they arise in the self, are as private and individualized as the self in which they reside. A sense of responsibility toward anyone outside the self dies, as does integrity- that moral quality which secures continuity between what is said or done in one moment and what is said or done in the future."[1]

The outcome of repressed emotions is an inner upheaval that rebels against us physically and emotionally in pain and in a darkened, deadened, perverted mind or process of thought. Instead of lifting up our worth as created in the image of I AM, we relate worth to subjective thought and perceived beneficial activity. Paradoxically, lifting up self invites us to devalue other people and more often than not devalue ourselves. Looking away from ourselves, outward to love I AM and love others, forgetting self. Mar 12:29-31 Jesus answered, "The most important is, 'Hear, O Israel: The Lord our God, the Lord is one. And you shall love the Lord your God with all your heart and with all your soul and with all your mind and with all your strength.' The second is this: 'You shall love your neighbor as yourself.' There is no other commandment greater than these."

The setting up of our own idea of health and happiness has been the greatest failure to achieve what we seek as mankind.

Richard Keyes says; "Idolatry may not involve explicit denials of God's existence or character. It may well come in the form of over attachment to something that is, in itself, perfectly good. The crucial warning is this: As soon as our loyalty to anything else leads us to disobey God, we are in danger of making it an idol.

As we will see, an idol need not be a full-sized replacement for God, for nothing can be. An Idol is something or someone we become increasingly attached to until it comes between us and God, making God remote and His commandments irrelevant or unrealistically prohibitive. In this society, our idols tend to be in clusters. They are inflationary, have short shelf lives, change, adapt, and multiply quickly as if by mitosis, or cell division. An idol can be a physical object, a property, a person, an activity, a role, an institution, a hope, an image, a pleasure, a hero –anything that can substitute for God. …

To summarize, idols will inevitably involve self-centeredness, self-inflation and self-deception. Idolatry begins with counterfeiting of God, because only with a counterfeit God can people remain the center of their lives and loyalties, autonomous architects of their futures. …But a counterfeit is a lie, not the real thing. It must present itself through self-deception, often with images suggesting that the idol will fulfill promises for the good life."[2]

In our pursuit of happiness, we look outside of ourselves in humility, humility is the first step on the way to love. We as creatures look to I AM, as our creator to find fulfillment the kind of joy and happiness that doesn't come from anything outside of Him. Likewise, I AM looks only within Himself to find, happiness, love, fulfillment.

John Piper writes; "How we view God will determine our idea of how we can please God. And how a person decides to try to please God is the most fateful decision a person can ever make. What if you discovered (like the Pharisees did), that you had devoted your whole life to trying to please God, but all the while you had been doing things that in God's sight were abominations (Luke 16:14-15)? Someone may say, "I don't think that's possible; God wouldn't reject a person who has been trying to please him." But do you see what the questioner has done? He has based his conviction about what would please God on His idea of what God is like. That is precisely why we must begin with the character of God. That is why we begin with the pleasures of God in Himself.

…God has no deficiencies that I might be required to supply. He is complete in himself. He is overflowing with happiness in the fellowship of the Trinity. The upshot of this is that God is a mountain spring, not a watering trough. A mountain spring is self-replenishing. It constantly overflows and supplies others. But a watering trough needs to be filled with a pump or bucket brigade. So if you want to glorify the worth of the watering rough you work hard to keep it full and useful. But if you want to glorify the worth of the spring you do it by getting down on your hands and knees and drinking to your heart's satisfaction, until you have the refreshment and strength to go back down in the valley and tell the people what you've found. You do not glorify a mountain spring by dutifully hauling water up the path from the river below and dumping it in the spring. What we have seen is God is like a mountain spring, not a watering trough. And since God is the way God is, we are not surprised to learn from Scripture- and our faith is strengthened to hold fast- that the way to please God is to come to him to get and not to give, to drink and not to water. He is most glorified in us when we are most satisfied in him.

My hope as a desperate sinner, who lives in a Death Valley desert of unrighteousness, hangs on this biblical truth that Gods the kind of God who will be pleased with the one thing I have to offer- my thirst. That is why the sovereign freedom and self-sufficiency of God are so precious to me:

they are the foundation of my hope that God is delighted not by the resourcefulness of bucket brigades, but by the bending down of broken sinner to drink at the fountain of grace. . . .

In other words, this unspeakable good news for helpless sinners- that God delights not when we offer him our strength but when we wait for his- this good news that I need to hear so badly again and again, is based firmly on a vision of God as sovereign, self-sufficient and free. If we do not have this foundational vision of God in place when we ask how we can please him, it is almost certain that our efforts to please him will become subtle means of self-exaltation, and end in the oppressive bondage of legalistic strivings."[3]

Jonathan Edwards in an unpublished essay on the Trinity lays out for us a clear picture of how the one God, I AM is perfectly content in the belief and trust of Himself.

"And this I suppose to be that blessed Trinity that we read of in the Holy Scriptures. The Father is the Deity subsisting in the prime, un-originated and most absolute manner, or the Deity in its direct existence. The Son is the Deity generated by God's understanding, or having an idea of Himself and subsisting in that idea. The Holy Ghost is the Deity subsisting in act, or the Divine essence flowing out and breathed forth in God's Infinite love to and delight in Himself. And I believe the whole

Divine essence does truly and distinctly subsist both in the Divine idea and Divine love, and that each of them are properly distinct Persons."…

"Hereby we see how the Father is the fountain of the Godhead, and why when He is spoken of in Scripture He is so often, without any addition or distinction, called God, which has led some to think that He only was truly and properly God. Hereby we may see why in the economy of the Persons of the Trinity the Father should sustain the dignity of the Deity, that the Father should have it as His office to uphold and maintain the rights of the Godhead and should be God not only by essence, but as it were, by His economical office. Hereby is illustrated the doctrine of the Holy Ghost. Proceeding [from] both the Father and the Son. Hereby we see how that it is possible for the Son to be begotten by the Father and the Holy Ghost to proceed from the Father and Son, and yet that all the Persons should be Co-eternal. Hereby we may more clearly understand the equality of the Persons among themselves, and that they are every way equal in the society or family of the three.

They are equal in honor: besides the honor which is common to them all, viz., that they are all God, each has His peculiar honor in the society or family. They are equal not only in essence, but the

Father's honor is that He is, as it were, the Author of perfect and Infinite wisdom. The Son's honor is that He is that perfect and Divine wisdom itself the excellency of which is that from whence arises the honor of being the author or Generator of it. The honor of the Father and the Son is that they are infinitely excellent, or that from them infinite Excellency proceeds; but the honor of the Holy Ghost is equal for He is that Divine excellency and beauty itself.

'Tis the honor of the Father and the Son that they are infinitely holy and are the fountain of holiness, but the honor of the Holy Ghost is that holiness itself. The honor of the Father and the Son is [that] they are infinitely happy and are the original and fountain of happiness and the honor of the Holy Ghost is equal for He is infinite happiness and joy itself.

The honor of the Father is that He is the fountain of the Deity as He from Whom proceed both the Divine wisdom and also excellency and happiness. The honor of the Son is equal for He is Himself the Divine wisdom and is He from Whom proceeds the Divine excellency and happiness, and the honor of the Holy Ghost is equal for He is the beauty and happiness of both the other Persons.

By this also we may fully understand the equality of each Person's concern in the work of redemption, and the equality of the Redeemed's concern with them and dependence upon them, and the equality and honor and praise due to each of them. Glory belongs to the Father and the Son that they so greatly loved the world: to the Father that He so loved that He gave His Only Begotten Son: to the Son that He so loved the world as to give up Himself.

But there is equal glory due to the Holy Ghost for He is that love of the Father and the Son to the world. Just so much as the two first Persons glorify themselves by showing the astonishing greatness of their love and grace, just so much is that wonderful love and grace glorified Who is the Holy Ghost. It shows the Infinite dignity and excellency of the Father that the Son so delighted and prized His honor and glory that He stooped infinitely low rather than [that] men's salvation should be to the injury of that honor and glory.

It showed the infinite Excellency and worth of the Son that the Father so delighted in Him that for

His sake He was ready to quit His anger and receive into favor those that had [deserved?] infinitely ill at His Hands, and what was done shows how great the excellency and worth of the Holy Ghost Who is that delight which the Father and the Son have in each other: it shows it to be Infinite. So great as the worth of a thing delighted in is to any one, so great is the worth of that delight and joy itself which he has in it.

Our dependence is equally upon each in this office. The Father appoints and provides the Redeemer, and Himself accepts the price and grants the thing purchased; the Son is the Redeemer by offering Himself and is the price; and the Holy Ghost immediately communicates to us the thing purchased by communicating Himself, and He is the thing purchased. The sum of all that Christ purchased for men was the Holy Ghost: (Gal. 3:13,14) "He was made a curse for us... that we might receive the promise of the Spirit through faith."

What Christ purchased for us was that we have communion with God [which] is His good, which consists in partaking of the Holy Ghost: as we have shown, all the blessedness of the Redeemed consists in their partaking of Christ's fullness, which consists in partaking of that Spirit which is given not by measure unto him: the oil that is poured on the head of the Church runs down to the members of His body and to the skirts of His garment (Ps. 133:2). Christ purchased for us that we should have the favor of God and might enjoy His love, but this love is the Holy Ghost.

Christ purchased for us true spiritual excellency, grace and holiness, the sum of which is love to

God, which is [nothing] but the indwelling of the Holy Ghost in the heart. Christ purchased for us spiritual joy and comfort, which is in a participation of God's joy and happiness, which joy and happiness is the Holy Ghost as we have shown. The Holy Ghost is the sum of all good things. Good things and the Holy Spirit are synonymous expressions in Scripture: (Matt. 7:11) "How much more shall your Heavenly Father give the Holy Spirit to them that ask Him." The sum of all spiritual good which the finite have in this world is that spring of living water within them which we read of (John 4:10), and those rivers of living water flowing out of them which we read of (John 7:38,39), which we are there told means the Holy Ghost; and the sum of all happiness in the other world is that river of water of life which proceeds out of the throne of God and the Lamb, which we read of (Rev. 22:1), which is the River of God's pleasures and is the Holy Ghost and therefore the sum of the Gospel invitation to come and take the water of life (verse 17).

The Holy Ghost is the purchased possession and inheritance of the saints, as appears because that little of it which the saints have in this world is said to be the earnest of that purchased inheritance.

(Eph. 1:14) Tis an earnest of that which we are to have a fullness of hereafter. (II Cor. 1:22; 5:5) The

Holy Ghost is the great subject of all Gospel promises and therefore is called the Spirit of promise.

(Eph. 1:13) This is called the promise of the Father (Luke 24:49), and the like in other places. (If the

Holy Ghost be a comprehension of all good things promised in the Gospel, we may easily see the force of the Apostle's arguing (Gal. 3:2), "This only would I know, Received ye the Spirit by the works of the law or by the hearing of faith?") So that it is God of Whom our good is purchased and it is God that purchases it and it is God also that is the thing purchased.

Thus all our good things are of God and through God and in God, as we read in Romans 11:36: "For of Him and through Him and to Him (or in Him as *eis* is rendered, I Cor. 8:6) are all things." "To Whom be glory forever." All our good is of God the Father, it is all through God the Son, and all is in the Holy Ghost as He is Himself all our good. God is Himself the portion and purchased inheritance of His people. Thus God is the Alpha and the Omega in this affair of redemption.

If we suppose no more than used to be supposed about the Holy Ghost, the concern of the Holy Ghost in the work of redemption is not equal with the Father's and the Son's, nor is there an equal part of the glory of this work belonging to Him: merely to apply to us or immediately to give or hand to us the blessing purchased, after it was purchased, as subservient to the other two Persons, is but a little thing [compared] to the purchasing of it by the paying an Infinite price, by Christ offering up Himself in sacrifice to procure it, and it is but a little thing to God the Father's giving His infinitely dear Son to be a sacrifice for us and upon His purchase to afford to us all the blessings of His purchased.

But according to this there is an equality. To be the love of God to the world is as much as for the Father and the Son to do so much from love to the world, and to be the thing purchased was as much as to be the price. The price and the thing bought with that price are equal. And it is as much as to afford the thing purchased, for the glory that belongs to Him that affords the thing purchased arises from the worth of that thing that He affords and therefore it is the same glory and an equal glory; the glory of the thing itself is its worth and that is also the glory of him that affords it.

There are two more eminent and remarkable images of the Trinity among the creatures. The one is in the spiritual creation, the soul of man. There is the mind, and the understanding or idea, and the spirit of the mind as it is called in Scripture, i.e., the disposition, the will or affection. The other is in the visible creation, viz., the Sun. The father is as the substance of the Sun. (By substance I don't mean in a philosophical sense, but the Sun as to its internal constitution.) The Son is as the brightness and glory of the disk of the Sun or that bright and glorious form under which it appears to our eyes. The Holy Ghost is the action of the Sun which is within the Sun in its intestine heat, and, being diffusive, enlightens, warms, enlivens and comforts the world. The Spirit as it is God's Infinite love to Himself and happiness in Himself, is as the internal heat of the Sun, but as it is that by which

God communicates Himself, it is as the emanation of the sun's action, or the emitted beams of the sun.

The various sorts of rays of the sun and their beautiful colors do well represent the Spirit. They well represent the love and grace of God and were made use of for this purpose in the rainbow after the flood, and I suppose also in that rainbow that was seen round about the throne by Ezekiel (Ezek.

1:28; Rev. 4:3) and round the head of Christ by John (Rev. 10:1), or the amiable excellency of God and the various beautiful graces and virtues of the Spirit. These beautiful colors of the sunbeams we find made use of in Scripture for this purpose, viz., to represent the graces of the Spirit, as (Ps.

68:13) "Though ye have lien among the pots, yet shall be as the wings of a dove covered with silver, and her feathers with yellow gold," i.e., like the light reflected in various beautiful colors from the feathers of a dove, which colors represent the graces of the Heavenly Dove." Public Domain*

From these thoughts, derived from revealed truth about I AM, His oneness in three persons, an entity of three, a community of oneness, absolute LOVE is the essence, nature of I AM.

We see that God believes and trusts in Himself as each personhood of the one looks upon the other, with no thought of self.

This is absolute love, this is the humility of not taking thought of self, eternally looking outward with care for another, this is total belief and trust. We can then fully believe and trust in I AM, because there is no motivation of selfishness or need within I AM.

Love overflows between and within the persons of I AM, I AM is absolute love. I AM is the same yesterday, today and forever. I AM is the Alpha and the Omega, the first and the last, the beginning and the end, eternal. I AM is overflowing, abundant in loving kindness, mercy and faithfulness; Exo 34:5-7 "The LORD descended in the cloud and stood with him there, and proclaimed the name of the LORD. The LORD passed before him and proclaimed, "The LORD, the LORD, a God merciful and gracious, slow to anger, and abounding in steadfast love and faithfulness, keeping steadfast love for thousands, forgiving iniquity and transgression and sin, but who will by no means clear the guilty, visiting the iniquity of the fathers on the children and the children's children, to the third and the fourth generation." He will not let the guilty go unpunished, justice is part of love. Heb 10:30 For we know him who said, "Vengeance is mine; I will repay." And again, "The Lord will judge his people." Yet He continues to come back generation after generation on rescue missions to give grace and forgiveness to those devastated by selfish rebellion, perversion and the sickness of sin.

In graduate school I focused on counseling. In studying family therapy theory and reading from Carl Whitaker and Virginia Satir, I learned about family systems and dysfunctions. Our rescue missions- attempts at helping/saving others often end up badly; we often end up enabling others in unhealthy behaviors. We also can end up scapegoating other individuals by projecting unwanted feelings towards those we are trying to help onto individuals or even groups of individuals. When these unhealthy mechanisms of defense multiply or overwhelm, we can become very sick antisocial, narcissistic, even paranoid. As groups these defense mechanisms can turn into mobbing, bullying, victimizing and stereotyping.

However, if we look to I AM, we can begin to believe and trust. We first of all learn through looking at I AM how to believe and trust in ourselves. Through unfailing loving kindness and forgiveness, we can believe in I AM and see that I AM believes and trusts in us. This is the only way to maintain that belief and trust by looking away from self to I AM.

We all slip into unhealthy-sinful ways of relating to others, we look at ourselves to know good and evil, not to I AM. We all in many ways have been involved in enabling, scapegoating, stereotyping and other sinful behaviors that inhibit and destroy our relationship with I AM and with those around us. The mercy, loving kindness and forgiveness of I AM can release us from those so that we can believe in ourselves and others.

It is then necessary to see that belief and trust mainly flow through looking to and passionately abiding in I AM. This is where we fail to love God and love others as ourselves, as Adam and Eve failed. We can only believe and trust in ourselves to the extent that we keep focus on I AM. One of the greatest truths the best psychiatrists and psychologists know is that we have an unceasing ability to deceive ourselves, to hide and distort truth. Psychology did not first discover this fact though it is revealed through the study of the nature of man, I AM revealed this. Of Jesus of Nazareth, I AM incarnate it is revealed; "Joh 2:23-25 Now when he was in Jerusalem at the Passover Feast, many believed in his name when they saw the signs that he was doing. But Jesus on his part did not entrust himself to them, because he knew all people and needed no one to bear witness about man, for he himself knew what was in man." Yeshua, Jesus, Isa is The Word (I AM, the three in one): yet He lived a life as a Jewish man (the Messiah or anointed one) who affirmed celebrating Passover, (indeed it was a celebration of Himself and His coming substitutionary sacrifice), yet love for others flowed from belief and trust in The Father(I AM, the three in one) and The Holy Spirit (I AM, the three in one). He was not entrusting himself to man, he knew what was in mankind; deception and hiding. He was believing and trusting in the Father and the Holy Spirit.

Other encounters in the life of Jesus records how even enemies of I AM can desire the blessings and benefits of I AM without wanting to live in intimate relationship with him. We often want to reduce faith and love to temporal satisfaction without seeing the benefit of turning away from everything else to only looking to I AM.

A young man of the ruling class in Palestine once came to Jesus looking to hold on to everything else and still have the benefit and blessing of I AM. "Luke 18:18-27 And a ruler asked him, "Good Teacher, what must I do to inherit eternal life?" And Jesus said to him, "Why do you call me good? No one is good except God alone. You know the commandments: 'Do not commit adultery, Do not murder, Do not steal, Do not bear false witness, Honor your father and mother.'" And he said, "All these I have kept from my youth." When Jesus heard this, he said to him, "One thing you still lack. Sell all that you have and distribute to the poor, and you will have treasure in heaven; and come, follow me." But when he heard these things, he became very sad, for he was extremely rich. Jesus, seeing that he had become sad, said, "How difficult it is for those who have wealth to enter the kingdom of God! For it is easier for a camel to go through the eye of a needle than for a rich person to enter the kingdom of God." Those who heard it said, "Then who can be saved?" But he said, "What is impossible with men is possible with God." It is totally turning away from self to I AM that allows us to really live, to have abundant, eternal life. This kind of life is only from I AM not from ourselves. "The deepest healing occurs not in the mind, but in the soul. And if the heart is 'hardened,' no words can penetrate it."[4] Writes M. Scott Peck M.D..

In another place it is revealed Jesus was with those who had given up everything to follow after Him. "Mat 14:22 Immediately he made the disciples get into the boat and go before him to the other side, while he dismissed the crowds.

Mat 14:23-33 And after he had dismissed the crowds, he went up on the mountain by himself to pray. When evening came, he was there alone, but the boat by this time was a long way from the land, beaten by the waves, for the wind was against them. And in the fourth watch of the night he came to them, walking on the sea. But when the disciples saw him walking on the sea, they were terrified, and said, "It is a ghost!" and they cried out in fear. But immediately Jesus spoke to them, saying, "Take heart; it is I. Do not be afraid." And Peter answered him, "Lord, if it is you, command me to come to you on the water." He said, "Come." So Peter got out of the boat and walked on the water and came to Jesus. But when he saw the wind, he was afraid, and beginning to sink he cried out, "Lord, save me." Jesus immediately reached out his hand and took hold of him, saying to him, "O you of little faith, why did you doubt?" And when they got into the boat, the wind ceased. And those in the boat worshiped him, saying, "Truly you are the Son of God."

Even those who are seen as most in touch with and focused on God can fail when they take their eyes off of I AM. This should be a strong warning to us not to be thrown off by failures of others, and then to let those failures of man to cause us to lose belief and trust in God.

Yet again another encounter with Jesus should help us to see that our perception should not be the basis of belief and trust. Jesus had been teaching across the land and healing many people from Israel. Then he was approached by a Roman soldier, a centurion. "Mat 8:5-13 When he entered Capernaum, a centurion came forward to him, appealing to him, "Lord, my servant is lying paralyzed at home, suffering terribly." And he said to him, "I will come and heal him." But the centurion replied, "Lord, I am not worthy to have you come under my roof, but only say the word, and my servant will be healed. For I too am a man under authority, with soldiers under me. And I say to one, 'Go,' and he goes, and to another, 'Come,' and he comes, and to my servant, 'Do this,' and he does it." When Jesus heard this, he marveled and said to those who followed him, "Truly, I tell you, with no one in Israel have I found such faith. I tell you, many will come from east and west and recline at table with Abraham, Isaac, and Jacob in the kingdom of heaven, while the sons of the kingdom will be thrown into the outer darkness. In that place there will be weeping and gnashing of teeth." And to the centurion Jesus said, "Go; let it be done for you as you have believed." And the servant was healed at that very moment."

Often those who we believe to be enemies or those who we think are outside of the focus of I AM are exactly the opposite, they are more clearly focused on I AM or at least have the potential to be focused on I AM. As we have already seen with man this is impossible but with God all things are possible.

This is the dilemma of trying to go it without God, it brings impossibility, it brings death. Hence as I AM teaches we should love our enemies; Mat 5:38-48 "You have heard that it was said, 'An eye for an eye and a tooth for a tooth.' But I say to you, Do not resist the one who is evil. But if anyone slaps you on the right cheek, turn to him the other also. And if anyone would sue you and take your tunic, let him have your cloak as well. And if anyone forces you to go one mile, go with him two miles. Give to the one who begs from you, and do not refuse the one who would borrow from you. "You have heard that it was said, 'You shall love your neighbor and hate your enemy.' But I say to you, Love your enemies and pray for those who persecute you, so that you may be sons of your Father who is in heaven. For he makes his sun rise on the evil and on the good, and sends rain on the just and on the unjust. For if you love those who love you, what reward do you have? Do not even the tax collectors do the same?" And if you greet only your brothers, what more are you doing than others? Do not even the Gentiles do the same? You therefore must be perfect, as your heavenly Father is perfect."

To be focused on I AM is to follow Him and mirror His character. This is the essence of absolute love, it is love that flows from within the one who loves, not love that is generate from the loveliness of the object to which love overflows toward.

This is the way the absolute love within I AM has been poured out to us: "Rom 5:6-11 For while we were still weak, at the right time Christ died for the ungodly. For one will scarcely die for a righteous person--though perhaps for a good person one would dare even to die-- but God shows his love for us in that while we were still sinners, Christ died for us. Since, therefore, we have now been justified by his blood, much more shall we be saved by him from the wrath of God. For if while we were enemies we were reconciled to God by the death of his Son, much more, now that we are reconciled, shall we be saved by his life. More than that, we also rejoice in God through our Lord Jesus Christ, through whom we have now received reconciliation."

It is clear now that believe and trust in others, and belief and trust in ourselves, is a result of a clear focus upon I AM. We are created in the Image of God, but that is not the center of the intrinsic worth of people, we are still creatures.

The center of the intrinsic worth of individuals is their relationship to I AM. I AM will have mercy upon whom He will have mercy. Worth is grounded in the direction of relationship to I AM and being made in His image the potential of that relationship, for with God nothing is impossible. The belief and trust is in I AM and towards I AM. Tit 3:1-7 "Remind them to be submissive to rulers and authorities, to be obedient, to be ready for every good work, to speak evil of no one, to avoid quarreling, to be gentle, and to show perfect courtesy toward all people. For we ourselves were once foolish, disobedient, led astray, slaves to various passions and pleasures, passing our days in malice and envy, hated by others and hating one another. But when the goodness and loving kindness of God our Savior appeared, he saved us, not because of works done by us in righteousness, but according to his own mercy, by the washing of regeneration and renewal of the Holy Spirit, whom he poured out on us richly through Jesus Christ our Savior, so that being justified by his grace we might become heirs according to the hope of eternal life."

We all come from the same place of being former enemies of I AM, to being followers focused on Him; Col 1:13-22 "He has delivered us from the domain of darkness and transferred us to the kingdom of his beloved Son, in whom we have redemption, the forgiveness of sins. He is the image of the invisible God, the firstborn of all creation. For by him all things were created, in heaven and on earth, visible and invisible, whether thrones or dominions or rulers or authorities--all things were created through him and for him. And he is before all things, and in him all things hold together. And he is the head of the body, the church. He is the beginning, the firstborn from the dead, that in everything he might be preeminent. For in him all the fullness of God was pleased to dwell, and through him to reconcile to himself all things, whether on earth or in heaven, making peace by the blood of his cross. And you, who once were alienated and hostile in mind, doing evil deeds, he has now reconciled in his body of flesh by his death, in order to present you holy and blameless and above reproach before him,"

Belief is an overwhelming sense of hope based on understanding of past actions and in the fulfillment of future promises that gives encouragement, so that we can be enthusiastic and self-stretching, in order that we might grow through developing (God given) potential.

Trust is the characteristic outgrowth of believing that gives us the ability to be open and share who we are and what we have been given so that we can be catalysts in the development of openness and candor in others.

Amman (Believe, confirm, support, nourish, make firm, establish, sure, lasting, trust)

Gen 15:6, 42:20, 45:26,

Exo 4:1, 4:5, 4:8, 4:9, 4:31, 14:31, 19:9,Num 11:12, 12:7, 14:11, 20:12,Deu 1:32, 7:9, 9:23, 28:59, 28:66,Judg 11:20,Ruth 4:16,1 Sam 2:35, 3:20, 22:14, 25:28, 27:12,2,Sam 4:4, 7:16, 20:19,1 Ki 8:26, 10:7, 11:38,2 Ki 10:1, 10:5, 17:14, 1 Chr 17:23, 17:24,2 Chr 1:9, 6:17, 9:6, 20:20, 32:15,Neh 9:8, 13:13,Est 2:7, 2:20,

Job 4:18, 9:16, 12:20, 15:15, 15:22, 15:31, 24:22, 29:24, 39:12, 39:24,Psa 12:1, 19:7, 27:13, 31:23, 78:22, 78:32, 89:28, 89:37, 93:5, 101:6, 106:12, 106:24, 111:7, 116:10, 119:66,Prov 8:30, 11:13, 14:15, 25:13, 26:25, 27:6,Isa 1:21, 1:26, 7:9, 8:2, 22:23, 22:25, 28:16, 33:16, 43:10, 49:7, 49:23, 53:1, 55:3, 60:4,Jer 12:6, 15:18, 40:14, 42:5,Lam 4:5, 4:12,Hosea 5:9, 11:12,Jonah 3:5,Micah 7:5,Hab 1:5.

Batach Trust, extend, lie face down, lie down extended, secure, rely upon, and be confident)

Deu 28:52,

Judg 9:26, 18:7, 18:10, 18:27, 20:36,

2 Ki 18:5, 18:19, 18:20, 18:21, 18:22, 18:24, 18:30, 19:10,

1 Chr 5:20,

2 Chr 32:10,

Job 6:20, 11:18, 39:11, 40:23,

Psa 4:5, 9:10, 13:5, 21:7, 22:4, 22:5, 22:9, 25:2, 26:1, 27:3, 28:7, 31:6, 31:14, 32:10, 33:21, 37:3, 37:5, 40:3, 41:9, 44:6, 49:6, 52:7, 52:8, 55:23, 56:3, 56:4, 56:11, 62:8, 62:10, 78:22, 84:12, 86:2, 91:2, 112:7, 115:8, 115:9, 115:10, 115:11, 118:8, 118:9, 119:42, 125:1, 135:18, 143:8, 146:3,

Prov 3:5, 11:15, 11:28, 14:16, 16:20, 28:1, 28:25, 28:26, 29:25, 31:11,

Isa 12:2, 26:3, 26:4, 30:12, 31:1, 32:9, 32:10, 32:11, 36:4, 36:5, 36:6, 36:7, 36:9, 36:15, 37:10, 42:17, 47:10, 50:10, 59:4,

Jer 5:17, 7:4, 7:8, 7:14, 9:4, 12:5, 13:25, 17:5, 17:7, 28:15, 29:31, 39:18, 46:25, 48:7, 49:4, 49:11,

Ezek 16:15, 33:13,

Hosea 10:13,

Amos 6:1,

Micah 7:5,

Hab 2:18,

Zep 3:2.

Pistueo (believe, be convinced of, give credence to, be influenced by,)

Mat 8:13, 9:28, 18:6, 21:22, 21:25, 21:32, 24:23, 24:26, 27:42,

Mark 1:15, 5:36, 9:23, 9:24, 9:42, 11:23, 11:24, 11:31, 13:21, 15:32, 16:13, 16:14, 16:16, 16:17,

Luke1:20, 1:45, 8:12, 8:13, 8:50, 16:11, 20:5, 22:67, 24:25, **John**1:7, 1:12, 1:50, 2:11, 2:22, 2:23, 2:24, 3:12, 3:15, 3:16, 3:18, 3:36, 4:21, 4:39, 4:41, 4:42, 4:48, 4:50, 4:53, 5:24, 5:38, 5:44, 5:46, 5:47, 6:29, 6:30, 6:35, 6:36, 6:40, 6:47, 6:64, 6:69, 7:5, 7:31, 7:38, 7:39, 7:48, 8:24, 8:30, 8:31, 8:45, 8:46, 9:18, 9:35, 9:36, 9:38, 10:25, 10:26, 10:37, 10:38, 10:42, 11:15, 11:25, 11:26, 11:27, 11:40, 11:42, 11:45, 11:48, 12:11, 12:36, 12:37, 12:38, 12:39, 12:42, 12:44, 12:46, 12:47, 13:19, 14:1, 14:10, 14:11, 14:12, 14:29, 16:9, 16:27, 16:30, 16:31, 17:8, 17:20, 17:21, 19:35, 20:8, 20:25, 20:29, 20:31,

Acts 2:44, 4:4, 4:32, 5:14, 8:12, 8:13, 8:37, 9:26, 9:42, 10:43, 11:17, 11:21, 13:12, 13:39, 13:41, 13:48, 14:1, 14:23, 15:5, 15:7, 15:11, 16:31, 16:34, 17:12, 17:34, 18:8, 18:27, 19:2, 19:4, 19:18, 21:20, 21:25, 22:19, 24:14, 26:27, 27:25,

Rom 1:16, 3:2, 3:22, 4:3, 4:5, 4:11, 4:17, 4:18, 4:24, 6:8, 9:33, 10:4, 10:9, 10:10, 10:11, 10:14, 10:16, 13:11, 14:2, 15:13,

1 Cor 1:21, 3:5,1 9:17, 11:18, 13:7, 14:22, 15:2, 15:11,

2 Cor 4:13,

Gal 2:7, 2:16, 3:6, 3:22,

Eph 1:13, 1:19,

Phil 1:29,

1 Th 1:7, 2:4, 2:10, 2:13, 4:14,2

Th 1:10, 2:11, 2:12,

1 Tim 1:11, 1:16, 3:16,

2 Tim 1:12,

Titus 1:3, s 3:8,

Heb 4:3, 11:6,

James 2:19, 2:23,

1 Pet 1:8, 1:21, 2:6, 2:7,

1 John 3:23, 4:1, 4:16, 5:1, 5:5, 5:10, 5:13,Jude 1:5.

Pistis

Mat 8:10,9:2,9:22,9:29, 15:28, 17:20, 21:21,23:23,

Mark 2:5,4:40,5:34, 10:52, 11:22,

Luke 5:20,7:9,7:50,8:25, 8:48,17:5, 17:6,17:19,18:8,18:42,22:32,

Acts 3:16, 6:5,6:7,6:8,11:24,13:8,14:9,14:22, 14:27,15:9,16:5,17:31,20:21,24:24,26:18,

Rom 1:5,1:8,1:12,1:17, 3:3,3:22, 3:25,3:26, 3:27,3:28,3:30,3:31, 4:5,4:9,4:11, 4:12,4:13,4:14,4:16,4:19,4:20,5:1,5:2,9:30,9:32, 10:6,10:8,10:17,11:20, 12:3,12:6, 14:1,14:22,14:23,16:26,1 Cor 2:5,12:9,13:2, 13:13,15:14,15:17,16:13,

2 Cor 1:24,4:13, 5:7,8:7,10:15,13:5,Gal 1:23,2:16,2:20,3:2,3:5, 3:7,3:8,3:9,3:11,3:12,3:14,3:22,3:23,3:24,3:25,3:26,5:5,5:6,5:22,6 :10,

Eph 1:15,2:8, 3:12,3:17, 4:5,4:13,6:16,6:23,

Phil 1:25,1:27,2:17,3:9,Col 1:4,1:23,2:5, 2:7,2:12,

1 Th 1:3,1:8,3:2,3:5,3:6,3:7,3:10,5:8, 2 Th 1:3,1:4,1:11,2:13,3:2,1 **Tim** 1:2,1:4,1:5,1:14, 1:19, 2:7, 2:15,3:9,3:13, 4:1,4:6,4:12, 5:8,5:12,6:10,6:11,6:12,6:21,2

Tim 1:5,1:13,2:18, 2:22, 3:8,3:10,3:15,4:7,

Titus 1:1,1:4, 1:13,2:2,2:10,3:15,

Phile 1:5,1:6,

Heb 4:2,6:1,6:12, 10:22 ,10:38,10:39, 11:1,11:3,11:4,11:5,11:6, 11:7,11:8,11:9, 11:11,11:13,11:17, 11:20,11:21, 11:22,11:23, 11:24,11:27,11:28,11:29,11:30,11:31,11:33,11:39,12:2,13:7,

James 1:3,1:6 ,2:1,2:5,2:14,2:17,2:18,2:20,2:22,2:24,2:26,5:15,1 **Pet** 1:5,1:7,1:9,1:21, 5:9,

2 Pet 1:1,1:5,

1 John 5:4,

Jude 1:3,1:20,

Rev 2:13,2:19,:10,14:12

Peitho (trust, persuaded, depend upon, set at ease, put confidence in, be convinced, certain, sure, follow, obey)

Mat 27:20, 27:43, 28:14,

Mark 10:24,Luke 11:22, 16:31, 18:9, 20:6,

Acts 5:36, 5:37, 5:40, 12:20, 13:43, 14:19, 17:4, 18:4, 19:8, 19:26, 21:14, 23:21, 26:26, 26:28, 27:11, 28:23, 28:24,

Rom 2:8, 2:19, 8:38, 14:14, 15:14,

2 Cor 1:9, 2:3, 5:11, 10:7,

Gal 1:10, 3:1, 5:7, 5:10,Phil 1:6, 1:14, 1:25, 2:24, 3:3, 3:4,2 Th 3:4,

2 Tim 1:5, 1:12,

Phile 1:21,

Heb 2:13, 6:9, 11:13, 13:17, 13:18,

James 3:3,

1 John 3:19.

1. Wells, David., *LOSING OUR VIRTUE; Why the Church Must Recover Its Moral Vision,* Wm. B. Eerdmans Publishing Co. , Grand Rapids, MI. , 1998, Pages 127,128.

2. Keyes, Richard written in, *NO GOD; BUT GOD; Breaking With the Idols of Our Age.*, ed. Os Guiness and John Seel; Moody Press, Chicago, IL. , 1992, Page 33.
3. Piper, Dr. John., *THE PLEASURES OF GOD; Meditations on God's Delight in Being God.*, Multnomah Publishing, Sister, OR. , pages 215-216
4. Edwards, Jonathan, *An Unpublished Essay on the Trinity;*, www.monergism.com
5. Peck, M. Scott M.D. *THE ROAD LESS TRAVELED AND BEYOND.* New York, NY, Touchstone Publishing; 1997, Page 270

CHAPTER SEVEN

Acceptance and Confidence

(Eph 3:11-12)

This was according to the eternal purpose that he has realized in Christ Jesus our Lord, in whom we have boldness and access with confidence through our faith in him.

Harvard psychology professor Daniel Gilbert in his bestselling book STUMBLING ON HAPPINESS, describes how human beings are the only being (earth bound animal) with a highly developed frontal lobe in as part of their brain. It seems that this part of the brain enables people to plan and project futures and how they feel about those futures that they imagine. The problem is more often than not we are wrong about the envisioning of those futures and how we will feel, (how happy we will be) in those futures we envision.

Gilbert writes' "The greatest achievement of the human brain is its ability to imagine objects and episodes that do not exist in the realm of the real, and it is this ability that allows us to think about the future. As one philosopher noted, the human brain is an 'anticipation machine' and 'making future' is the most important thing it does."[1] Yet the problem is that our future imaginings are often flawed and outright wrong. Why do we look at things especially in this seemingly deceptive way? Gilbert says; "How do we manage to think of ourselves as great drivers, talented lovers, and brilliant chefs when the facts of our lives include a pathetic parade of dented cars, disappointed partners and deflated soufflés? The answer is simple: we cook the facts."[2]

Dr. Gilbert lays out four barriers to we human, having the ability to accurately imagine our future and especially barriers to accurately imagining how we will feel about the futures we imagine.

The barriers are subjectivity, realism, presentism and rationalization. So, we imagine and plan for futures that we don't really want and imagine those futures making us happy when they won't. His remedy is very utilitarian, which is find someone who has the future we imagine and ask them how they feel. This it seems to me to be bringing us right back to the very naiveté that Dr. Gilbert outlines in his book. "One person might be very happy in their life with a spouse, two children, a dog and a successful business venture and another person may be even more exceptionally fulfilled living in an area of immense need and caring for the needs of those around them without having all the amenities of others. In fact, a case could be made that at any particular time either person described above may be intensely satisfied and at other times be intensely dissatisfied."[3]

Dr. Gilbert is right that we have a way of looking at things wrongly so that our choices are often misjudged and our planning for the future is very often wrongheaded. We have only our own subjective view, we need something, someone who can be unbiased, objective. We cannot discern the reality of what we imagine. There holes in our imagining and we cannot imagine all of the contingencies that would add to or take away from our happiness by the future we imagine. Still again we fill in past emotional reactions to being in a certain situation with how we feel now about that situation.

We tend to be overly nostalgic about the good old days, when as we were living the good old days we did not have quite the good feelings about that time that we hold in our memories. While at the same time we have a exceptional ability to rationalize to imagine things that we are predisposed to favorably and likewise things we have no objective experience with unfavorably.

James the earthly half-brother of Jesus, Jesus did not have a birth father on earth) Yeshua, Isa says; Jas 4:1-2 "What causes quarrels and what causes fights among you? Is it not this, that your passions are at war within you? You desire and do not have, so you murder. You covet and cannot obtain, so you fight and quarrel. You do not have, because you do not ask.

Os Guiness says; "If we were not marked by the results of the Fall, we would experience an unconscious natural harmony between our understanding, willing and feeling. All our actions and reactions would be whole. But none of us enjoy that perfect balance now, and alienation of sin means that we are alienated not only from God and each other but also from ourselves. The deep harmony within each of us has been lost. For some people, the alienation is so extreme that it leads to severe emotional disorder. For most of us the hassle of living with our contradictory 'selves' and struggling with our conflicting emotions, is a run-of-the-mill aspect of living. We are so used to putting up with the brokenness of our fallen human nature that we tend to accept it as normal and take it for granted."[4]

Jas 4:3 You ask and do not receive, because you ask wrongly, to spend it on your passions."

Our passions are misaligned

Here is the real crux of our unhappiness, our passions are misplaced. We have a real inability to accept ourselves, and deep down we lack confidence in our choices. Sooner or later we come to the realization that we have been duped or more likely we have duped ourselves, in looking for happiness we have gone the wrong way. If we are honest we can see that we are at odds with ourselves, weaving the wrong trail. The objective, absolute I AM, the three in one is the only way to find our way to aligning our passions with what will truly bring happiness, where we will find the future we desire, the future we were made for.

I AM has been building that future for us. When the people of the book had sunk to their lowest, they were again captives. They had built for themselves a future based on their own passions, this future had brought division, war and exile. I AM came with a promise of His absolute LOVE: **Jer 29:11-12** "For I know the plans I have for you, declares the LORD, plans for welfare and not for evil, to give you a future and a hope. Then you will call upon me and come and pray to me, and I will hear you."

Just as belief and trust come from looking away from self to looking at I AM, the three in one, acceptance of ourselves and confidence in ourselves runs through looking to I AM. To be made in the image of God is not intrinsic to us it is intrinsic to I AM and the image is lost apart from I AM.

Ever since Eden our attempts to find fulfillment, to become who we really want to be has been hampered by our own wrong sense of the future. Namely a future apart from I AM that brings death and destruction to our lives. The constant looking away to I AM is how we image forth the absolute image of God. This absolute love for us can most clearly be seen in Jesus, Isa, Yeshua of whom it is written; Col 1:15-20 "He is the image of the invisible God, the firstborn of all creation. For by him all things were created, in heaven and on earth, visible and invisible, whether thrones or dominions or rulers or authorities--all things were created through him and for him. And he is before all things, and in him all things hold together. And he is the head of the body, the church. He is the beginning, the firstborn from the dead, that in everything he might be preeminent. For in him all the fullness of God was pleased to dwell, and through him to reconcile to himself all things, whether on earth or in heaven, making peace by the blood of his cross."

I AM, the three in one is the essence of acceptance and confidence. When Isa, Yeshua, Jesus began to teach and lead he went to be baptized as a way to demonstrate humility, belief and trust. When he was baptized a voice from heaven that many people heard said: Mat 3:16 -17 "And when Jesus was baptized, immediately he went up from the water, and behold, the heavens were opened to him, and he saw the Spirit of God descending like a dove and coming to rest on him; and behold, a voice from heaven said, "This is my beloved Son, with whom I am well pleased."

Here all three of the one I AM stand forth in full acceptance of one another and confidence in one another. Millard Erickson writes; "The closeness of these three is accentuated through the fact that the goals, intentions, values, and objectives of each of the three is the same as those of each of the others. ... There is also a closeness to the relationship due to the fact that each knows that there is no option of separation. Sometimes love among humans becomes tentative because there is the fear that the other will somehow turn away from the relationship or against the person himself/herself. This cannot be in the case of the three members of the Trinity, however. They are eternally and permanently one with the others."[5] I AM the three in one is bathed in full acceptance and the confidence of that acceptance within Himself.

We cannot experience this level of acceptance outside of looking to I AM. Our plans for the future and future happiness are muddied in the mire of subjectivity, realism, presentism and rationalization.

Writes Adrio König "The goal of the proclamation can be summed up as faith. As we proceed, it will become clear that much is contained in this one word. . . . We did not discuss personal faith . . . when we spoke about the goal being realized "for us". There we saw that Christ achieved God's goal for us without our faith- indeed even before we were able to believe. Enmity was annihilated, peace restored, the new humanity created, the world redeemed, access to the Father obtained- all through Christ alone, without our faith. . . .

But when the eschaton is attained in the second mode (i.e. in us), the call to faith is "added" in quotation marks, for the moment, because it is not yet clear how anything could be added to the completeness of our salvation, justification, righteousness, peace and access to the Father obtained by Jesus. Nevertheless, it is unmistakable that there is an addition, and that it is of decisive importance.

. . .   Before the proclamation's goal can be broadly outlined, it is necessary to show that this "addition" of faith is no addition at all, and that because of the nature of faith there is agreement in reformation theology on the emptiness of faith. This does not mean that faith is unimportant, but rather that its importance- even indispensability- lies in that it is nothing on its own, is not autonomous, is no human contribution, but must receive its content and its meaning from the other side: in fact, from God in Christ through the Spirit. In faith, we confess God as the subject and ourselves as the object of salvation. Salvation means that Christ has fully attained God's goal for us. And when a person believes this, God's goal is attained in that person. Proclamation has as its goal to bring people to this knowledge and trust. How radically this faith involves our whole life is shown by the New Testament's equation of faith with obedience. So it is clear that by the nature of faith no tension can exist between "Christ alone" and the "addition" of faith. Faith lives solely from Christ, and is filled by what he has done. Stated in eschatological terms, Christ's attainment of the goal for us (but without us) and his attainment of the goal in us. Are not concurrent.

Yet it is this very emptiness of faith in itself which leads to its decisive character. Because it is directed solely to Christ and his work for us, faith is necessary- and its lack excludes one from salvation... Without faith, God's goal in us is not reached. Precisely because faith is neither a human accomplishment nor a human contribution but rather a confession that everything has been done for us by Christ, we have no Christ if we have no faith. This is why Scripture speaks so strongly about the necessity, value, and power of faith. Faith receives value only from its object. And because of faith's necessity, we are bound to speak of the mortal peril of unbelief."[6]

Acceptance is the characteristic outgrowth of believing that gives us the ability to forgive ourselves and others so that healing and understanding can take place.

Confidence is the characteristic outgrowth of believing that gives us assurance of our being accepted and gives us the ability to look past self-promotion to the promotion of others so that their confidence is built up.

Given the fact that we so often make wrong choices and project for ourselves unhappy futures, it is no wonder that we often find it difficult to accept ourselves and lack confidence. Or confidence is misplaced in ourselves and we eventually find out, sometimes devastatingly, that our confidence was placed in someone that could not live up to that level of confidence. This is the real flaw in asking someone who is in the future that we imagine or plan for ourselves, that person may not as yet come to realization that they have put their confidence in something that is ultimately unsatisfying.

Dietrich Bonhoeffer said; "Human love has little regard for truth. It makes the truth relative, since nothing, not even truth, must come between it and the beloved person. Human love desires the other person, his company, his answering love, but it does not serve him. On the contrary, it continues to desire even when it seems to be serving. There are two marks, both of which are one in the same thing, that manifest the difference between spiritual and human love: Human love cannot tolerate the dissolution of fellowship that has become false for the sake of genuine fellowship, and human love cannot love an enemy, that is, one who seriously and stubbornly resists it. Both spring from the same source: human love is by its very nature desire--desire for human community. So long as it can satisfy this desire in some way, it will not give it up, even for the sake of truth, even for the sake of genuine love to others. But where it can no longer expect its desire to be fulfilled, there it stops short--namely in the face of an enemy. There it turns to hatred, contempt and calumny.

Right here is the point where spiritual love begins. This is why human love becomes personal hatred when it encounters genuine spiritual love, which does not desire but serves. Human love makes itself an end in itself. It creates of itself an end, an idol which it worships, to which it must subject everything. It nurses and cultivates an ideal, it loves itself, and nothing else in this world. Spiritual love, however, comes from Jesus Christ, it serves him alone; it knows that it has no immediate access to other persons.

Jesus Christ stands between the lover and the others he loves. I do not know in advance what love to others means on the basis of the general idea of love that grows out of my human desires--all this may rather be hatred and an insidious kind of selfishness in the eyes of Christ. What love is, only Christ tells in his Word. Contrary to all my own opinions and convictions, Jesus Christ will tell me what love toward the brethren really is. Therefore, spiritual love is bound solely to the Word of Jesus Christ. Where Christ bids me to maintain fellowship for the sake of love, I will maintain it. Where his truth enjoins me to dissolve fellowship for love's sake, there I will dissolve it, despite all the protests of my human love. Because spiritual love does not desire but rather serves, it loves an enemy as a brother. It originates neither in the brother nor in the enemy but in Christ and his Word. Human love can never understand spiritual love, for spiritual love is from above; it is something completely strange, new, and incomprehensible to all earthly love.

Because Christ stands between me and others, I dare not desire direct fellowship with them. As only Christ can speak to me in such a way that I may be saved, so others, too, can be saved only by Christ himself. This means that I must release the other person from every attempt of mine to regulate, coerce, and dominate him with my love. The other person needs to retain his independence of me; to be loved for what he is, as one for whom Christ became a man, died, rose again, for whom Christ brought forgiveness of sins and eternal life. Because Christ has long since acted decisively for my brother, before I could begin to act, I must leave him the freedom to be Christ's; I must meet him only as the person that he already is in Christ's eyes. This is the meaning of the proposition that we can meet others through the mediation of Christ. Human love constructs its own image of the other person, of what he is and what he should become. It takes the life of the other person into its own hands. Spiritual love recognizes the true image of the other person which he has received from Jesus Christ; the image that Jesus Christ himself embodied and would stamp upon all men.

Therefore, spiritual love proves itself in that everything it says and does commends Christ. It will not seek to move others by all too personal, direct influence, by impure interference in the life of another. It will not take pleasure in pious, human fervor and excitement. It will rather meet the other person with the clear Word of God and be ready to leave him alone with this Word for a long time, willing to release him again in order that Christ may deal with him. It will respect the line that has been drawn between him and us by Christ, and it will find full fellowship with him in the Christ who alone binds us together. Thus this spiritual love will speak to Christ about a brother more than to a brother about Christ. It knows the most direct way to others is always through prayer to Christ and that love of others is wholly dependent upon truth in

Christ. It is out of this love that John the disciple speaks. "I have no greater joy than to hear that my children walk in truth"(III John 4)

Human love lives by uncontrolled and uncontrollable dark *desires*; spiritual love lives in the clear light of service ordered by *truth*. Human love produces human subjection, dependence, constraint; spiritual love creates *freedom* of the brethren under the Word. Human love breeds hothouse flowers; spiritual love creates the *fruits* that grow healthily in accord with God's good will in the rain and storm and sunshine of God's outdoors. The existence of any Christian life together depends on whether it succeeds at the right time in bringing out the ability to distinguish between a human ideal and God's reality, between spiritual and human community. "[7]

Earlier we found out that what we do outwardly is really nothing, but the only thing that really matters is "faith working through love". Furthermore, we found that there are only three things that remain ultimately in our lives faith, hope and love, "the greatest of these is love". In the book it is written; Heb 11:1 Now, faith is the assurance of things hoped for, the conviction of things not seen. Further it says; Heb 11:6 "And without faith it is impossible to please him, for whoever would draw near to God must believe that he exists and that he rewards those who seek him."

What sets us as human beings apart from other creatures here on earth is our ability to plan and dream of future. If we can accept and have confidence that what I AM will give us as reward for believing and trusting in Him is better than the future happiness we could imagine for ourselves then we can truly accept and have confidence that He is absolute LOVE, this will bring us a greater ability to accept and have confidence in others. We will not have our gaze focused on them, our faith in them, hope in future happiness fixed in them, but only fixed on I AM, absolute Love. I AM says: Jer 29:13 "You will seek me and find me, when you seek me with all your heart." A.W. Tozer states; "From all this we learn that faith is not a once-done act, but a continuous gaze of the heart at the Triune God."[8]

Acceptance is the characteristic outgrowth of believing that gives us the ability to forgive ourselves and others so that healing and understanding can take place.

Confidence is the characteristic outgrowth of believing that gives us assurance of our being accepted and gives us the ability to look past self-promotion to the promotion of others so that their confidence is built up.

Ratsah (Acceptable, be pleased with, favorable to,)**Gen** 33:10,**Lev** 1:4, 7:18, 19:7, 22:23, 22:25, 22:27, 26:34, 26:41, 26:43,**Deu** 33:11,**1 Sam** 29:4,**2 Sam** 24:23,**1 Chr** 28:4, 29:3, 29:17,**2 Chr** 10:7, 36:21,**Est** 10:3,Job 14:6, 20:10, 34:9,**Psa** 40:13, 50:18, 51:16, 62:4, 102:14, 119:108, 147:10,147:11, 149:4,**Prov** 3:12, 16:7,**Eccl** 9:7,**Isa** 40:2,42:1,**Jer**14:10, 14:12,**Ezek** 20:40, 20:41, 43:27,**Hosea** 8:13,**Amos** 5:22,**Micah** 6:7,**Hag** 1:8,**Mal** 1:8, 1:10, 1:13 **Ratson Gen** 49:6,**Exo** 28:38 ,**Lev** 1:3, 19:5, 22:19, 22:20, 22:21, 22:29, 23:11,**Deu** 33:16, 33:23, 33:24, **2 Chr** 15:15 ,**Ezra** 10:11,**Neh** 9:37,**Est** 1:8,**Psa** 5:12, 19:14, 30:5, 30:7, 40:8, 51:18, 69:13, 89:17, 103:21, 106:4, 143:10, 145:16, 145:19,**Prov** 8:35, 10:32, 11:1, 11:20, 11:27, 12:2, ,12:22, 14:9, 14:35, 15:8, 16:13,16:15, 18:22, 19:12,**Isa** 49:8, 56:7, 58:5, 60:7, 60:10, 61:2,**Jer** 6:20,**Dan** 8:4, 11:3, 11:16, 11:36,**Mal** 2:13.**Kecel** (confidence, loins, stupidity)**Lev** 3:4, 3:10,**Lev** 3:15, 4:9, 7:4,**Job** 8:14, 15:27, 31:24,**Psa** 38:7, 49:13, **78:7,Prov** 3:26,**Eccl** 7:25. **Kiclah Job** 4:6, **Psa** 85:8

Proslambano(Accept, take with, receive)**Mat**16:22,**Mark** 8:32,**Acts**17:5,18:26,27:33,27:34,27:36,28:2,**Rom**14:1,14:3,15: 7**Phile**1:12,1:17

Dechomai(Approve,Accept,take,receive)

Mat10:14,10:40,11:14,18:5,**Mark**6:11,9:37,10:15,**Luk**e2:28,8:1
3,9:5,9:11,9:48,9:53,10:8,10:10,16:4,16:6,16:7,16:9,18:17,22:17,
John4:45,**Acts**3:21,7:38,7:59,8:14,11:1,17:11,21:17,22:5,28:21,
1Cor2:14,**2Cor**6:1,7:15,8:4,8:17,11:4,11:16,**Gal**4:14,**Eph**6:17,**P
hil** 4:18,**Col** 4:10, **1 Th** 1:6,2:13,**2 Th 2:10,Heb** 11:31,**James**
1:21

Parrhesia(confidence, frankness, plainness of speech,
courage, boldness, fearlessness, joyousness)

Mark8:32,John7:4,7:13,7:26,10:24,11:14,11:54,16:25,16:29,18:
20,**Acts**4:13,4:29,4:31,9:27,28:31,**2Cor**3:12,7:4,**Eph**3:12,6:19,
Phil1:20,**Col**2:15,**1Tim**3:13,**Phile**1:8,**Heb3:6,**4:16,10:19,10:3
5,**1John**2:28,3:21,4:17,5:14

Pepoithesis(confidence, trust, faith)

2Cor 1:15, 3:4,8:22,10:2,**Eph** 3:12,**Phil** 3:4

1. Gilbert, Daniel., *STUMBLING ON HAPPINESS*,
   Vintage Books a division of Random House, New
   York, NY., 2006, Page 5
2. Ibid., Page 179
3. Guiness, Os., *GOD IN THE DARK;* Crossway Books,
   Wheaton, IL. , A division of Good News Publishers,
   1996, Page 127
4. Erickson, Millard J.., *GOD IN THREE PERSONS; A
   Contemporary Interpretation of the Trinity,* Baker Books,
   Grand Rapids, MI., 1995, Page 226
5. Koenig, Adrio., *THE ECLIPSE OF CHRIST IN
   ESCHATOLOGY; Toward a Christ Centered Approach.,*
   Wm. B. Eerdmans Publishing, Grand Rapids, MI.
   1989, Pages 157-159, Adapted from Jesus die Laaste,
   Gelowig Nage Dink, Deel 2 Pretoria, DBC Bookshop,
   Marshall, Morgan and Scott, London, England, 1980.
6. Bonhoeffer, Dietrich., *LIFE TOGETHER; A
   Discussion of Christian Fellowship,* Harper and Row

Publishers, Inc. 1954, Pages 34-37, Published in Germany under Gemeinsames Leben

7. Tozer, A.W.., *THE PURSUIT OF GOD,* Christian Publications Inc., Harrisburg, PA., Tyndale House Publishers, Wheaton, IL., 1982,83, Page 90

CHAPTER EIGHT

Gratitude and Compassion

Isa_63:7

I will recount the steadfast love of the LORD, the praises of the LORD, according to all that the LORD has granted us, and the great goodness to the house of Israel that he has granted them according to his compassion according to the abundance of his steadfast love.

The development and popularity of what has been identified as "Positive Psychology" has become an accepted form of the social sciences. "Positive Psychology" focuses on the ways to improve the social and psychological health of individuals in order to increase productivity and happiness. In fact, the most of the research involves an attempt to discover in what manner true, complete or persistent happiness may be developed.

Moving away from the negative

Psychologists have come to discover that human beings have a bent toward, we might say a natural disposition toward the bad or negative. In an article in AMERICAN Psychologist November 2006 Martin E. P. Seligman, Tayyab Rashid and Acacia C. Parks of the Positive Psychology Center at the University of Pennsylvania write; "The negative quite easily attract human attention and memory, and the larger literature on "bad is stronger than good" (Baumeister, Bratlavsky, Finkenauer, & Vohs, 2001) testifies to this. It makes evolutionary sense that negative emotions, tied as they are to threat, loss and trespass, should trump happiness".[1]

It is a wonder here again that the scientific bias towards attributing a disposition that is naturally intent on the bad and negative to natural selection, as opposed to the fall of mankind in the garden where threat, loss and trespass ruined happiness. However, the authors continue; "Human beings are naturally biased to remembering the negative, attending to the negative, and expecting the worst."[2] It is this tendency that is the inevitable cause of unhappiness, depression and the progression to other psychological and physical maladies leading further to disease and psychosis.

The connection between our current inescapable disposition toward, might I say "cursedness", is a barrier to our inability to lasting happiness (blessedness) or I might say everlasting happiness. People of the Book might well remember the words of the law giver Moses; Deu 30:15-20 "See, I have set before you today life and good, death and evil. "If you obey the commandments of the LORD your God that I command you today, by loving the LORD your God, by walking in his ways, and by keeping his commandments and his statutes and his rules, then you shall live and multiply, and the LORD your God will bless you in the land that you are entering to take possession of it. But if your heart turns away, and you will not hear, but are drawn away to worship other gods and serve them, Deu 30:18 I declare to you today, that you shall surely perish. You shall not live long in the land that you are going over the Jordan to enter and possess. I call heaven and earth to witness against you today, that I have set before you life and death, blessing and curse. Therefore choose life, that you and your offspring may live, loving the LORD your God, obeying his voice and holding fast to him, for he is your life and length of days."

Positive Psychology though has discovered an antidote to our predicament; psychologists have discovered that there are three paths or environments for happiness. The three paths are seemingly integrated, progressive and cumulative.

The first path is "the Pleasant Life" it consist of pleasures or the more hedonic emotions associated with pleasures. These emotions brought on by pleasurable activities produce positive feelings about the future and build hope, faith, trust and confidence. The happiness elicited by "the Pleasant Life" also include positive emotions about the past including satisfaction, contentment, fulfillment and serenity.

A second path or level of happiness is "the Engaged Life" where happiness is experienced through strong engagements with life that pursues involvement and absorption with others and the world around us. The main idea is a focus beyond oneself where it is said; "the self is lost".

A third path and level of happiness is "the Meaningful Life" involving the pursuit of meaning. At the level of "the Meaningful Life" the author's say; "This consists in using one's signature strengths and talents to belong and serve something that one believes is bigger than self. It is then as all three of these paths convene and fully intertwine that we find "the Full Life".

The research concludes that it is really only activities that help individuals to focus on "meaning" and "engagement" to be significantly impactful and correlated highly to a higher level of life satisfaction and a lower incidence of depression. The center of the therapeutic interventions for moving towards "the Full Life" focus on three highly impactful areas; gratitude and forgiveness training, optimism and hope, love and attachment.[3]

In another paper published in the Journal of International Association of Applied Psychology 2008 Martin E. P. Seligman outlines physical and psycho social benefits of Positive Psychology. Effects were cited for positive results of positive affect in protection against disease such as coronary and cardiovascular events, stroke, depression, frailty measurements, hospitalization recovery time was seen to be reduced and even colds and influenza were seen as reduced. Many Psychologists see gratitude and gratitude intervention as one of the most helpful and positive affective treatments for Psychological health.[4]

Alex Wood, Stephen Joseph and Alex Liney write in The Psychologist January 2007 an article titled GRATITUDE-PARENT OF ALL VIRTUES in it they say; "the first reason that gratitude may be an important personality trait is because it seems to have one of the strongest links with mental health of any personality variable."[3]   Lawrence J. Crabb, Jr. & Dan B. Allender have written; "It is a mistake to think of encouragement as a set of specific words or phrases. Encouragement depends less on which words we use than on the motivation behind them. Words that encourage are (1) inspired by love, and (2) directed toward fear. These two conditions must be met for words to encourage. Let us look at these conditions in more detail.

Condition 1: Words that encourage are prompted by love, not by fear; that is, the words spoken must never function as a layer for the speaker;

Condition 2: Words that encourage are aimed not at another's layers with the intent of rearranging them, but rather at another's hidden fear with the intent of reducing it. . . .

To be encouraging, words must be prompted by love. That's the first condition. The second condition is equally important: they must be directed to fear. From my love to another's fear-- that's the formula. Words of rebuke, exhortation, suggestion, instruction, or sympathy must all meet these two conditions if they are to further God's purposes and qualify as words of encouragement.

Targeting our words toward fear of another is an easily stated but often misunderstood concept. Too many people reason like this: "All this encouragement business about warmth and supportiveness and acceptance is really off the mark. It fails to address the real problem and evidences a weak view of sin. People need less affirmation and more exhortation to put off the old man and put on the new."

People with "executive personalities"(who rarely have close friends) mercilessly pound others about their responsibilities. They apply pressure in every available way to compel others to have devotions, witness, attend church, and tithe. Some people, depending on their temperament, conform to the pressure and appear to move along nicely on the road to spiritual maturity. Others rebel. In either case, little heart movement toward God takes place.

The still popular cult of Christian self-love, whose cardinal teaching is "You must learn to love yourself," leads to the reaction to harsh exhorters by swinging to the other extreme. "We just need to be warm and unconditionally caring. Exhortation, calls to discipline, and pressure to make commitments are all counterproductive to spiritual growth. People need an atmosphere of loving acceptance for growth to occur. Only in the context of love will personal maturity develop."

These people come dangerously close to buying into humanism, an unbiblical philosophy that affirms the inherent goodness of man and argues that problems result when society thwarts the expression of that goodness by an oppressive system of laws and sanctions. Christians need to divorce themselves from this idea by recognizing the radical results of mankind's fall into sin. The truth is, people have no natural tendency to conform their lives to the character of God. Straying from the path of righteousness is as natural to us as bucking is to a bronco.

Spiritual regeneration by the Holy Spirit provides us with new motivation and goals, but our sinful tendencies remain. Therefore we do require exhortation, rebuke discipline-- and the Bible is filled with it. The prophet Amos would have scorned the notion that Jews of his day were essentially cooperative people needing only a loving environment for their real selves to blossom with love and good deeds. The Bible instructs us to "stimulate" each other to greater love and better behavior (Heb. 10:24). Passively accepting people where they are until they get around to godly living is not a biblical strategy for encouragement.

Encouragement, therefore, must not be defined as either rigorous exhortation or accepting warmth. Both will be involved in the work of encouragement, but neither gets at the essence of what encouragement is. Encouragement depends on loving motivation in the encourager as well as wisdom to discern the needs of the person accurately. The actual words used may be admonishing, rebuking, correcting, reproving, instructing, explaining, sympathizing, reflecting, affirming or self-disclosing. If the motive is love and the target is fear, the words will be encouraging."[6]

Against these there is no need for laws; love, joy, peace, patience, kindness, goodness, faithfulness, gentleness and self-control Gal. 5:22-23. Of course this is not a new declaration, it is the outworking of I AM the three in ONE, through the personal life of the Spirit of I AM the three in one as we look to Him.

As scientific data is gathered and analyzed it is clear how much I AM the three in one and His Word to us is vindicated and verified. It is also true that the presuppositions we bring to scientific proofs will seem to verify our conclusions whether naturally developed or divinely initiated and governed.

Giving in to Absolute Love

J.I. Packer and Thomas Howard say; "The question of esteem and identity now appear in a new light. What the psychologists and gurus offered us was self-discovery through introspection, self-scrutiny, and self-love. What Christ in the gospel offers us is, in effect, self-discovery through self-abandonment to God's love. This is self-discovery not in isolation, but in relationship; not by shutting oneself up to keep the world out and withdrawing in to some inner sanctum of the psyche, but by opening oneself up to the invading Savior and letting him lead one's heart out into the world in sympathetic care and concern for others. The esteem which creates and shapes our identity, and thereby leads us to a strong and joyful sense of identity, is the redeeming love of our creator to us his sinful creatures. We deserve to be shaken off into hell, as one shakes an insect off one's hand into the fire, and here is God seeking to love us into heaven at the cost of the death of his Son. And the gospel affirms that all avenues to self-discovery apart from opening myself to God's approach are blind alleys, for the notion of myself to which they lead me, however agreeable, consoling, bracing, and fascinating it may be (and what can be more fascinating to sinners than the study of themselves?) is precisely not "me," any more than the notion of myself which by its collapse sent me flying to the shrinks and gurus was "me." In telling me how I function in terms of my make-up the counselors are *not* telling me who I am; that is something which only God makes known to me. There is no way in heaven, earth or hell that I know myself without knowing the One who made me, and for whom I was made in the first instance, and from whom I should never have lapsed.

But there is more to the matter of my identity than just this. From Jesus Christ I receive a new identity, which is henceforth my true identity as a sinner now redeemed, an identity which I may truly know as the real "me." This new identity has two aspects, just as my natural identity does: namely, the relational and the dispositional. The relational aspect has to do with commitment and identification. As Christian marriage changes a woman's identity, because she commits herself to her husband as leader and identifies with the task of furthering his welfare and his interests, so Christian faith changes the believers identity; for having committed myself to follow Christ. I am now bidden to identify myself with him in such a way that the pattern of his life, death, and resurrection become the pattern of my own existence henceforth. His laying aside of his prerogatives, rights, dignities, and interests, here on earth and his laying down of his life for others must be reproduced in me here and now at the level of motives, goals and strategies. I am, in short, to imitate Christ, to model myself on him, to walk as he walked, indeed to *be* Christ in my attitudes to other people.

The dispositional aspect of our new identity springs from the reality of our new creation. People who become Christians may look the same from the outside as they did before, but they are not the same inside. They are new people, radically altered-- though they themselves may not fully at first appreciate this. Deep down within them, however, deeper than depth psychology can plumb or sustained introspection can reach, God has changed the motivational core of their personality-- what Scripture calls the "heart"-- in such a way that now there moves within them a longing and love for God: God's will, God's truth, God's service, God's fellowship, God's honor and glory. It is a desire to know and please and enjoy and share the God of one's salvation, and only as this desire is satisfied is their heart at all contented. So, whereas before it was one's nature to live to oneself, it is now what may almost be called and instinctual drive to live for God, and worship becomes the deepest joy of one's heart."[7]

I AM the three in one **is** the happiest being of all, He does whatever He pleases; **Psa 135:6-7** "Whatever the LORD pleases, he does, in heaven and on earth, in the seas and all deeps. "He it is who makes the clouds rise at the end of the earth, who makes lightnings for the rain and brings forth the wind from his storehouses."

Where to find happiness

In His abundant uncontained happiness, He overflows with Absolute Love to people, He has no needs because everything belongs to Him and was created by Him. If a need would arise He would create the satisfier of the need. His love to us overflows out of the Absolute Love within Himself. Deu 10:14-15 "Behold, to the LORD your God belong heaven and the heaven of heavens, the earth with all that is in it. Yet the LORD set his heart in love on your fathers and chose their offspring after them, you above all peoples, as you are this day."

The Absolute Love of I AM the three in one flows from the Father to the Son and the Son to the Father and is transmitted between the three by the Spirit. Each person within the one having a distinct role in the overflowing LOVE that comes to us as we are established by love to hope in Him; **Psa 147:10-11** "His delight is not in the strength of the horse, nor his pleasure in the legs of a man, but the LORD takes pleasure in those who fear him, in those who hope in his steadfast love." His personal delight, His gratitude is reflected in the activity of His Son Jesus, Yeshua, Isa; Mat 17:1-5 "And after six days Jesus took with him Peter and James, and John his brother, and led them up a high mountain by themselves. And he was transfigured before them, and his face shone like the sun, and his clothes became white as light. And behold, there appeared to them Moses and Elijah, talking with him. And Peter said to Jesus, "Lord, it is good that we are here. If you wish, I will make three tents here, one for you and one for Moses and one for Elijah." He was still speaking when, behold, a bright cloud overshadowed them, and a voice from the cloud said, "This is my beloved Son, with whom I am well pleased; listen to him."

The happy gratitude of I AM that flows out of the relational Absolute Love of I AM. He eternally enjoys the relationship of the three Absolute Love flows out in compassion toward His creation. His overflowing compassionate love allows Him to be slow to anger and to forgive thousands to overflow with steadfast love. I AM needs no gratitude or forgiveness therapy, it is the core of His existence, it is His Glory revealed.

Gratitude is the characteristic outgrowth of believing that gives us the ability to look at all good things as gifts from God and causes us give in return so the gifts can be shared by all. Compassion is the characteristic outgrowth of believing that gives us the ability to be gracious (giving undeserved favor) and merciful (not demanding retribution) so that we might live in a way that will be most beneficial to ourselves and others and glorifying to God.

The irony of much thinking about man is that the elimination of a creator makes the creature think more highly of self than we ought to think, putting ourselves into the place where we believe by our own mechanistic, social and psychological designs we can make the kind of world we desire; that we believe will make us happy. The studies indicated that at the longest the positive results of the gratitude and forgiveness therapy lasted only about six months. On the other hand, we throw away any hope of lasting happiness or everlasting happiness by not having an absolute mooring from which happiness is imparted.

Francis A. Schaeffer writes; "One of the problems with humanists is that they tend to "love" humanity as whole-- Man with a capital M, Man as an idea-- but forget about man as an individual, as a person. Christianity is to be the exact opposite. Christianity is not to love in abstraction, but to love the individual who stands before me in a person to person relationship. He must never be faceless to me or I am denying everything I say I believe. This concept will always involve some cost: it is no cheap thing, because we live in a fallen world, and we ourselves are fallen.

Now we must ask, what happens when someone has been hurt by my sin? The Bible teaches that the moment we have confessed this sin to God, the shed blood of Jesus is enough to cleanse the moral guilt. As Christians, we insist that all sin is ultimately against God. When I hurt the man, I sin against God. But let us never forget that this does not change the fact that because man has been made in the image of God, the man I have hurt has real value. And this must be important to me, not only as a concept but in my practice and demonstration. My fellowman is not unimportant: he is God's image-bearer. That is true of the non-Christian man as well as of the Christian. He is lost, but he is still a man. Thus when God says," My child, this sin is different; in this sin you have hurt another person," I respond, "What shall I do LORD?" And the answer is clear from the Word of God: "Make it right with the man you have hurt. The man you have hurt is not a zero."

But what is the usual reaction when God says to me, "Go make it right"? It is to answer, "But that would be humiliating." Yet surely, if I have been willing to tell God I am sorry when I have sinned, I must be willing to tell this to the man I have hurt. How can I say, "I am sorry" to God, if I am not willing to say, "I am sorry" to the man I have hurt, when he is my equal, my fellow creature, my kind? Such repentance is meaningless hypocrisy. We cannot just trample human relationships and expect our relationship to God to be lovely, beautiful and open. This is not only a matter of what is legally right, but of a true relationship of person to person on the basis of who I am and who the man is.

In James 5:16 we are told, "Confess your faults one to another." We are not told to confess our faults to a priest, nor to the group, unless the group has been harmed, but to the person we have harmed. This is a very simple admonition, but in our present imperfect state, very difficult to obey. To go and say, "I am sorry" is to enter by the low door; first in confessing to God, and then to the individual harmed. Let me emphasize, this is a *person* before me, a human being, made in God's image. So, it is not such a low door after all, all it involves is being willing to admit our equality with the one we have hurt. Being his equal it is perfectly right that I should want to say, "I am sorry." Only a desire to be superior makes me afraid to confess and apologize.

If I am in living relationship with the Trinity, my human relationships become more important in one way, because I see the real value of man, but less important in another way because I do not need to be God in these relationships any longer. So now I can go up to the man and say, "I am sorry for such and such a specific harm I have done you," without smashing the integration point of my universe, because it is no longer myself, but God. "[8]

Acknowledging, loving, worshipping a creator and realizing ourselves as being created allows us as creatures to think rightly about ourselves and become happy, everlastingly happy. Everlastingly happy only as we everlastingly keep our focus upon I AM the three in one from whom happiness overflows, gratitude is constantly exuded and forgiveness is poured out.

Yadah (Gratitude, throw, cast, confess, give thanks, praise, laud)

Gen29:35,49:8,**Lev**5:5,16:21,26:40,**Num**5:7,**2Sam**22:50,**1Ki**8:33,8:35,**1Chr**16:4,16:7,16:8,16:34,16:35,16:41,23:30,25:3,29:13,**2Chr**5:13,6:24,6:26,7:3,7:6,20:21,30:22,31:2,**Ezra**3:11,10:1,**Neh**1:6,9:2,9:3,11:17,12:24,12:46,**Job**40:14,**Psa**6:5,7:17,9:1,18:49,28:7,30:4,30:9,30:12,32:5,33:2,35:18,42:5,42:11,43:4,43:5,44:8,45:17,49:18,52:9,54:6,57:9,67:3,67:5,71:22,75:1,76:10,79:13,86:12,88:10,89:5,92:1,97:12,99:3,100:4,105:1,106:1,106:47,107:1,107:8,107:15,107:21,107:31,108:3,109:30,111:1,118:1,118:19,118:21,118:28,118:29,119:7,119:62,122:4,136:1,136:2,136:3,136:26,138:1,138:2,138:4,139:14,140:13,142:7,145:10,**Prov**28:13,**Isa**12:1,12:4,25:1,38:18,38:19,**Jer**33:11,50:14,**Lam**3:53,**Dan**9:4,9:20,**Zec** 1:21

Rakam (Compassion, love)**Gen** 43:14, 49:25,**Exo** 33:19,**Lev** 11:18,**Deu**13:17,14:17,30:3,**Judg** 5:30, **2 Sam** 24:14,**1 Ki** 8:50,**2 Ki**13:23,**1Chr**2:44,21:13,**2Chr**30:9,**Neh**1:11,9:19,9:27,9:28,9:31,**Psa**18:1,25:6,40:11,51:1,69:16,77:9,79:8,102:13,103:4,103:13,106:46,**116:5**,119:77,119:156,145:9,**Prov**12:10,28:13,30:16,**Isa**

9:17,13:18,14:1,27:11,30:18,46:3,47:6,49:10,49:13,49:15,54:7,5
4:8,54:10,55:7,60:10,63:7,63:15,**Jer**6:23,12:15,13:14,16:5,21:7,3
0:18,31:20,33:26,42:12,50:42,**Lam**3:22,3:32,**Ezek**20:26,39:25,
Dan9:9,9:18,**Hosea**1:6,1:7,2:1,2:4,2:19,2:23,14:3,**Amos**1:11,
Micah7:19,**Hab**3:2,**Zec**1:12,1:16,7:9,10:6

Rakum (compassion, softness, gentleness)**Exo34:6**,**Deu**
4:31,**2Chr**30:9,**Neh**9:17,9:31,**Psa**78:38,86:15,103:8,111:4,112:
4,145:8, **Joel** 2:13,**Jonah** 4:2

Eucharistia (Gratitude, thankfulness)**Acts** 24:3, **1 Cor** 14:16,2
Cor 4:15,9:11,9:12,**Eph** 5:4, **Phil** 4:6,**Col** 2:7,4:2,1 Th 3:9,**1
Tim** 2:1,**4:3,4:4,Rev** 4:9,7:12

Eucharisteo (be thankful,   feel obligated, give or return
thanks)**Mat**15:36,26:27,**Mark**8:6,14:23,**Luke**17:16,18:11,22:7,
22:19,**John**6:11,6:23,11:41,**Acts**27:35,28:15,**Rom**1:8,1:21,7:25,
14:6,16:4,**1Cor**1:4,1:14,10:30,11:24,14:17,14:18,**2Cor** 1:11,**Eph**
1:16,5:20, **Phil** 1:3,**Col** 1:3,1:12 ,3:17,**1 Th** 1:2, 2:13,5:18,**2 Th**
1:3,2:13, **Phil**e 1:4,**Rev** 11:17

Eleos (Compassion, mercy, pity,) **Mat** 9:13,12:7,23:23,**Luke**
1:50,1:54,1:58,1:72,1:78,10:37,**Rom**9:23,11:31,15:9,**Gal**6:16,**E
ph** 2:4,1 **Tim** 1:2,2 **Tim** 1:2,1:16,1:18,**Titus** 1:4,3:5,**Heb**
4:16,**James** 2:13,3:17,**1 Pet** 1:3,**2 John** 1:3, **Jude** 1:2,1:21

1. Seligman, Martin E.P., Rashid, Tayyab and Parks,
   Acacia C. , American Psychologist, Nov. 2006
2. Ibid.
3. Ibid
4. Seligman, Martin E.P., Journal of International
   Association of Applied Psychology, 2008
5. Wood, Alex, Joseph, Stephen, and Liney, Alex, The
   Psychologist, January, 2007.
6. Crabb, Lawrence J. and Allender, Dan B..,
   ENCOURAGEMENT THE KEY TO CARING,
   Pyranee Books, Zondervan Publishing House, Grand
   Rapids, NMI. 1984, Pages 71-79.

7. Packer, J.I. and Howard, Thomas. *CHRISTIANITY:THE TRUE HUMANISM,* Word Inc., Waco, TX. 1985, Pages 233-234

8. Schaeffer, Francis A., *TRUE SPIRITUALITY,* Tyndale House Publishers, Wheaton, IL. 1971, Pages 157, 158.

CHAPTER NINE

Freedom, Stewardship and Servanthood

Joh 8:32 and you will know the truth, and the truth will set you free ."

Rom 6:22 But now that you have been set free from sin and have become slaves of God, the fruit you get leads to sanctification and its end, eternal life.

1Co 9:17 For if I do this of my own will, I have a reward, but if not of my own will, I am still entrusted with a stewardship.

Mat 20:28 even as the Son of Man came not to be served but to serve, and to give his life as a ransom for many."

Gal 5:13 For you were called to freedom, brothers. Only do not use your freedom as an opportunity for the flesh, but through love serve one another.

The United States of America, Declaration of Independence is a definitive cry against tyrannical rule that limits the very nature of being humans. The famous words "we hold these truths to be self-evident, that all men are created equal that they are endowed by their Creator with certain unalienable Rights, that among these are Life, Liberty and the pursuit of Happiness."

The words to follow may be known or at least noted less, "That to secure these rights, Governments are instituted among Men, deriving their just powers from the consent of the governed, --That whenever any Form of Government becomes destructive of these ends, it is the Right of the People to alter or to abolish it, and to institute new Government, laying its foundation on such principles and organizing its powers in such form, as to them shall seem most likely to affect their Safety and Happiness. Prudence, indeed, will dictate that Governments long established should not be changed for light and transient causes; and accordingly all experience hath shewn, that mankind are more disposed to suffer, while evils are sufferable, than to right themselves by abolishing the forms to which they are accustomed. But when a long train of abuses and usurpations, pursuing invariably the same Object evinces a design to reduce them under absolute Despotism, it is their right, it is their duty, to throw off such Government, and to provide new Guards for their future security."

Tyrannical governments and Despotic rulers, whether under the name of a so called "god" or to make themselves to be god, is the wasteland of human history. The carnage flows back to the fall and our eviction from standing in the presence of I AM the three in one.

You shall be free indeed

The loss of life, liberty and everlasting happiness is inevitably the result of separation from Him. Thinking that I AM might be withholding some pleasure or benefit from us we seek to find benefit elsewhere. In seeking freedom from the creator the creature has become trapped in the prisons of our own making. There is no absolute apart from Him. The inalienable rights of life, liberty and the pursuit of happiness being self-evident also evidence the purpose of I AM in the way He created the world.

Consider the words of Daniel Fuller; "In looking back over redemptive history, therefore, it should be plain that the earth will render proper worship to God not only to the extent that it is filled with those who worship him but also to the extent of the zeal with which they worship him. Had it not been vital for God to order holy history so that later generations would worship him the more fervently, it is conceivable that there would have been no need for a redemptive history that consists in an extended overlap between this evil age and the glorious age to come. However, we know that God's own intense love for his glory cannot settle for anything less from the world he has created, for Jesus said that he would spit out of his mouth those who had mere lukewarm love for him (Rev. 3:16). Therefore God ordained a redemptive history whose sequence fully displays his glory so that, at the end, the greatest possible number of people would have had the historical antecedent necessary to engender fervent love for God. Thus Paul sums it all up in Romans 11:32: "God has bound all men over to disobedience so that he may have mercy on them all." Viewing redemptive history in this light then evokes in Paul the doxology of verses 33-36.

But some might ask, Why does God not use his omnipotence to make everyone sing such a doxology from the start and thus avoid the extended overlap and the problem of evil that redemptive history entails? The answer is that God could find no delight in a creation that, puppet like, was forced to love him. His love for himself arises freely, that is, because he sees clearly that he is indeed worthy of all his own worship. And unless creation's delight in God is also a free act, arising from the full display of all his glory in the sequence of redemptive history, creation would not be consonant with God's delight in himself, and God could not tolerate it.

The one thing, therefore, that God is doing in all of redemptive history is to show forth his mercy in such a way that the greatest number of people will throughout eternity delight in him with all their heart, strength, and mind. When the earth of the new creation is filled with such people, then God's purpose in showing forth his mercy will have been achieved. The "glorious freedom" (Rom. 8:21) that will then be enjoyed by the children of God and the complete orderliness of all creation, in contrast to the "frustration" that now prevails (v. 20), will represent the fullness of God's glory by showing that he was so sufficient in himself that he could find complete fulfillment and blessedness simply in mercifully imparting the ultimate blessing to creation, with no ulterior purpose beyond that. All the events of redemptive history and their meaning as recorded in the Bible compose a unity in that they conjoin to bring about this goal."[1]

The clear evidence of mankind is that we have chosen a liberty, freedom from I AM's absolute love, to find ourselves imprisoned by our own limitedness. We are the creatures and I AM is the Creator, we are finite in resource and I AM is infinite in resource, we are vulnerable and prone to error, I AM is invulnerable and the one who establishes truth. Human history is a history of futility in finding liberty, of destroying life of heartache and immense toil in the pursuit of happiness. What did I AM say? "You will surely die." The promise of increased pain, toil, sweat, thorns, thistles and loss of freedom and happiness is a reality and all of us return to the dust from which we were formed.

If as has been said, "the chief end of man is to glorify God and enjoy Him forever", we have gone astray from that exponentially. Freedom, true liberty is found in becoming what we were meant to be as creatures. As I have said it is ironic that the more we realize our place as creatures before a creator the more we are likely to hold up one another as significant and unique, valued. We are equal in place as creatures but distinct in role and I AM has created each of us to be everlastingly happy as that role is fulfilled by us and in us.

J.I. Packer writes in contrasting the world's idea of freedom as absence of restraint with the Bible's idea of freedom; "The second approach to freedom is distinctly Christian. It is evangelical, personal and positive. It defines freedom persuasively, that is, in terms which (so it urges) all should recognize as expressing what they are really after. The terms relate not to externals, which vary from age to age and person to person, but to unchanging realities of the inner life.

This definition starts with freedom from and freedom not to--- in this case, freedom from the guilt and power of sin, and freedom not to be dominated by tyrannical self-will--- but it centers on freedom for: freedom for God and godliness, freedom to love and serve one's Maker and fellow creatures, freedom for the joy, hope and contentment which God gives to sinners who believe in Christ. The essence of freedom(so the claim runs) lies in these inward qualities of the heart, of which modern secular man knows nothing.

This approach sees freedom as an inner state of all who are fulfilling the potential of their own created nature by worshipping and serving their Savior-God from the heart. Their freedom is freedom not to do wrong, but to do right; not to break the moral law, but to keep it, not to forget God, but to cleave to him every moment, in every endeavor and relationship; not to abuse and exploit others, but to lay down one's life for them (cf. John 15:12,13; 1 John 3:16)). Freedom for such free service and self-giving is beyond the capacity, even the comprehension, of fallen human nature. At first sight few can recognize it as freedom at all. Though it is really the way of life for which we were made, it so negates the self-absorbed lifestyle which we all instinctively choose that it seems to us anti-human and frightens us off. In fact, the only way anyone comes to know it at all is as a gift of the risen Christ, who affirms his penitent disciples in their self-denial and imparts his life to us as we give away our own.

One aspect of this freedom is integrity that simplicity and purity of heart which, as Kierkegaard analyzed it, consists in willing one thing, namely the will and glory of God, so that one's motives are freed from the taint of self-regard.

A second aspect is spontaneity. Unlike the rule-ridden Pharisees, whom Jesus pictured living(as it were) by numbers, the free person in Christ invests creative enterprise and resourcefulness in the task of pleasing and praising God and doing good to one's fellows. Where Pharisees concern is simply to avoid doing wrong, the free person seeks to make the most and best of every situation, thus becoming lively and sometimes breathtaking company.

A final aspect is contentment, the fruit of God's gift of a joy within that increases all life's pleasures, stays with one whatever is present or lacking in one's outward circumstances, and enables one to accept without bitterness the most acute forms of suffering and pain. In short, the real Christian-- for that is the person I am describing-- is free for holiness, humanness and happiness-- a freedom which surely merits its name."[2]

Now this is a twist on freedom, not being free to do anything at all, being free to become exactly what we were created for, glorifying I AM. We were each of us born to uniquely image forth I AM. It will take an infinite number of us infinitely with individual roles to image forth what is infinite. In order to realize this kind of freedom we must be captivated by I AM the three in one.

It is only through being willingly captivated and passionately enamored by the infinite I AM who is absolute love that we can fully find freedom to be what through us fully reflects back to Him what will make us everlastingly happy. This freedom only comes from being willingly captive to I AM the three in one who is the only absolutely free being, uncreated, eternal, all knowing, all wise, all loving, all powerful, without beginning or end, and unchangeable. We can only say along with Paul who was miraculously changed from a despotic murdering religious bigot to find happiness in being captivated by I AM; Rom 11:29-36 "For the gifts and the calling of God are irrevocable. For just as you were at one time disobedient to God but now have received mercy because of their disobedience, so they too have now been disobedient in order that by the mercy shown to you they also may now receive mercy. For God has consigned all to disobedience, that he may have mercy on all. Oh, the depth of the riches and wisdom and knowledge of God! How unsearchable are his judgments and how inscrutable his ways! "For who has known the mind of the Lord, or who has been his counselor?" "Or who has given a gift to him that he might be repaid?" For from him and through him and to him are all things. To him be glory forever. Amen."

So also, the history of mankind is the history of I AM, the three in one, coming again and again to show mercy, pour out grace and bring freedom to anyone who will have it.

Freedom requires constraints and in an environment of separateness from absolute love it requires restraints. I AM the three in one is constrained by absolute love, He is absolutely self-controlled. There are no controls outside of the being of I AM that could restrain Him. He is slow to anger, He forestalls His anger in the face of rebellious creatures.

The fruit of looking only to I AM three in one includes self-control. "2Co 5:14 For the love of Christ controls us, because we have concluded this: that one has died for all, therefore all have died; 2Co 5:15 and he died for all, that those who live might no longer live for themselves but for him who for their sake died and was raised." The love of I AM controls or elsewhere it says constrains us apart from this love are needed restraints. Then it must be clear that we are not absolutely free, we do not have that capacity, we are not all knowing or all powerful. We are only free in full, perfected relationship to I AM.

Richard Lovelace says; "Patients tested for glaucoma are shown a circle which represents their visual field and then asked to point out the areas they can see. The disease typically darkens the center of the field, while leaving some vision on the periphery. The fallen mind's view of the world is like that of a glaucoma patient. Its view of all things is darkened and distorted by sin, but it has sort of twilight vision of the periphery of life. In the inner circle of ultimate concerns, however, it is in deeper darkness. It has at best only a dim apprehension of the grandeur of God, the depth of its own need, and the real significance of its relationship to other people.

The gift of faith is a divine healing of this central blindness of the soul. It is an exact reversal of the entrance into darkness which was the essence of the Fall. Through faith in the Messiah, the soul is able to face reality again with cleared vision. As T.S. Elliot said, "Humankind cannot bear very much reality." But through the light shed by the Holy Spirit on the Messiah and his saving work, the soul can take in at a glance the truth about its own standing before God. It can bear the bad news about the justice of God and the depth of its sin, because it can see in the same glance the good news of the grace of Christ available simply through faith.

The blaze of this illumination, faith necessarily involves repentance. The Greek word for repentance, metanoia, literally means "a change of mind"- toward God, toward oneself and toward others. It is a Copernican revolution in which the self is evicted from the center of life, and the Messiah is enthroned instead. Sorrow for sin and gratitude for the amazing mercy of God replace self-assertion, evasion of God and the soul's fallen motives. Optimum spiritual health simply involves remaining in the focused light of truth concerning our needs and their fulfillment in Jesus' redemptive work(1 John 1:5-7) An honest assessment of our spiritual state and a deepening trust in the Messiah are qualities which guarantee our continued spiritual growth.

The heart which is illuminated by the Holy Spirit's application of truth is progressively set free from its bondage of sin and error. . .. As our hearts, the subconscious root of our personality, are increasingly filled with light, our minds are freed to discover and affirm truth, our wills are freed to obey God, and our emotions are released to feel about all things as God feels about them. . .. This fellowship will of course lead to works, to thoughts and words and acts on behalf of the kingdom of God. But these works will emerge primarily out of our fellowship with Christ. And we will be clearly aware that in the deepest sense they are his works and not ours- the acts of the risen Christ."[3]

The history of mankind is full of the fact that mankind in making gods in our own image have become less free. Your complaint might be one often voiced if I AM is all loving why would He allow or even command the death of so many people in the Law and Writings of the Tanakh (Old Testament)?

The development of man's imagined religion was a bloody, vicious and enslaving circle of violence and human abuse. In ancient Canaan and surrounding societies, the worship of Baal and Molech included sacrificing of babies and young children, they were burned alive. The cannibalistic practice of eating one's children and the bloody sacrificing of young virgins was among the rituals of these religious communities.

In addition, ancient temples were filled with enslaved prostitutes to use in the worship of gods that demanded impurity and enslavement. I AM the three in one stood against this withholding anger, yet in loving-kindness and mercy holding out a different way a choice that the people were unwilling to make. They continually shunned His forgiveness. Gen 6:5-6 "The LORD saw that the wickedness of man was great in the earth, and that every intention of the thoughts of his heart was only evil continually. And the LORD was sorry that he had made man on the earth, and it grieved him to his heart."

Yet I AM spares and forgives even if there are a few who still refrain from evil and continue to act rightly. Gen 18:20-32 Then the LORD said, "Because the outcry against Sodom and Gomorrah is great and their sin is very grave, I will go down to see whether they have done altogether according to the outcry that has come to me. And if not, I will know." So the men turned from there and went toward Sodom, but Abraham still stood before the LORD. Then Abraham drew near and said, "Will you indeed sweep away the righteous with the wicked? Suppose there are fifty righteous within the city. Will you then sweep away the place and not spare it for the fifty righteous who are in it? Far be it from you to do such a thing, to put the righteous to death with the wicked, so that the righteous fare as the wicked! Far be that from you! Shall not the Judge of all the earth do what is just?" And the LORD said, "If I find at Sodom fifty righteous in the city, I will spare the whole place for their sake." Abraham answered and said, "Behold, I have undertaken to speak to the Lord, I who am but dust and ashes. Suppose five of the fifty righteous are lacking. Will you destroy the whole city for lack of five?" And he said, "I will not destroy it if I find forty-five there." Again he spoke to him and said, "Suppose forty are found there." He answered, "For the sake of forty I will not do it." Then he said, "Oh let not the Lord be angry, and I will speak. Suppose thirty are found there." He answered, "I will not do it, if I find thirty there." He said, "Behold, I have undertaken to speak to the Lord. Suppose twenty are found there." He answered, "For the sake of twenty I will not destroy it." The leaders of Israel even fell into the entrapments of these horrific activities. Gen Then he said, "Oh let not the Lord be angry, and I will speak again but this once. Suppose ten are found there." He answered, "For the sake of ten I will not destroy it."

Still mankind continues to follow after destructive, deadly, vicious and enslaving practices. 2Ki 16:2-3 Ahaz was twenty years old when he began to reign, and he reigned sixteen years in Jerusalem. And he did not do what was right in the eyes of the LORD his God, as his father David had done, but he walked in the way of the kings of Israel. He even burned his son as an offering, according to the despicable practices of the nations whom the LORD drove out before the people of Israel. Jer 7:30-36 "For the sons of Judah have done evil in my sight, declares the LORD. They have set their detestable things in the house that is called by my name, to defile it. And they have built the high places of Topheth, which is in the Valley of the Son of Hinnom, to burn their sons and their daughters in the fire," For the children of Israel and the children of Judah have done nothing but evil in my sight from their youth. The children of Israel have done nothing but provoke me to anger by the work of their hands, declares the LORD. This city has aroused my anger and wrath, from the day it was built to this day, so that I will remove it from my sight because of all the evil of the children of Israel and the children of Judah that they did to provoke me to anger--their kings and their officials, their priests and their prophets, the men of Judah and the inhabitants of Jerusalem. They have turned to me their back and not their face. And though I have taught them persistently, they have not listened to receive instruction. They set up their abominations in the house that is called by my name, to defile it. They built the high places of Baal in the Valley of the Son of Hinnom, to offer up their sons and daughters to Molech, though I did not command them, nor did it enter into my mind, that they should do this abomination, to cause Judah to sin. "Now therefore thus says the LORD, the God of Israel, concerning this city of which you say, 'It is given into the hand of the king of Babylon by sword, by famine, and by pestilence''.

It would be completely against the character and nature of Absolute Love to not let the anger of His love destroy these evil cultures. Absolute LOVE will not ignore or tolerate the injustice of the strong preying upon the weak. Absolute Love defends the child, the widow, the fatherless, and the humble who cry out for His mighty arm to save them from evil men.

A.W. Tozer declares; "One mighty fact there is which for us men overwhelms all other considerations and gives significance to everything we do. It is that the human race has left its first estate and is morally fallen.

Since the fall of man the earth has been a disaster area and everyone lives with a critical emergency. Nothing is normal. Everything is wrong and everyone is wrong until made right by the redeeming work of Christ and effective operation of the Holy Spirit.

The universal disaster of the Fall compels us to think differently about our obligation to our fellow men. What would be entirely permissible under normal conditions becomes wrong in the present situation, and many things not otherwise required are necessary because of abnormal conditions.

It is in view of this that all our Christian service must be evaluated. The needs of the people, not our own convenience, decide how far we should go and how much we shall do. Had there been no disaster there would have been no need for the Eternal Son to empty Himself and descend to Bethlehem's manger. Had there been no Fall there would have been no incarnation, no thorns, no cross. These resulted when divine goodness confronted the human emergency.

While Christ was the perfect example of the healthy normal man, He yet did not live a normal life. He sacrificed many pure enjoyments to give Himself to the holy work of moral rescue. His conduct was determined not by what was legitimate or innocent, but by our human need. He pleased not Himself but lived for the emergency; and as He was so are we in this world.

Before the judgment seat of Christ my service will be judged not by how much I have done but by how much I could have done. In God's sight my giving is measured not by how much I have given but by how much I could have given and how much I had left after my gift. The needs of the world and my total ability to minister to those needs decide the worth of my service.

Not by its size is my gift judged, but by how much of me there is in it. No man gives at all until he has given all. No man gives anything acceptable to God until he has first given himself in love and sacrifice.

The hero is sighted by his country not for the number of persons he has saved only, but for the degree of danger to himself present in his act. Service that can be done without peril, that carries no loss, no sacrifice, does not rate high in the sight of men or God.

In the work of the church the amount one man must do to accomplish a given task is determined by how much or how little the rest of the company is willing to do. It is a rare church whose members all put their shoulders to the wheel. The typical church is composed of the few whose shoulders are bruised by their faithful labors and the many who are unwilling to raise a blister in the service of God and their fellow men. There may be a bit of wry humor in all this, but it is quite certain that there will be no laughter when each of us gives account to God of the deeds done in the body.

I think that most Christians would be better pleased if the LORD did not inquire into their personal affairs too closely. They want Him to save them, keep them happy and take them to heaven at last, but not to be too inquisitive about their conduct or service. But He has searched us and known us; He knows our down sitting and our uprising and understands our thoughts afar off. There is no place to hide from those eyes that are as a flame of fire and there is no way to escape from the judgment of those feet that are fine brass. It is the part of wisdom to live with these things in mind."[4]

Instead of this enslavement mankind was meant to be a steward and a servant. Mankind was to care for one another and the creation. In the beginning, I AM made a park or a garden for mankind. In it man was to glorify I AM by enjoying Him forever. In the park was beauty untold and every plant and tree that was good for food. Gen 2:15 " The LORD God took the man and put him in the garden of Eden to work it and keep it." The Hebrew word for work in this voice also means serve, worship or cultivate and the Hebrew word for keep also means guard or protect. All things are from I AM and belong to I AM.

We are free when we become what we were created for, to be worshipers of I AM and protectors of one another and the creation. We are free when we become more loving.

Joh 8:31-36 So Jesus said to the Jews who had believed in him, "If you abide in my word, you are truly my disciples, and you will know the truth, and the truth will set you free." They answered him, "We are offspring of Abraham and have never been enslaved to anyone. How is it that you say, 'You will become free'?" Jesus answered them, "Truly, truly, I say to you, everyone who commits sin is a slave to sin. The slave does not remain in the house forever; the son remains forever. So if the Son sets you free, you will be free indeed**." Freedom is the characteristic outgrowth of believing that gives us the ability to set aside personal desires and postpone pleasure, (i.e. physical, emotional gratification), in order** that we be liberated to find complete satisfaction in God and be separated from enslaving entanglements.

Stewardship is the characteristic of believing that gives us the ability to be inter-connected with each other in a truly loving manner. We do not lose any integral parts of ourselves or disintegrate into another person, yet we value and need each other's gifts and uniqueness for the full use and completion of our own giftedness Servanthood is the characteristic of believing that gives us the ability to worship in everything that we do by looking to God to fill us and overflow through us into the lives of others for thoughtful attentiveness to God's desires for them.

R. C. Sproul writes; "How do we know if our faith is authentic? There are two basic tests for genuine faith. The first is our own inner disposition. A regenerate person has received the internal operation of the Holy Spirit, by which the inclination or disposition of the soul has been changed. The regenerate heart has a love and desire for Christ that is not found in the unbeliever. . . . In addition to the question of the heart, we must face the question of the presence or absence of the fruit of faith. Again, it is not a question of whether our fruit is perfect, but whether there is any fruit at all. No fruit means no faith. Some fruit means some faith. The Bible tells us we will know them by their fruit.

The fruit we are looking for is the fruit of obedience. . ..This is where works fit into the Christian life. We are not justified by our works, but we are justified unto works. The indispensable evidence of true faith is the presence of works. The works add nothing to the merit of Christ, by whose merit we are justified. But faith inevitably and necessarily produces works or it is not saving faith. . . .

Faith is shown or demonstrated by works. If no works are demonstrated, saving faith is absent. To have assurance of salvation we need objective evidence of the fruit in our lives. A regenerate person is a changed person. Two vital changes have taken place. The first change is a disposition of the soul affected by the Holy Spirit. The second change is the indwelling of the Spirit.

If a person goes through two such alterations-- regeneration and indwelling-- it is simply impossible that there be no change in the individuals life. It is a root change, so radical that it is called a new creation. The change in the root produces change in the fruit."[5]

Rom 12:1 I appeal to you therefore, brothers, by the mercies of God, to present your bodies as a living sacrifice, holy and acceptable to God, which is your spiritual worship. Absolute Love transforms us to freely become captive to a life of sacrifice to others, serving others as a stewardship to I AM.

Kopshiy(Freedom)**Exo**21:2,21:5,21:26,21:27,**Deu**15:12,15:13
,15:18,**1Sam**17:25,**Job**3:19,39:5,**Psa**88:5,**Isa**58:6,**Jer**34:9,34:10
,34:11,34:14,34:16

Kapash Lev 19:20

Nakah (Free, pure, clean, empty, exempt, innocent, acquitted)
Gen24:8,24:41,**Exo**20:7,21:19,34:7,**Num** 5:19,5:28,5:31,14:18,
Deu 5:11,**Judg** 15:3,**1 Sam** 26:9,**1 Ki** 2:9,**Job** 9:28, 10:14,   **Psa**
19:12,19:13,51:2,**Prov** 6:29,11:21,16:5,17:5,19:5,19:9,28:20,**Isa**
3:26,**Jer** 2:35, 25:29, 30:11, 46:28, 49:12,**Joel** 3:21,**Nahum**
1:3,**Zec** 5:3

Nakiy Gen 24:41,44:10, **Exo** 21:28, 23:7, **Num** 32:22,**Deu**
19:10,19:13,21:8,21:9,24:5,27:25,**Josh**2:17,2:19,2:20,**1Sam**19:5,
2Sam3:28,14:9,**1Ki**15:22,**2Ki**21:16,24:4,**Job**4:7,9:23,17:8,22:19
,22:30,27:17,**Psa**10:8,15:5,24:4,94:21,106:38,**Prov**1:11,6:17,**Isa**
59:7, **Jer** 2:34,7:6, 19:4,22:3, 22:17,26:15,**Joel** 3:19,**Jonah** 1:14

Eleutheria (Freedom, liberty) **Rom** 8:21,**1 Cor** 7:39,10:29,**2**
Cor 3:17,Gal 2:4, 5:1,5:13,**James** 1:25, 2:12,**1 Pet** 2:16,**2 Pet**
2:19

Eleutheros (free, independent, not bound)Mat 17:26,**John**
8:33,8:36,**Rom** 6:20,7:3,**1 Cor** 7:21,7:22,7:39,9:1,9:19,12:13,
Gal 3:28,4:22,4:23,4:26,4:30,4:31,**Eph** 6:8,**Col** 3:11,**1 Pet**
2:16,**Rev** 6:15,13:16,19:18

Eleutheroo John 8:32,8:36,**Rom** 6:18,6:22, 8:2,8:21,**Gal** 5:1

Abad (Serve, work, obey, worship, cultivate, till) **Gen**
2:5,2:15,3:23,4:2,4:12,14:4,15:13,15:14,25:23,27:29,27:40,29:15
,29:18,29:20,29:25,29:27,29:30,30:26,30:29,31:6,31:41,49:15,**E**
xo1:13,1:14,3:12,4:23,5:18,6:5,7:16,8:1,8:20,9:1,9:13,10:3,10:7,
10:8,10:11,10:24,10:26,12:31,13:5,14:5,14:12,20:5,20:9,21:2,21:
6,23:24,23:25,23:33, **Lev** 25:39,25:40,25:46,**Num** 3:7,3:8,4:23,
4:24,4:26,4:30,4:37,4:41,4:47,7:5,8:11,8:15,8:19,8:22,8:25,8:26,1
6:9,18:6,18:7,18:21,18:23,**Deu**4:19,4:28,5:9,5:13,6:13,7:4,7:16,8

:19,10:12,10:20,11:13,11:16,12:2,12:30,13:2,13:4,13:6,13:13,15:
12,15:18.15:19,17:3,20:11,21:3,21:4,28:14,28:36,28:39,28:47,28
:48,28:64, 29:18,29:26, 30:17,31:20,**Josh** 16:10,22:5,22:27,23:7,
23:16,24:2,24:14,24:15,24:16,24:18,24:19,24:20,24:21,24:22,24:
24,24:31,Judg 2:7, 2:11, 2:13, 2:19,3:6,3:7,3:8,3:14, 9:28,9:38,
10:6,10:10,10:13,10:16,1**Sam**4:9,7:3,7:4,8:8,10:7,11:1,12:10,12:
14,12:20,12:24,17:9,26:19,**2Sam** 9:10,10:19,15:8,16:19,22:44, **1
Ki**4:21,9:6,9:9,9:21,12:4,12:7,16:31,22:53,2**Ki**10:18,10:19,10:21
,10:22,10:23,17:12,17:16,17:33,17:35,17:41,18:7,21:3,21:21,25:
24,**1Chr**19:19,28:9,**2Chr**2:18,7:19,7:22,10:4,24:18,30:8,33:3,33:
16,33:22,34:33,35:3,**Neh**9:35,**Job**21:15,36:11,39:9,**Psa**2:11,18:
43,22:30,72:11,97:7,**100**:2,102:22,106:36,**Prov**12:11,28:19,**Eccl**
5:9,5:12,**Isa**14:3,19:9,19:21,19:23,28:21,30:24,43:23,43:24,60:**1
2,Jer**2:20,5:19,8:2,11:10,13:10,16:11,16:13,17:4,22:9,22:13,25:6
,25:11,25:14,27:6,27:7,27:8,27:9,27:11,27:12,27:13,27:14,27:17,
28:14,30:8,30:9,34:9,34:10,34:14,35:15,40:9,44:3,**Ezek**20:39,20
:40,29:18,29:20,34:27,36:9,36:34,48:18,48:19,**Hosea**12:12,**Zep**
3:9,Zec 2:9,13:5, **Mal** 3:14,3:17,3:18

Douleuo (serve, obey) **Mat** 6:24,**Luke**15:29,16:13,**John**
8:33,**Acts**7:7,20:19,**Rom**6:6,7:6,7:25,9:12,12:11,14:18,16:18,**G
al** 4:8.4:9,4:25,5:13,**Eph** 6:7,**Phil 2:22**,Col 3:24, **1 Th** 1:9,**1 Tim**
6:2,**Titus** 3:3

Doulos Mat 8:9.10:24,10:25,13:27,13:28,18:23, 18:26,18:27,
18:28,18:32,20:27,21:34,21:35,21:36,22:3,22:4,22:6,22:8,22:10,
24:45,24:46,24:48,24:5,25:14,25:19,25:21,25:23,25:26,25:30,26:
51,**Mark**10:44,12:2,12:4,13:34,14:47,**Luke**2:29,7:2,7:3,7:8,7:10
,12:37,12:38,12:43,12:45,12:46,12:47, 14:17,14:21, 14:22, 14:23,
15:22,17:7,17:9,17:10,19:13,19:15,19:17,19:22,20:10,20:11,22:5
0,**John**4:51,8:34,8:35,13:16,15:15,15:20,18:10,18:18,18:26,**Acts**
2:18,4:29,16:17,**Rom**1:1,6:16,6:17,6:19,6:20,**1Cor**7:21,7:22,7:2
3,12:13,**2 Cor** 4:5,**Gal** 1:10,3:28, 4:1,4:7, **Eph** 6:5,6:6,6:8,**Phil**
1:1,2:7,**Col** 3:11,3:22,4:1,4:12,**1 Tim** 6:1,**2 Tim** 2:24, **Titus**
1:1,2:9, **Phile** 1:16,**James** 1:1,**1 Pet** 2:16,**2 Pet** 1:1,2:19,**Jude**
1:1,**Rev**1:1,2:20,6:15,7:3,10:7,11:18,13:16,15:3,19:2,19:5,19:18,
22:3,22:6

Latreuo (Serve, Worship) **Mat** 4:10,**Luke** 1:74,2:37,4:8,**Acts** 7:7,7:42,24:14,26:7,27:23, **Rom**1:9,1:25,**Phil**3:3,**2Tim** 1:3,**Heb** 8:5,9:9,9:14,10:2,12:28,13:10,**Rev** 7:15,22:3

Latreia John 16:2,**Rom** 9:4,12:1,**Heb** 9:1,9:6

Leitourgeo Acts 13:2,**Rom** 15:27,**Heb** 10:11

Leitourgia Luke 1:23,**2 Cor** 9:12,**Phil** 2:17,2:30, **Heb** 8:6, 9:21

 Leitourgos Rom 13:6,15:16,**Phil** 2:25,**Heb** 1:7,8:2

Diakonia (Serve, help, support, minister, care for, aid) **Luke** 10:40,**Acts**1:17,1:25,6:1,6:4,11:29,12:25,20:24,21:19,**Rom**11:1 3,12:7,15:31,**1Cor**12:5,16:15,**2Cor**3:7,3:8,3:9,4:1,5:18,6:3,8:4,9: 1,9:12,9:13,11:8,**Eph**4:12,**Col**4:17,**1Tim**1:12,**2Tim**4:5,4:11,**H** eb1:14,**Rev**2:19

Diakoneo   **Mat**4:11,8:15,**20:28,25:44**,27:55,**Mark** 1:13,1:31,10:45,15:41,**Luke**4:39,8:3,10:40,12:37,17:8,22:26,22: 27,**John**12:2,12:26,**Acts**6:2,19:22,**Rom**15:25,**2Cor**3:3,8:19,8:2 0,1 Tim 3:10,3:13,**2 Tim** 1:18,**Phile** 1:13,**Heb** 6:10,**1 Pet** 1:12,4:10,4:11

1. Fuller, Daniel P.., *THE UNITY OF THE BIBLE; Unfolding God's Plan for Humanity,* 1992   Pages 453-454
2. Packer, J.I.., *TRUTH AND POWER,* Harold Shaw Publishers, Wheaton, IL. 1996. Pages 22-24
3. Lovelace, Richard., *RENEWAL AS A WAY OF LIFE; A Guide For Spiritual Growth.,* Intervarsity Press, Downers Grove, IL., 1985, Pages 134-135.
4. Tozer, A.W., *THAT INCREDIBLE CHRISTIAN,* Christian Publications, Inc. Harrisburg, PA. 1964, 104-106

5. Sproul, R. C., *THE SOUL'S QUEST FOR GOD;
    Satisfying the Hunger for Spiritual Communion With God.*,
    1992, Pages 216-219

CHAPTER TEN

Loyalty, Purity and Justice

Pro 22:11 He who loves purity of heart, and whose speech is gracious, will have the king as his friend.

2Co 6:4 - 6 but as servants of God we commend ourselves in every way: by great endurance, in afflictions, hardships, calamities, beatings, imprisonments, riots, labors, sleepless nights, hunger;

By purity, knowledge, patience, kindness, the Holy Spirit, genuine love;

Deu 10:18   He executes justice for the fatherless and the widow, and loves the sojourner, giving him food and clothing.

Deu 16:19 You shall not pervert justice. You shall not show partiality, and you shall not accept a bribe, for a bribe blinds the eyes of the wise and subverts the cause of the righteous.

Luk 11:42 "But woe to you Pharisees! For you tithe mint and rue and every herb, and neglect justice and the love of God. These you ought to have done, without neglecting the others.

I AM the three in one, is not a man-made idol, His anger cannot be appeased by anything we could do. There is nothing that we could give Him that He could need. There is no desire in Him for us to abuse others or be abused. Eze 18:23 Have I any pleasure in the death of the wicked, declares the Lord GOD, and not rather that he should turn from his way and live? Eze 33:11 Say to them, As I live, declares the Lord GOD, I have no pleasure in the death of the wicked, but that the wicked turn from his way and live; turn back, turn back from your evil ways, for why will you die, O house of Israel? The sacrifices I AM the three in one instituted were to point to the gifts He gives, gifts of sustenance, forgiveness, cleansing and life. The sacrifices were to point people to His care for us not as a means to gain His love, He is Absolute love. 1Sa 15:22 "And Samuel said, "Has the LORD as great delight in burnt offerings and sacrifices, as in obeying the voice of the LORD? Behold, to obey is better than sacrifice, and to listen than the fat of rams." Psa 40:6 "In sacrifice and offering you have not delighted, but you have given me an open ear. Burnt offering and sin offering you have not required." Psa 50:23 "The one who offers thanksgiving as his sacrifice glorifies me; to one who orders his way rightly I will show the salvation of God!" Psa 51:17 "The sacrifices of God are a broken spirit; a broken and contrite heart, O God, you will not despise." Pro 21:3 To do righteousness and justice is more acceptable to the LORD than sacrifice."

The Tanakh (Old Testament) has five major offerings: burnt offering, meal offering, peace offering, sin offering, and the trespass offering.

The offerings or sacrifices were to draw attention first to I AM and His forgiveness, secondly to His salvation from slavery, third to the provisions He supplies, fourth to the peace and rest that He brings and fifth to the relationships that He restores.

However, two specific things about the detail of how these acts of worship were to be performed pointed to a further mystery not yet revealed. The perfection or unblemished nature of the animals sacrificed or the grains offered pointed to the need of a perfect unblemished sacrifice that had to be made. Secondly it was to be of the first born of the animals or the first fruits of the harvest that were required which pointed to the need for a totally unique nature that belonged to the offering as the only one of it's kind the first born, there can only be one first born.

The offerings were to be orderly and worshipful, sanctifying and cleansing, but not abusive or cruel. If a bull was not available or could not be afforded a lamb could be offered, if not a lamb a goat and if not a goat a bird. The point of the offering was for the person to see the provision of I AM not to gain favor. The favor was found in the worshipful and grateful attitude of the offering, I AM desired to give them all that was needed. Psa 37:4 "Delight yourself in the LORD, and he will give you the desires of your heart." **Psa 147:10** "His delight is not in the strength of the horse, nor his pleasure in the legs of a man, Psa 147:11 but the LORD takes pleasure in those who fear him, in those who hope in his steadfast love."

The condition is a gift given

Louis Berkhof writes "On the one hand the covenant is unconditional. There is in the covenant of grace no condition that can be considered meritorious…

On the other hand, the covenant may be called conditional. There is a sense in which the covenant is conditional. If we consider the basis of the covenant, it is clearly conditional on the surety of Jesus Christ. In order to introduce the covenant of grace, Christ had to, and actually did, meet the conditions originally laid down in the covenant of works, by his active and passive obedience. Again, it may be said that the covenant is conditional as far as the first conscious entrance into the covenant as a real communion of life is concerned. This entrance is contingent on faith, a faith, however, which is itself a gift of God."[1]

The contrast between the love and care of I AM and the bloodthirsty, abusive enslaving cultures in the ancient near east is stark. It is amazing that I AM must constantly warn not to follow after those brutal uncaring ways of making idols that we can serve rather that follow after Him. 2Ki 17:15 "They despised his statutes and his covenant that he made with their fathers and the warnings that he gave them. They went after false idols and became false, and they followed the nations that were around them, concerning whom the LORD had commanded them that they should not do like them."

Abuse tears at the very nature of the one being abused as well as the abuser. There is a logical disconnect between reality and what is experienced while abusing someone or being abused by someone. It is common for psychiatrists and psychologists to talk about dissociative disorders. Dissociative orders or syndromes are characterized by disruptions or lapses, long or short, in consciousness, identity, memory, motor behavior, and environmental awareness. People literally become torn apart or not themselves from abusing and being abused. Sometimes the abuse is buried latent deep inside so that it is not even remembered by the one who was abused, only to know that something is terribly wrong but not consciously being able to face or deal with whatever it might be. Sometimes multiple selves emerge, often abused individuals end up abusing others.

Of course, that is all in the past? No one knows of idol worshippers who sacrifice or eat their own children? No one knows of people forced into slavery and prostitution as temple worship?

Today it is estimated by Unicef that there are 1.2 million people kidnapped and sold into human trafficking every year. The majority of those taken are between the ages of 18 to 24 years old, 95% are taken for the purpose of physically abusive labor or sexual violence. Every 9 seconds in the U.S. alone a woman is assaulted or beaten. There are 95,000 rapes reported each year in the U. S. and no one knows how many go unreported. Minnesota Citizens Concerned For Life reports that in the U. S. a baby is aborted every 26 seconds. Five children die each day of child abuse and child neglect.[2]

Sexual gratification is not an end in itself and at the same time it is not a means to initiate or establish a relationship. Love is not sex and sexual gratification is not love.

Sexual intercourse is a gift from I AM and He established its bounds, the bounds of one committed, caring relationship of a man to a woman. In the garden there was one man and one woman made one flesh, and it was very good. This was the pattern of goodness and love, yet sexual union is one of the gifts of I AM that is most perverted by people in our world.

It is clear in nature that sexual gratification though achievable was not designed by the creator to be male with male, nor female with female nor in an unloving, uncommitted relationship male to female. Learning that whatever feels good is not necessarily good is a part of becoming a loving and caring individual.

Sexual sin is a unique form of sin because it is within our bodies. 1Co 6:18-20 "Flee from sexual immorality. Every other sin a person commits is outside the body, but the sexually immoral person sins against his own body." Or do you not know that your body is a temple of the Holy Spirit within you, whom you have from God? You are not your own, for you were bought with a price. So glorify God in your body."

Sexual union only is safe and sanctioned by this one flesh relationship, in lifelong commitment of one man to one woman. This relationship was uniquely to image forth I AM and His relationship to us. Eph 5:31-32 "Therefore a man shall leave his father and mother and hold fast to his wife, and the two shall become one flesh." This mystery is profound, and I am saying that it refers to Christ and the church."

It is difficult to find anyone these days who is not touched by the devastating effects of divorce, the tearing apart of families and damage to children of broken relationships.

What is holding the fabric of purity and justice together in this world? Pope John Paul II has written; ". . . Today, as a result of advances in medicine and in a cultural context frequently closed to the transcendent, the experience of dying is marked by new features.

When the prevailing tendency is to value life only to the extent that it brings pleasure and well-being, suffering seems like an unbearable setback, something from which one must be freed at all costs. Death is considered "senseless" if it suddenly interrupts a life still open to a future of new and interesting experiences. But it becomes a "rightful liberation" once life is held to be no longer meaningful because it is filled with pain and inexorably doomed to even greater suffering.

Furthermore, when he denies or neglects his fundamental relationship to God, man thinks he is his own rule and measure, with the right to demand that society should guarantee him the ways and means of deciding what to do with his life in full and complete autonomy. It is especially people in the developed countries who act in this way: they feel encouraged to do so also by the constant progress of medicine and its ever more advanced techniques. By using highly sophisticated systems and equipment, science and medical practice today are able not only to attend to cases formerly considered untreatable and to reduce or eliminate pain, but also to sustain and prolong life even in situations of extreme frailty, to resuscitate artificially patients whose basic biological functions have undergone collapse and to use special procedures to make organs available for transplanting.

In this context the temptation grows to have recourse to euthanasia, that is, to take control of death and bring it about before its time, "gently" ending one's own life or the life of others. In reality, what might seem logical and humane, when looked at more closely is seen to be senseless and inhumane. Here we are faced with one of the more alarming symptoms of the "culture of death", which is advancing above all in prosperous societies, marked by an attitude of excessive preoccupation with efficiency and which sees the growing number of elderly and disabled people as intolerable and too burdensome. These people are very isolated by their families and by society, which are organized almost exclusively on the basis of criteria of productive efficiency, according to which a hopelessly impaired life no longer has value. . ..

Quite different from this is the way of love and true mercy, which our common humanity calls for, and upon which faith in Christ the Redeemer, who died and rose again, sheds ever new light. The request which arises from the human heart in the supreme confrontation with suffering and death, especially when faced with the temptation to give up in utter desperation, is above all a request for companionship, sympathy and support in time of trial. It is a plea for help to keep on hoping when all human hopes fail. . . .

This natural aversion to death and this incipient hope of immortality are illumined and brought to fulfillment by Christian faith, which both promises and offers a share in the victory of the Risen Christ: it is the victory of the One who, by his redemptive death, has set man free from death, "the wages of sin" (Rom. 6:23), and has given him the Spirit, the pledge of the resurrection and of life (cf. Rom. 8:11). The certainty of future immortality and hope in the promised resurrection cast new light on the mystery of suffering and death, and fill the believer with an extraordinary capacity to trust fully in the plan of God."[3]

I AM, the three, in one keeps loyalty and faithfulness. He is slow to anger and forgives rebellion, perversion and unfaithfulness, but He will not let the guilty go unpunished. He is overflowing with loving-kindness and mercy. Yet He will have mercy upon who He will have mercy. Deu 10:17-20 For the LORD your God is God of gods and Lord of lords, the great, the mighty, and the awesome God, who is not partial and takes no bribe. "He executes justice for the fatherless and the widow, and loves the sojourner, giving him food and clothing. Love the sojourner, therefore, for you were sojourners in the land of Egypt. You shall fear the LORD your God. You shall serve him and hold fast to him, and by his name you shall swear." Psa 10:17-18 "O LORD, you hear the desire of the afflicted; you will strengthen their heart; you will incline your ear to do justice to the fatherless and the oppressed, so that man who is of the earth may strike terror no more."

Jas 1:27 "Religion that is pure and undefiled before God, the Father, is this: to visit orphans and widows in their affliction, and to keep oneself unstained from the world." The Absolute Love of I AM is just that Absolute. It cannot be earned but it is demanding and just. It is not unconditional it is uncompromising, sacrificial and absolute. We cannot do a thing to deserve His forgiveness, but justice demands repayment.

The offerings I AM required in the Tanakh though, point to His forgiveness, His salvation from slavery, the provisions He supplies, the peace and rest that He brings and fifth to the relationships that He restores. He provides the sacrifice, the perfect and only sacrifice He could accept. Heb 9:11-28 "But when Christ appeared as a high priest of the good things that have come, then through the greater and more perfect tent (not made with hands, that is, not of this creation) he entered once for all into the holy places, not by means of the blood of goats and calves but by means of his own blood, thus securing an eternal redemption. For if the blood of goats and bulls, and the sprinkling of defiled persons with the ashes of a heifer, sanctify for the purification of the flesh, how much more will the blood of Christ, who through the eternal Spirit offered himself without blemish to God, purify our conscience from dead works to serve the living God. Therefore he is the mediator of a new covenant, so that those who are called may receive the promised eternal inheritance, since a death has occurred that redeems them from the transgressions committed under the first covenant. For where a will is involved, the death of the one who made it must be established. For a will takes effect only at death, since it is not in force as long as the one who made it is alive. Therefore, not even the first covenant was inaugurated without blood. For when every commandment of the law had been declared by Moses to all the people, he took the blood of calves and goats, with water and scarlet wool and hyssop, and sprinkled both the book itself and all the people, saying, "This is the blood of the covenant that God commanded for you." And in the same way he sprinkled with the blood both the tent and all the vessels used in worship. Indeed, under the law almost everything is purified with blood, and without the shedding of blood there is no forgiveness of sins. Thus it was necessary for the copies of the heavenly things to be purified with these rites, but the heavenly things themselves with better sacrifices than these. For Christ has entered, not into holy places made with hands, which are copies of the true things, but into heaven itself, now to appear in the presence of God on our behalf. Nor was it to offer himself repeatedly, as the high priest enters the holy places every year with blood not his own, for then he would have had to suffer repeatedly since the foundation of the world. But as it is, he has appeared once for all at the end of the ages to put away sin by the sacrifice of himself. And just as it is appointed for man to die once, and after that comes judgment, so Christ, having been offered once to bear the sins of many, will appear a second time, not to deal with sin but to save those who are eagerly waiting for him."

Moses and the Tanakh point to Jesus Christ, Isa AL-Masih, Yeshua the long-awaited Messiah. He is one who makes all things new, who has satisfied the justice of I AM, by taking on the robes of humanity and humility. This is what Absolute Love is, I AM the three in one is actively loyal to His creation and His beloved creatures, He restores purity because He is pure and brings about justice because He is absolutely just. 2Co 5:14-21 "For the love of Christ controls us, because we have concluded this: that one has died for all, therefore all have died; and he died for all, that those who live might no longer live for themselves but for him who for their sake died and was raised. From now on, therefore, we regard no one according to the flesh. Even though we once regarded Christ according to the flesh, we regard him thus no longer. Therefore, if anyone is in Christ, he is a new creation. The old has passed away; behold, the new has come. All this is from God, who through Christ reconciled us to himself and gave us the ministry of reconciliation; that is, in Christ God was reconciling the world to himself, not counting their trespasses against them, and entrusting to us the message of reconciliation. Therefore, we are ambassadors for Christ, God making his appeal through us. We implore you on behalf of Christ, be reconciled to God. For our sake he made him to be sin who knew no sin, so that in him we might become the righteousness of God."

Jesus, Isa Al-Misah, Yeshua the promised Messiah is now our perfect mediator and way to purity, wholeness and integrity, our way to being made whole. Heb 7:22-28 "This makes Jesus the guarantor of a better covenant. The former priests were many in number, - were prevented by death from continuing in office, but he holds his priesthood permanently, because he continues forever. Consequently, he is able to save to the uttermost those who draw near to God through him, since he always lives to make intercession for them. For it was indeed fitting that we should have such a high priest, holy, innocent, unstained, separated from sinners, and exalted above the heavens. He has no need, like those high priests, to offer sacrifices daily, first for his own sins and then for those of the people, since he did this once for all when he offered up himself." For the law appoints men in their weakness as high priests, but the word of the oath, which came later than the law, appoints a Son who has been made perfect forever."

Without the Absolute Love of I AM, the three in one, justice would fade and die and purity and wholeness would disappear. **Joh 1:14** And the Word became flesh and dwelt among us, and we have seen his glory, glory as of the only Son from the Father, full of grace and truth."

Loyalty is the characteristic outgrowth of believing that gives us the ability to remain true or faithful to IAM, ourselves and others so that we are not pushed or led along by demands other than God's.

Purity is the characteristic outgrowth of believing that gives us the ability to be unmixed in our allegiance toward God so that we won't be driven by any other purpose than to love, glorify and enjoy God to the ultimate benefit, enjoyment and fulfillment of ourselves and others.

Justice is the characteristic outgrowth of believing that gives us the ability to act rightly on behalf of God so that despots (those who want to control, oppress and use others for personal gain) are not allowed to triumph and the defenseless are defended.

Bernard of Clairvaux has written; "Nothing can be so restless and fleeting- no part of my nature can be so changeful- than my heart. How exceedingly vain, trifling and unsettled is this vagabond. Never fixed on the will of God, never stirred by divine guidance and counsel, it follows instead its own whims. It is in perpetual motion, without any principle of rest within it. It is under a thousand different determinations at once and flies about after innumerable quests. It makes experiments but to no purpose. It seeks rest everywhere lies away from but it finds it not. Happiness flies away from it. …

So when the soul falls away from worthy causes, and it becomes bewildered by sordid affections- then vanity seizes it, curiosity distracts it, covetous desires allure it, pleasure seduces it, luxury defiles it, envy racks it, anger ruffles it and grief afflicts and depresses it. The soul is then overwhelmed and sinks into all manner of vice. All this happens because it forsakes God, for He alone is the answer to all the heart's wants and desires. Thus the mind is dissipated and scattered among a multitude of trifles. Although it seeks anxiously for satisfaction, yet it cannot attain any until it returns to the All-Sufficient object of the heart…

The conditions of my being are such that I cannot live in subjection to myself but only in being subject to Him. I can never have the mastery of my own heart. Only God has that. So long, then, as I am not united to God, I am divided within myself and at perpetual strife within myself. Now this union with God can only love. And the subjection to Him can only be grounded in humility. And the humility can only be the result of knowing and believing the truth, that is to say, having the right notions of God and of myself.

How necessary it is to inquire diligently about the true state of my soul. Then I will discover how vile, weak, fickle, and corruptible I am. Then I will discover also how vital t is to lay hold of God and to hold Him fast, for it is from Him that I derive my being and without Whom I am nothing."[4]

Emet (Loyal, True, Trustworthy, Firm, Faithful, Reliable, Stable, Certain,)

Gen 24:27,24:48, 24:49,32:10,42:16,47:29,**Exo** 18:21,34:6,**Deu** 13:14,17:4,22:20,**Josh**2:12,2:14,24:14,**Judg**9:15,9:16,9:19,**1Sa m** 12:24,**2 Sam** 2:6,7:28,15:20,**1 Ki** 2:4,3:6,10:6,17:24,22:16,**2 Ki**20:3,20:19,**2Chr**9:5,15:3,18:15,31:20,32:1,**Neh**7:2,9:13,9:33, **Est**9:30,**Psa**15:2,19:9, 25:5,25:10,26:3,30:9,31:5,40:10,40:11,43:3,45:4,**51:6**,54:5,57:3,5 7:10,61:7,69:13,71:22,85:10,85:11,86:11,86:15,89:14,91:4,108:4 ,111:7,111:8,115:1,117:2,119:43,119:142,119:151,119:160,132: 11,138:2,145:18,146:6,**Prov**3:3,8:7,11:18,12:19,14:22,14:25,16: 6,20:28,22:21,23:23,29:14,**Eccl** 12:10,Isa 10:20,16:5,38:3,38:18, 38:19,39:8,42:3,43:9,48:1,59:14,59:15,61:8,**Jer**2:21,4:2,9:5,10:1 0,14:13, 23:28,26:15,28:9 ,32:41,33:6,42:5,**Ezek 18:8,18:9,Dan** 8:12,8:26,9:13,10:1,10:21,11:2,**Hosea**4:1,**Micah**7:20,**Zec** 7:9,8:3,8:8,8:16,8:19,**Mal** 2:6

Aletheia (Loyal, True,Dependable,Upright,Fidelity,Real) **Mat** 22:16,5:33,12:14,12:32,**Luke**4:25,20:21,22:59,John1:14,1:17,3:21,4:23,4:24,5:33,8:32,8:40,8:44,8:45,8:46,14:6,14:17,15:26,16:7,16:13,17:17,17:19,18:37,18:38,**Acts**4:27,10:34,26:25,**Rom**1:18,1:25,2:2,2:8,2:20,3:7,9:1,15:8,**1Cor**5:8,**13:6**,**2Cor**4:2,6:7,7:14,11:10, 12:6,13:8, **Gal** 2:5,2:14, 3:1,5:7,**Eph** 1:13,4:21,4:24,2 **Th** 2:10,2:12,2:13,**1Tim**2:4,2:7,3:15,4:3,6:5,**2Tim**2:15,2:18,2:25,3:7,3:8,4:4,**Titus** 1:1,1:14,**Heb** 10:26,**James** 1:18,3:14, 5:19,**1 Pet** 1:22,**2 Pet** 1:12,2:2,**1 John** 1:6,1:8,2:4,2:21,3:18,3:19,4:6,5:6,**2 John**1:1,1:2,1:3,1:4,**3John**1:1,1:3,1:4,1:8,1:12

Alethes (Honest, Genuine)

Mat 22:16,**Mark** 12:14, 3:33, 4:18,5:31, 5:32,7:18, 8:13, 8:14, 8:16,8:17,8:26,10:41,19:35,21:24,**Acts**12:9,**Rom**3:4,**2Cor**6:8, **Phil** 4:8,**Titus** 1:13,**1 Pet** 5:12,**2 Pet** 2:22,**1 John** **2:8,2:27**,3 **John**1:12

Alethinos   **Luke**16:11,**John** 1:9,4:23,4:37,6:32,7:28,15:1,17:3,19:35,**1 Th** 1:9,**Heb** 8:2, 9:24, 10:22,**1John**2:8,5:20,**Rev**3:7,3:14,6:10,15:3,16:7,19:2,19:9,19:11, 21:5,22:6

Taher(Purity, empty, bright, clean)

Gen35:2**Lev**11:32,12:7,12:8,13:6,13:13,13:17,13:23,13:28,13:34,13:37,13:58,13:59,14:4,14:7,14:8,14:9,14:11,14:14,14:17,14:18,14:19,14:20,14:25,14:28,14:29,14:31,14:48,14:53,15:13,15:28,16:19,16:30,17:15,22:4,22:7,23:22,**Num**8:6,8:7,8:15,8:21,19:12,19:19,31:23,31:24,**Josh**22:17,**2Ki**5:10,5:12,5:13,5:14,**2Chr**29:15,29:16,29:18,30:18,34:3,34:5,34:8,**Ezra**6:20,**Neh**12:30,13:9,13:22,13:30,**Job**4:17,17:9,37:21,**Psa**51:7,**Prov**20:9,**Isa**66:17,**Jer**13:27,33:8,**Ezek**22:24,24:13,36:25,36:33,37:23,39:12,39:14,39:16,43:26,Mal 3:3 **Tehowr Prov** 22:11

Hagnos(Purity, holiness, innocence, chaste)

2 Cor 7:11,11:2,**Phil 1:16,4:8,1 Tim** 5:22,**Titus** 2:5,James 3:17,**1 Pet** 3:2, **1 John** 3:3

Hagnotes (Purity, sincerity),**2 Cor** 6:6

Hagneia 1 Tim 4:12,5:2

Katharos(Purity, clean, clear, free, guiltless) **Mat 5:8**,8:2,8:3,23:26,27:59,**Luke** 11:41, **John** 13:10,13:11,15:3, **Acts** 18:6,20:26,**Rom** 14:20,**1 Tim 1:5**,3:9,**2 Tim** 1:3,2:22, Titus1:15,Heb10:22,James1:27,**1Pet**1:22,Rev15:6,19:8,19:14, 21:18,21:21,22:1

Katharizo (Purify, cleanse, remove)

Mat8:2,8:3,10:8,11:5,23:25,23:26,**Mark**1:40,1:41,1:42,7:19,**Lu** ke4:27,5:12,5:13,7:22,11:39,17:14,17:17,**Acts** 10:15,11:9,15:9,**2 Cor** 7:1, **Eph** 5:26,**Titus** 2:14,**Heb** 9:14, 9:22, 9:23,James 4:8,**1 John** 1:7,1:9

Katharotes Heb 9:13

Katharismos Mark 1:44,**Luke** 2:22,5:14,John 2:6,3:25,**Heb 1:3, 2 Pet** 1:9

Zedakah(Righteousness, executed justice, truthfulness, justification, salvation, prosperous)

Gen 15:6,18:19,30:33,**Deu** 6:25,9:4,9:5,9:6,24:13,33:21, **Judg** 5:11,**1 Sam** 12:7,26:23, **2 Sam** 8:15,19:28,22:21,22:25,**1 Ki** 3:6,8:32,10:9,**1Chr**18:14,**2Chr**6:23,9:8,**Neh**2:20,27:6,33:26,**Job** 35:8,37:23,Psa 5:8,11:7,22:31,24:5,31:1,33:5,36:6, 36:10,40:10, 51:14,69:27,71:2,71:15,71:16,71:19,71:24,72:1,72:3,88:12,89:16 ,98:2,99:4,103:6,103:17,106:3,106:31,111:3,112:3,112:9,119:40, 119:142,143:1,143:11,145:7,**Prov**8:18,8:20,10:2,11:4,11:5,11:6, 11:18,11:19,12:28,13:6,14:34,15:9,16:8,16:12,16:31,21:3,21:21,I sa1:27,5:7,5:16,5:23,9:7,10:22,28:17,32:16,32:17,33:5,33:15,45: 8,45:23,45:24,46:12,46:13,48:1,48:18,51:6,51:8,54:14,54:17,56:

1,57:12,58:2,59:9,59:14,59:16,59:17,60:17,61:10,61:11,63:1,64:
6,**Jer**4:2,9:24,22:3,22:15,23:5,33:15,51:10,**Ezek**3:20,14:14,14:2
0,18:5,18:19,18:20,18:21,18:22,18:24,18:26,18:27,33:12,33:13,3
3:14,33:16,33:18,33:19,45:9, **Dan** 9:7,9:16,9:18,**Hosea** 10:12,
Joel2:23,**Amos**5:7,5:24,6:12,**Micah**6:5,7:9,**Zec** 8:8,**Mal** 3:3,4:2

Mispat (Justice, litigate, decision, sentence, right, rectify,
proper, fit,)

Gen18:19,18:25,40:13,**Exo**15:25,21:1,21:9,21:31,23:6,24:3,26:
30,28:15,28:29,28:30,**Lev**5:10,9:16,18:4,18:5,18:26,19:15,19:35,
19:37,20:22,24:22,25:18,26:15.26:43,26:46,**Num**9:3,9:14,15:16,
15:24,27:5,27:11,27:21,29:6,29:18,29:21,29:24,29:27,29:30,29:3
3,29:37,35:12,35:24,35:29,36:13,**Deu**1:17,4:1,4:5,4:8,4:14,4:45,
5:1,5:31,6:1,6:20,7:11,7:12,8:11,10:18,11:1,11:32,12:1,16:18,16:
19,17:8,17:9,17:11,18:3,21:17,24:17,25:1,26:16,26:17,27:19,30:
16,32:4,32:41,33:10,33:21**Josh**6:15,20:6,24:25**Judg**4:5,13:12,1
8:7,**1Sam**2:13,8:3,8:9,8:11,10:25.30:25,**2Sam**8:15,15:2,15:4,15:
6,22:23,**1Ki**2:3,3:11,3:28,4:28,6:12,6:38,7:7,8:45,8:49,8:58,8:59,
9:4,10:9,11:33,18:28,20:40,**2Ki**1:7,11:14,17:26,17:27,17:33,17:3
4,17:37,17:40,25:6,**1Chr**6:32,15:13,16:1,16:14,18:14,22:13,23:3
1,24:19,28:7,**2Chr**4:7,4:20,6:35,6:39,7:17,8:14,9:8,19:6,19:8,19:
10,30:16,33:8,35:13,**Ezra**3:4,7:10,**Neh**1:7,8:18,9:13,9:29,10:29,
Job8:3,9:19,9:32,13:18,14:3,19:7,22:4,23:4,27:2,29:14,31:13,32:
9,34:4,34:5,34:6,34:12,34:17,34:23,35:2,36:6,36:17,37:23,40:8,**P
sa**1:5,7:6,9:4,9:7,9:16,10:5,17:2,18:22,19:9,25:9,33:5,35:23,36:6,
37:6,37:28,37:30,48:11,72:1,72:2,76:9,81:4,89:14,89:30,94:15,9
7:2,97:8,99:4,101:1,103:,105:5,105:7,106:3,111:7,112:5,119:7,1
19:13,119:20,119:30,119:39,119:43,119:52,119:62,119:75,119:8
4,119:91,119:102,119:106,119:108,119:120,119:121,119:132,11
9:137,119:149,119:156,119:160,119:164,119:175,122:5,140:12,
143:2,146:7,147:19,147:20,149:9,**Prov**1:3,2:8,2:9,8:20,12:5,13:2
3,16:8,16:10,16:11,16:33,17:23,18:,19:28,21:3,21:7,21:15,24:23,
28:5,29:4,29:26,**Eccl**3:16,5:8,8:5,8:6,11:9,12:14,**Isa**1:17,1:21,1:
27,3:14,4:4,5:7,5:16,9:7,10:2,16:5,26:8,26:9,28:6,28:17,28:26,30:
18,32:1,32:7,32:16,33:5,34:5,40:14,40:27,41:1,42:1,42:3,42:4,49:
4,50:8,51:4,53:8,54:17,56:1,58:2,59:8,59:9,59:11,59:14,59:15,61:
8,**Jer**1:16,4:2,4:12,5:1,5:4,5:5,5:28,7:5,8:7,9:24,10:24,12:1,17:11,

21:12,22:3,22:13,22:15,23:5,30:11,30:18,32:7,32:8,33:15,39:5,4
6:28,48:21,48:47,49:12,51:9,52:9,**Lam**3:35,3:59,**Ezek**5:6,5:7,5:
8,7:23,7:27,11:12,11:20,16:38,18:5,18:8,18:9,18:17,18:19,18:21,
18:27,20:11,20:13,20:16,20:18,20:19,20:2,20:24,20:25,21:27,22:
29,23:24,23:45,33:14,33:16,33:19,34:16,36:27,37:24,39:21,42:1
1,44:24,45:9,**Dan**9:5,**Hosea**2:19,5:1,5:11,6:5,10:4,12:6,**Amos**5
:7,5:15,5:24,6:12,**Micah**3:1,3:8,3:9,6:8,7:9, **Hab** 1:4,1:7,1:12,
Zep 2:,3:5,3:8,3:15,**Zec** 7:9,8:16,**Mal** 2:17,3:5,4:4

Krino (Justice, Separate, Distinguish, Select, Prefer, Think,
Consider, Decide, Propose, Intend, Condemn, Criticize) **Mat**
5:40,7:1,7:2,19:28,**Luke**6:37,7:43,12:57,19:22,22:30,**John**3:17,
3:18,5:22,5:30,7:24,7:51,8:15,8:16,8:26,8:50,12:47,12:48,16:11,1
8:31,**Acts**3:13,4:19,7:7,13:27,13:46,15:19,16:4,16:15,17:31,20:1
6,21:25,23:3,23:6,24:6,24:21,25:9,25:10,25:20,25:25,26:6,26:8,2
7:1,**Rom**2:1,2:3,2:12,2:16,2:27,3:4,3:6,3:7,14:3,14:4,14:5,14:10,
14:13,**1Cor**2:2,4:5,5:3,5:12,5:13,6:1,6:2,6:3,6:6,7:37,10:15,10:29
,11:13,11:31,11:32,**2 Cor** 2:1,5:14,**Col** 2:16,**2 Th** 2:12,**2 Tim**
4:1,3:12,**Heb**10:30,13:4,**James**2:12,4:11,4:12,**1Pet**1:17,2:23,4:
5,4:6,**Rev**6:10,11:18,16:5,18:8,18:20,19:2,19:11,20:12,20:13

Krisis   **Mat**5:21,5:22,10:15,11:22,11:24,12:18,12:20,
12:36,12:41,12:42,23:23,23:33,**Mark**3:29,6:11,**Luke**10:14,11:3
1,11:32,11:42,

John3:19,5:22,5:24,5:27,5:29,5:30,7:24,8:16,12:31,16:8,16:11,**A
cts** 8:33,**2 Th** 1:5, **1 Tim** 5:24,**Heb** 9:27,10:27,**James 2:13**,2
Pet2:4,2:9,2:11,3:7,**1John**4:17,**Jude**1:6,1:9,1:15,**Rev**14:7,16:7,1
8:10,19:2

Dikaiosune(righteousness, uprightness, justice,)

Mat3:15,5:6,5:10,5:20,6:33,21:32,**Luke**1:75,**John**16:8,16:10,**A
cts**10:35,13:10,17:31,24:25,**Rom**1:17,3:5,3:21,3:22,3:25,3:26,4:
3,4:5,4:6,4:9,4:11,4:13,4:22,5:17,5:21,6:13,6:16,6:18,6:19,6:20,8:
10,9:28,9:30,9:31,10:3,10:4,10:5,10:6,10:1,14:17,**1Cor**1:30,**2Co
r**3:9,5:21,6:7,6:14,9:9,9:10,11:15,**Gal**2:21,3:6,3:21,5:5,**Eph**4:24,
5:9,6:14,**Phil**1:11,3:6,3:9,**1Tim**6:11,**2Tim**2:22,3:16,4:8,**Titus**3:

5,**Heb**1:9,5:13,7:2,11:7,11:33,12:11,**James** 1:20,2:23,3:18,**1 Pet** 2:24,3:14,2 Pet 1:1,2:5,2:21,3:13,**1 John** 2:29,3:7,3:10,**Rev** 19:11

Dikaioo (acquitted, made free, made pure, proved to be right)

Mat11:19,12:37,**Luke**7:29,7:35,10:29,16:15,18:14,Acts13:39,**R om**2:13,3:4,3:20,3:24,3:26,3:28,3:30,4:2,4:5,5:1,5:9,6:7,8:30,8:3 3,**1Cor**4:4,6:11,**Gal2:**16,2:17,3:8,3:11,3:24,5:4,**1Tim** 3:16,**Titus** 3:7,**James** 2:21,2:24,2:25,**Rev** 22:11

1. Berkhof, Louis., *SYSTEMATIC THEOLOGY,* Wm. B. Eerdmans Publishing Co., Grand Rapids, MI. 1996, page 280.
2. www.unicefusa.org
3. John Paul II., *THE GOSPEL OF LIFE.,* Times Books, Random House Publishing, Evangelium Vitae, 1995, 115-122
4. Bernard of Clairvaux; Abridged, Edited and Introduced by Houston, James M., *THE LOVE OF GOD AND SPIRITUAL FRIENDSHIP,* Multnomah Press, Portland, OR. 1983, pages 7 -8.

CHAPTER 11

Rest and Determination

<u>Heb 4:3</u> For we who have believed enter that rest, as he has said,"As I swore in my wrath, 'They shall not enter my rest,'" although his works were finished from the foundation of the world.

<u>Heb 4:10, 11</u> for whoever has entered God's rest has also rested from his works as God did from his. Let us therefore strive to enter that rest, so that no one may fall by the same sort of disobedience.

When we lose our sense of who we are, why we are and what our purpose is as human beings our lives lose congruency, integrity. We literally become sick because all health, all life flows from I AM the three in one. If you look around you can see we all are broken and in need. Everyone is seeking peace and rest at a break neck speed.

On a recent trip to my office three miles away from my house in a small university town of 50,000 people I took note of the anxiety of that brief journey of only about ten minutes. After pulling out from my relatively short street, two blocks long with a cul-de-sac at one end. I try to move from that quiet onto the main artery. The traffic is moving at more than 45 miles per hour on a street marked at a 30 mile per hour traffic zone. I wait for enough time to jump into the flow without making the person I pull in front of too angry. I accelerate as fast as I can in order to get in line.

Who knew you would need a car that went from zero to 50 within five seconds to travel small town streets? I drive a little Toyota not a Porsche! Traveling along the young woman behind me is so close to my rear window I can read her lips as she has one hand to her ear holding her cell phone, that is, if I could read lips. I am pretty sure she is agitated about something though as fast as she is talking.

As I pull up to the stop sign I wonder if she will actually stop as she gets even closer to my back window when I slow down. Keeping my eye on her and watching the road in front I have to stop short as the person turning across in front of me cuts a line across the corner clearing a big swath through my lane. Luckily the woman behind be stopped in time not to crunch my bumper from behind.

As we travel on the car behind me gives me a little room to breathe as she makes an attempt to look like she was going to stop for the stop sign also. Whew she's not so close no, oh not for long, there she is again so close I can see her glancing back anxiously as she tries to continue her conversation. I see the man behind her is as close maybe closed tailing her car. As I begin to come to the corner where I turn off the main artery I turn on my signal light. I try to slow down. I can't slow down too much because she keeps getting closer and closer. I take the corner at a speed far greater than I am comfortable with. The line of cars speeds past. Whew, what a 10 minute trip!

Bernard of Clairvaux writes, "Every rational person naturally desires to be always satisfied with what it esteems to be preferable. It is never satisfied with something which lacks the qualities it desires to have. So, if a man has chosen a wife because of her beauty, then he will look out with a roving eye for more beautiful women. Or if he is desirous of being well dressed he will look out for even more expensive clothes. No matter how rich he is, if wealth is his desire, he will envy those who are richer than he is.

… Likewise, men in high places are drawn are drawn on by insatiable ambitions to climb higher and higher still. Indeed there is no end to all this because unsatisfied desires have no final satisfaction if they cannot be defined as absolutely the best or highest.

Need we wonder that a man cannot find contentment with what is less or worse since he seeks peace and satisfaction in what is highest and best? So how stupid and mad it is to seek to find peace or satisfaction in that which cannot fulfill these needs. So no matter how many things one possesses, he will always be lusting for what is perceived to be still missing. Discontented, he will spend himself in restlessness and futility. Thus the restless heart runs to and fro looking for the pleasures of this life in weariness of the evanescent and the unreal. He is like a starving man who thinks anything he can stuff down his throat is not enough, for his eyes are still looking at what he has not eaten. Thus man craves continually for what is still lacking, with more anxiety in his preoccupation with what he lacks rather than having any joy or contentment in what he has already got.

… Yet foolishly they reject what would lead them to their true goal which is found not in consumption but in consummation. So they wear themselves out in futility without reaching their blessed consummation because they stake their happiness on earthly things instead of upon their Creator. They seek to try each one in turn rather than to think of coming to Him who is Lord of all the universe.

Suppose, even if they could succeed in the realization of their longings, so they possessed the whole world (Matthew 16:26). Yet without having God who is the Author of all being, then the same principle that makes them restless for more would still leave then dissatisfied.

Only God can give them that ultimate satisfaction"[1]

It is no wonder we are anxious, life whizzes by awfully fast. We all experience anxiety, become overstressed and sometimes overwhelmed by just day to day life. Some experience deeper anxiety and lose their ability to cope in a healthy manner.

According to the Baker Encyclopedia of Psychology about 4% of people suffer from some type of anxiety disorder.

A particularly disruptive disorder that is normally brought on by very severe distress is Post Traumatic Stress Disorder. Severe distressful situations such as atrocities in war, rape, witnessing murder, being abused or tortured psychologists find the commonality of events that bring on PTSD are that they are not common experiences, they are profoundly intense and severe and they involve a strong potential for physical harm.[2]

With all the strife and discord in the world it is a wonder that we are not all more anxious that what we appear on the outside to be.

The absolute love of I AM the three in one though permeates life, none of us would even be still here without love being poured out to all. I AM is overflowing with steadfast love that reaches to even those who hate Him.

This kind of love is an important part of imaging forth His glory. Mat 5:43-48 "You have heard that it was said, 'You shall love your neighbor and hate your enemy.' But I say to you, Love your enemies and pray for those who persecute you, so that you may be sons of your Father who is in heaven. For he makes his sun rise on the evil and on the good, and sends rain on the just and on the unjust. For if you love those who love you, what reward do you have? Do not even the tax collectors do the same? And if you greet only your brothers, what more are you doing than others? Do not even the Gentiles do the same? You therefore must be perfect, as your heavenly Father is perfect." Complete, perfect, absolute love does not love because love is deserved, love flows from within in spite of any barriers to love from without.

Striving and fighting result from being separated from Absolute Love

I have been researching to see if there was ever a prolonged period on earth when there was not a war being fought. It seems there have been recorded wars all the way back 5,000 years where some societal group or nation was trying to dominate by force another group or nation. The first sets of brothers were the first people to compete and had the desire to dominate and even kill each other. Nightmares, reliving the stressful event, lapses from reality, illusions and other interferences in cognitive congruence are some of the symptoms experienced in PTSD.

There are other forms of anxiety disorders that bring on different painful or disruptive symptoms however the point is that being over stressed can cause both physically harmful and emotionally disruptive effects. Not many of us experience stress related effects to this degree, but for many people around us stress induced insomnia, depression or anxiety is at least mildly disruptive.

Resting in His Love

I AM, the three in one, is the means to and provider of rest. Isa, Al-Masih, Jesus, Yeshua said; Mat 11:28-30 "Come to me, all who labor and are heavy laden, and I will give you rest. Take my yoke upon you, and learn from me, for I am gentle and lowly in heart, and you will find rest for your souls. For my yoke is easy, and my burden is light."

John Piper writes; "First, notice that all conditions are summed up in love. Paul said, concerning doing good and obeying God's commandments, that this is precisely what love does. Love does no wrong to a neighbor; therefore love is the fulfillment of the law" Romans 13:5). Forgiveness is clearly an expression of love (I Corinthians 13:5. Paul also says that love is the essence of holiness or sanctification: "May the Lord cause you to increase and abound in love… so that he may establish your hearts … in holiness" (I Thessalonians 3:12-13). In other words, all the behavior that is required of a Christian may be summed up in love. "Let all that you do be done in love" (I Corinthians 16:14).

What we have seen, then, is that the ten conditions of future grace … are all summed up in faith. And the behavioral conditions we have just discussed are all summed up in love. Which means we may now say the conditions a Christian must meet, to go on enjoying the blessings of future grace, are faith and love." [3]

Rest was instituted by I AM and in the beginning a pattern was set up through creation of creativity and rest. Gen 2:2-3 "And on the seventh day God finished his work that he had done, and he rested on the seventh day from all his work that he had done. So God blessed the seventh day and made it holy, because on it God rested from all his work that he had done in creation."

The pattern of creation and rest is highlighted throughout the history of followers of I AM. A servant purchased for work in a household was to be set free for no price on the seventh year of service (Ex. 21:2). Land that produced crops were to be worked for six years but every seventh year was not to be harvested the land was to rest. The ebb and flow of creativity was to be observed weekly one out of seven days was a day of rest and renewal through concentrated focus on I AM. Annually one out of every months was to be observed as rest and one out of every seven years was to be observed as rest. Rest was to benefit all: Exo 23:6 12 "You shall not pervert the justice due to your poor in his lawsuit. Keep far from a false charge, and do not kill the innocent and righteous, for I will not acquit the wicked. And you shall take no bribe, for a bribe blinds the clear-sighted and subverts the cause of those who are in the right. "You shall not oppress a sojourner. You know the heart of a sojourner, for you were sojourners in the land of Egypt. "For six years you shall sow your land and gather in its yield, but the seventh year you shall let it rest and lie fallow, that the poor of your people may eat; and what they leave the beasts of the field may eat. You shall do likewise with your vineyard, and with your olive orchard. "Six days you shall do your work, but on the seventh day you shall rest; that your ox and your donkey may have rest, and the son of your servant woman, and the alien, may be refreshed."

The loving character of I AM, the three in one, is to be reflected to all through the days and seasons of rest and creativity. Rest is to be observed as a time to focus on I AM. Resting is to reflect on the ultimate rest from sin and sadness that will come for all who look to I AM and rest in Him for comfort and solace. Heb 3:15-4:11 "As it is said, "Today, if you hear his voice, do not harden your hearts as in the rebellion." For who were those who heard and yet rebelled? Was it not all those who left Egypt led by Moses? And with whom was he provoked for forty years? Was it not with those who sinned, whose bodies fell in the wilderness? And to whom did he swear that they would not enter his rest, but to those who were disobedient? So we see that they were unable to enter because of unbelief. Therefore, while the promise of entering his rest still stands, let us fear lest any of you should seem to have failed to reach it. For good news came to us just as to them, but the message they heard did not benefit them, because they were not united by faith with those who listened. For we who have believed enter that rest, as he has said, "As I swore in my wrath, 'They shall not enter my rest,'" although his works were finished from the foundation of the world. For he has somewhere spoken of the seventh day in this way: "And God rested on the seventh day from all his works." And again in this passage he said, "They shall not enter my rest." Since therefore it remains for some to enter it, and those who formerly received the good news failed to enter because of disobedience, again he appoints a certain day, "Today," saying through David so long afterward, in the words already quoted,

"Today, if you hear his voice, do not harden your hearts." For if Joshua had given them rest, God would not have spoken of another day later on. So then, there remains a Sabbath rest for the people of God, for whoever has entered God's rest has also rested from his works as God did from his. Let us therefore strive to enter that rest, so that no one may fall by the same sort of disobedience."

Rest is not merely inactivity

In a different manner, the lack of enough stimuli, activity or stress can also be harmful in many ways. In fact, physical and mental activities that provide adequate stress to body and mind are necessary for health. Without physical exercise and mental stimuli our bodies and our brains diminish in capacity. Exercise stimulates capacity for both the body and brain, it increases blood circulation and oxygen supplies which enhance energy and waste removal.

According to the Franklin Institute; exercise can be observed to increase cerebral blood vessels, improve memory skills, concentration and abstract reasoning. Studies have shown that exercise contributes to new brain cell growth. Inactive were individuals were twice as likely to develop Alzheimer's disease or dementia. Similar studies have also shown that exercise is just as effective as medication in treating major depression. The ebb and flow of exercise and rest are essential parts of health yet it is worthy to note that rest does not necessarily mean inactivity. It can be restful and relaxing to go on a hike, take a bicycle ride or walk the dogs around the neighborhood. In fact exercise releases chemicals that cause feelings of well-being and calm that allow us to be more creative and productive.[4]

There is a reason that creative activity is emphasized to us in a ratio of 6 to 1 in relation to rest. It may well be that the creativity of imaging forth I AM through the productive activity of work, if focused on working through the power He supplies, is the most effective way to become more creatively loving. Rest in a different way refocuses us on Him as the power supply so that we can continue to be more and more productive through His empowerment. 1Pe 4:7-11 "The end of all things is at hand; therefore be self-controlled and sober-minded for the sake of your prayers. Above all, keep loving one another earnestly, since love covers a multitude of sins. Show hospitality to one another without grumbling. As each has received a gift, use it to serve one another, as good stewards of God's varied grace: whoever speaks, as one who speaks oracles of God; whoever serves, as one who serves by the strength that God supplies--in order that in everything God may be glorified through Jesus Christ. To him belong glory and dominion forever and ever. Amen."

In regard to the contribution of both rest and determination Anthony Hoekema says; "No protestant creed has a better or more complete statement of the doctrine of the perseverance of true believers than the Canons of Dordt (1618-19). . . .

After the first two articles . . . have described the inclination of believers to fall into daily sins of weakness, Article 3 states that the converted, if left to their own resources, would not be able to remain standing in the grace of God. "But", the article continues, "God is faithful, mercifully strengthening them in the grace once conferred on them and powerfully preserving them in it to the end."

Article 4 goes on to indicate that true believers may indeed fall into serious sins if they fail to watch and pray. But article 6 affirms that: "God, who is rich in mercy according to his unchangeable purpose of election does not take his Holy Spirit from his own completely, even when they fall grievously. Neither does he let them fall down so far that they forfeit the grace of adoption and the state of justification, or commit the sin which leads to death (the sin against the Holy Spirit), and plunge themselves, entirely forsaken by him, into eternal ruin."

In Article 7 the Canons maintain that God will by his Word and Spirit certainly and effectually renew to repentance those of his people who have fallen into serious sins. Then follows Article 8, which underscores the fact that the preservation of God's people is due entirely to God's grace: "So it is not by their own merits or strength but by God's undeserved mercy that they (true believers) nether forfeit faith and grace totally nor remain in their own downfalls to the end and are lost. With respect to themselves this not only easily could happen, but also undoubtedly would happen; but with respect to God it cannot possibly happen, since his plan cannot be changed, his promise cannot fail, the calling according to his purpose cannot be revoked, the merit of Christ as well as his interceding and preserving cannot be nullified, and the sealing of the Holy Spirit can neither be invalidated nor wiped out." It would be hard to compose a more beautiful statement of this doctrine. Once again, the thought is repeated that the perseverance of true believers is due not to their merits or strength but only to God's undeserved mercy. And once again the real heartbeat of this doctrine comes home to us: God's unchanging faithfulness to his promises. This is what we lean on-weak, changeable, and fickle sinners that we are- when we profess to believe in the perseverance of God's true people.

It should further be observed, however, that the Canons of Dordt do not in any way support the erroneous understanding of this doctrine that some seem to have: namely, "Once saved, always saved, regardless of how we live." Articles 12 and 13 make clear that the assurance of our preservation by God, far from being an occasion for carelessness in living or in morals, is actually an incentive to godliness: "The assurance of perseverance, however, so far from making true believers proud and carnally self-assured, is rather the true root of humility, of childlike respect, of genuine godliness, of endurance in every conflict, of fervent prayers, of steadfastness in cross bearing and in confessing the truth, and of well-founded joy in God. Reflecting on this benefit provides an incentive to a serious and continual practice of thanksgiving and good works, as is evident from the testimonies of scripture and the examples of the saints.

Neither does the renewed confidence of perseverance produce immorality or lack of concern for godliness in those put back on their feet after a fall, but it produces a much greater concern to observe carefully the ways of the Lord which he prepared in advance."

The teaching of the perseverance of true believers is one of the most comforting teachings of Scripture. We learn from it that God by his power keeps his people from falling away from him, that Christ will never permit anyone to snatch them out of his hand, and that the Holy Spirit seals them for the day of redemption. Our heavenly Father holds us securely in his grasp, that is our ultimate comfort in life and death. We rest finally not in our hold of God but on God's hold of us.

Yet this teaching also urges us to persevere in the faith- and this is our challenge. We can only persevere through God's strength and by his grace. But to teach this doctrine in such a way as to present only its comfort and not its challenge, only the security and not the exhortation, is to teach it one-sidedly. And the Bible constantly warns us against such one sidedness.

. . . The doctrine of the perseverance of true believers, therefore, is both a comfort and a challenge. But the challenge is based on the comfort. We can be certain that we shall persevere to the end only because God has promised to enable us to do so. And so we rest in him, for time and eternity, knowing that he will never let us go."[5]

I AM, the three in one, is eternally active yet always at rest.

He is constantly ruling, supplying, creating, recreating and yet never is tired. He is always described as sitting yet he is never inactive. I have heard it said that He is never in a hurry but He is always on time. It is striking how His steadfast love is associated with strength. Psa 59:16-17 " But I will sing of your strength; I will sing aloud of your steadfast love in the morning. For you have been to me a fortress and a refuge in the day of my distress. O my Strength I will sing praises to you, for you, O God, are my fortress, the God who shows me steadfast love."

It is in and by His strength that we are empowered and renewed as we rest in Him and wait for His strength. Isa 40:28-31 "Have you not known? Have you not heard? The LORD is the everlasting God, the Creator of the ends of the earth. He does not faint or grow weary; his understanding is unsearchable. He gives power to the faint, and to him who has no might he increases strength. Even youths shall faint and be weary, and young men shall fall exhausted; but they who wait for the LORD shall renew their strength; they shall mount up with wings like eagles; they shall run and not be weary; they shall walk and not faint."

However, waiting and resting are not the same as inactivity. 2Pe 1:2-10 "May grace and peace be multiplied to you in the knowledge of God and of Jesus our Lord. His divine power has granted to us all things that pertain to life and godliness, through the knowledge of him who called us to his own glory and excellence, by which he has granted to us his precious and very great promises, so that through them you may become partakers of the divine nature, having escaped from the corruption that is in the world because of sinful desire. For this very reason, make every effort to supplement your faith with virtue, and virtue with knowledge, and knowledge with self-control, and self-control with steadfastness, and steadfastness with godliness, and godliness with brotherly affection, and brotherly affection with love. For if these qualities are yours and are increasing, they keep you from being ineffective or unfruitful in the knowledge of our Lord Jesus Christ. For whoever lacks these qualities is so nearsighted that he is blind, having forgotten that he was cleansed from his former sins. Therefore, brothers, be all the more diligent to make your calling and election sure, for if you practice these qualities you will never fall."

Rest is the characteristic of believing that gives us the ability see past obstacles to our own well-being and the well-being of others so that we can peacefully work to overcome those obstacles and overthrow those who are setting them up.

Determination is the characteristic of believing that gives us the ability to persist until that which has been started is completed.

Shabat (Rest, cease, desist, be completed, remove, exterminate, destroy)

Gen 2:2,2:3,**8:22**, **Exo** 5:5,12:15,16:30,23:12,31:17,34:21,**Lev** 2:13,23:32, 26:6,26:34,26:35,**Deu** 32:26, **Josh** 5:12,22:25,**Ruth** 4:14,**2 Ki** 23:5,23:11, **2 Chr** 16:5, 36:21, **Neh** 4:11,6:3,32:1, **Psa**8:2,46:9,89:44,119:119,**Prov**18:18,22:10,**Isa**13:11,14:4,16:1 0,17:3,21:2,24:8,30:7,30:11,33:8,**Jer**7:34,16:9,31:36,36:29,48:33 ,48:35,**Lam**5:14,5:15,**Ezek**6:6,7:24,12:23,16:41,23:27,23:48,26: 13,30:10,30:13,30:18,33:28,34:10,34:25,**Dan**9:27,11:18 ,**Hosea** 1:4,2:11,7:4,**Amos** 8:4

Shabbaton **Exo**16:23,31:15,35:2,**Lev**16:31,23:3,23:24, 23:32,23:39,25:4,25:5

Shalom (Peacefulnesss, wholeness, completeness, soundness, welfare, health, prosperity, wellness, tranquility, contentment)

Gen15:15,26:29,26:31,28:21,29:6,37:4,37:14,41:16,43:23,43:27, 43:28,44:17,**Exo** 4:18,18:7,18:23,**Lev** 26:6,**Num** 6:26, 25:12, **Deu**2:26,20:10,20:11,23:6,29:19,**Josh**9:15,10:21,**Judg**4:17,6:23 ,8:9,11:13,11:31,18:6,18:1519:20,21:13,**1Sam**1:17,7:14,10:4,16: 4,17:18,17:22,20:7,20:13,20:21,20:42,25:5,25:6,25:35,29:7,30:2 1,**2Sam**3:21,3:22,3:23,8:10,11:7,15:9,15:27,17:3,18:28,18:29,18:

32,19:24,19:30,20:9,**1Ki**2:5,2:6,2:13,2:33,4:24,5:12,20:18,22:17, 22:27,22:28,**2Ki**4:23,4:26,5:19,5:21,5:22,9:11,9:17,9:18,9:19,9:22, 9:31, 10:13,20:19,22:20,**1 Chr** 12:17,12:18,18:10,22:9,**2 Chr** 15:5,18:16,18:26,18:27,19:1,34:28,**Ezra**9:12,**Est**2:11,9:30,10:3, **Job**5:24,15:21,21:9,25:2,**Psa**4:8,28:3,29:11,34:14,35:20,35:27,37:11,37:37,38:3,41:9,55:18,55:20,69:22,72:3,72:7,73:3,85:8,85:10,119:165,120:6,120:7,122:6,122:7,122:8,125:5,128:6,147:14,**Prov**3:2,3:17,12:20,**Eccl**3:8,**Song**8:10,**Isa**9:6,9:7,26:3,26:12,27:5, 32:17,32:18,33:7,38:17,39:8,41:3,45:7,48:18,48:22,52:7,53:5,54:10,54:13,55:12,57:2,57:19,57:21,59:8,60:17,66:12,**Jer**4:10,6:14, 8:11,8:15,9:8,12:5,12:12,13:19,14:13,14:19,15:5,16:5,20:10,23:17,25:37,28:9,29:7,29:11,30:5,33:6,33:9,34:5,38:4,38:22,43:12,**Lam** 3:17,**Ezek**7:25,13:10,13:16, 34:25,37:26,**Dan** 10:19, **Oba** 1:7,**Micah** 3:5,5:5, **Nahum** 1:15,**Hag** 2:9,**Zec** 6:13, 8:10, 8:12,8:16,8:19,9:10,**Mal**2:5,2:6

Shalem Gen 14:18, 15:16,33:18,34:21,**Deu** 25:15, 27:6, **Josh** 8:31,**Ruth** 2:12,**1 Ki** 6:7,8:61,11:4,15:3,15:14,**2 Ki** 20:3,**1 Chr** 12:38,28:19 ,29:9,29:19,**2 Chr** 8:16,15:17,**16:9**,19:9,25:2, **Psa** 76:2, **Prov** 11:1,**Isa** 38:3,**Amos** 1:6,1:9, **Nahum** 1:12

Anapauo (Rest, stop, cease, refresh, remain quiet, revive)

Mat 11:28,26:45,**Mark** 6:31,14:41, Luke 12:19,1 Cor 16:18,2

Cor7:13,**Phile**1:7,1:20,**1Pet** 4:14,**Rev** 6:11,14:13

Anapausis Mat11:29,12:43,**Luke**11:24,**Rev**4:8,14:11

Epanapauomai Luke 10:6,**Rom** 2:17

Sunanapauomai Rom 15:32

Katapausis Acts 7:49**, Heb** 3:11,3:18,4:1,4:3,4:5,4:10,4:11

Teleios(Completed, Whole, Perfected, finished, accomplished, performed, fulfilled, kept, concluded, reached the goal)

Mat **5:48**,19:21,**Rom** 12:2,**1 Cor** 2:6,13:10, 14:20,**Eph** 4:13,**Phil**3:15,**Col**1:28,4:12,**Heb**5:14,9:11,**James** 1:4,1:17,1:25,3:2,**1 Pet** 1:13,**1 John 4:18**

Teleiotes Col3:14,Heb6:1,**12:2**

Teleo Mat10:23,11:1,13:53,17:24,19:1,26:1,**Luke** 2:39,12:50,18:31,22:37,**John**19:28,19:30,**Acts**13:29,**Rom**2:27,1 3:6, **Gal** 5:16,**2 Tim** 4:7,**Heb** 2:10,9:9,10:1,**James**2:8,**Rev** 10:7,11:7,15:1,15:8,17:17,20:3,20:5,20:7

EpiteleoLuke 13:32,**Rom** 15:28,**2Cor**7:1,8:6,8:11,**Gal** 3:3,**Phil** 1:6, **Heb** 8:5,9:6, **1 Pet** 5:9

Irene(Peace, Quietness, Set at one again) **Mat**10:13,10:34 **Mark**5:34;Luke1:79;2:14,29;7:50;8:48;10:5,6;11:21;12:51;14:32 ,19:38,42;24:36

John14:27;16:33;20:19,21,26**Acts**7:26;9:31;10:36;12:20;15:33;1 6:36;24:2**Rom**1:7;2:10;3:17;5:1;8:6;10:15;14:17,19;15:13,33;16: 20 **1 Cor** 1:3;7:15;14:33; 16:11 **2 Cor** 1:2;13:11 **Gal** 1:3;5:22;6:16 **Eph** 1:2;2:14,15,17;4:3;6:15,23 **Phil** 1:2;4:7,9**Col** 1:2;3:15 **1 Th** 1:1;5:3,23 **2 Th** 1:2;3:16 **1 Tim** 1:2 **2 Tim** 1:2;2:22 **Titus** 1:4 **Phile** 1:3 **Heb** 7:2;11:31;12:14;13:20 **James** 2:16;3:18 **1 Pet** 1:2;3:11;5:14 **2 Pet** 1:2;3:14 **2 John** 1:3 **3 John** 1:14 **Jude** 1:2 **Rev** 1:4; 6:4

Cun (Determined, steadfast, be firm, be established, put right, correct, stable, secure, ready, prepared, ordered, upright, honest)

Gen 41:32,43:16,43:25,**Exo** 8:26,15:17,16:5,19:11,19:15, 23:20,34:2,**Num**21:27,23:1,23:29,**Deu**13:14,17:4,19:3,32:6, **Josh**1:11,3:17,4:3,4:4,8:4,**Judg**12:6,16:26,16:29,**1Sam**7:3,13:13 ,20:31,23:22,23:23,26:4,**2Sam**5:12,7:12,7:13,7:16, 7:24,7:26,**1Ki** 2:12,2:24,2:45,2:46,5:18,6:19,**1Chr**9:32,12:39,14:2,15:1,15:3,15: 12,16:30,17:11,17:12,17:1,17:24,18:8,22:3,22:5,22:10,22:14,28: 2,28:7,29:2,29:3,29:16,29:18,29:19,**2Chr**1:4,2:7,2:9,3:1,8:16,12:

1,12:14,17:5,19:3,20:33,26:14,27:6,29:19,29:35,29:36,30:19,31:
11, 35:4,35:6,35:10,35:14,35:15,35:16, 35:20,Ezra 3:3,7:10,Neh
8:10,**Est**6:4,7:10,**Job**8:8,11:13,12:5,15:23,15:35,18:12,21:8,27:1
6,27:17,28:27,29:7,31:15,38:41,42:7,42:8,**Psa**5:9,7:9,7:12,7:13,8
:3,9:7,10:17,11:2,21:12,24:2,**37:23**,38:17,40:2,48:8,51:10,57:6,5
7:7,59:4,65:6,65:9,68:9,68:10,74:16,78:8,78:20,78:37,89:2,89:4,
89:21,89:37,90:17,93:,93:2,96:10,99:4,101:7,102:28,103:19,107:
36,108:1,112:7,119:5,119:73,119:90,119:133,140:11,141:2,147:
8,**Prov**3:19,4:18,4:26,6:8,8:27,12:3,12:19,16:3,16:9,16:12,19:29,
20:18,21:29,21:31,22:18,24:3,24:27,25:5,29:14,30:25,**Isa**2:2,9:7,
14:21,16:5,30:33,40:20,45:18,51:13,54:14,62:7,**Jer**10:12,10:23,3
0:20,33:2,46:14,51:12,51:15,**Ezek**4:3,4:7,7:14,16:7,28:13,38:7,4
0:43,43:25,45:17,45:22,45:23,45:24,46:2,46:7,46:12,46:13,46:14
,46:15,**Hosea** 6:3,**Amos** 4:12, **Micah** 4:1,**Nahum** 2:3,2:5,**Hab**
2:12,**Zep** 1:7,**Zec** 5:11

Meno (Determined, Steadfast, continue, abide, persist, remain,
persevere, lasting, permanent) **Mat** 10:11,11:23,26:38,**Mark**
6:10,14:34,**Luke**1:56,8:27,9:4,10:7,19:5,24:29,**John**1:32,1:33,1:
38,1:39,2:12,3:36,4:40,5:38,6:27,6:56,7:9,8:31,8:35,9:41,10:40,1
1:6,12:24,12:34,12:46,14:10,14:16,14:17,14:25,**15:4,15:5,15:6,1
5:7,15:9,15:10,15:11,15:16**,19:31,21:22,**Acts**5:4,9:43,16:15,18:3,
18:20,20:5,20:15,20:23,21:7,21:8, 27:31,27:41,28:16,28:30,**Rom**
9:11,**1Cor**3:14,7:8,7:11,7:20,7:24,7:40,13:13,15:6,**2Cor**3:11,3:1
4,9:9,**Phil**1:25,**1Tim**2:15,**2Tim**2:13,3:14,4:20,**Heb**7:3,7:24,10:
34,12:27,13:1,13:14,**1Pet**1:23,1:25,**1John**2:6,2:10,2:14,2:17,2:1
9,2:24,2:27,3:6,3:9,3:14,3:15,3:17,3:24,4:12,4:13,4:15,4:16,**2
John** 1:2,1:9,**Rev** 17:10

Epimeno

John8:7,**Acts**10:48,12:16,13:43,**15:34**,21:4,21:10,28:12,28:14,**R
om** 6:1,11:22, 11:23,**1 Cor** 16:7,16:8,**Gal** 1:18,Phil 1:24,**Col**
1:23,**1 Tim4:16**

Hupomeno Mat 10:22, 24:13, **Mark** 13:13,**Luke** 2:43,**Acts**
17:14,**Rom**12:12,**1Cor**13:7,**2Tim**2:10,2:12,**Heb**10:32,12:2,12:
3,12:7,**James**1:12,5:11,**1Pet** 2:20

Hupomone Luke 8:15,21:19,**Rom** 2:7,5:3,5:4,8:25,15:4,15:5,2 **Cor** 1:6,6:4,12:12,**Col** 1:11,**1 Th** 1:3,**2 Th** 1:4,3:5,**1 Tim** 6:11,**2 Tim** 3:10,**Titus** 2:2,**Heb** 10:36,12:1, **James** 1:3,1:4,**5:11,2 Pet** 1:6, **Rev** 1:9,2:2,2:3,2:19,3:10,13:10,14:12

1. Bernard of Clairvaux; Abridged, Edited and Introduced by Houston, James M., *THE LOVE OF GOD AND SPIRITUAL FRIENDSHIP,* Multnomah Press, Portland, OR. 1983, pages 149-151.
2. Benner, David G. ed., *BAKER ENCYCLOPEDIA OF PSYCHOLOGY,* Baker Book House, Grand Rapids, MI. 1985 Pages 857-858.
3. Piper, Dr. John., *Future Grace,* Multnomah Books, a part of the Questar publishing family, Sisters, OR.,1995, Page 254
4. The Franklin Institute., www.fi.edu/brainexercise.
5. Hoekema, Anthony, H. , *SAVED BY GRACE,* Wm. B. Eerdmans Publishing, Grand Rapids, MI., 1989, Pages 253-254

CHAPTER 12

Love Never Fails

1Co 13:4-8 Love is patient and kind; love does not envy or boast; it is not arrogant or rude. It does not insist on its own way; it is not irritable or resentful; it does not rejoice at wrongdoing, but rejoices with the truth.

Love bears all things, believes all things, hopes all things, endures all things. Love never ends.* *Other translations say "Love Never Fails"

1Co 13:13 So now faith, hope, and love abide, these three; but the greatest of these is love.

Our world, earth, and its inhabitants, have from creation, been racing toward a beginning. I AM the three in one has planned from before the creation of the world a perfect world, a world of fullness and fulfillment.

A world where absolute love will transform those who love I AM here by His overflowing, steadfast, loving kindness because they will keep their eyes on him and not look away. We will love Him and He will transform us by His love. 1Co 13:12 'For now we see in a mirror dimly, but then face to face. Now I know in part; then I shall know fully, even as I have been fully known." When He returns we will become like Him in His love: 1Jn 3:2- 3 "Beloved, we are God's children now, and what we will be has not yet appeared; but we know that when he appears we shall be like him, because we shall see him as he is." And everyone who thus hopes in him purifies himself as he is pure."

Look ahead but keep yourself in Loves pathway

The race is a dangerous one filled with lots of land mines and enemy attacks. The difference between mankind and the rest of creation according to Daniel Gilbert is; "The human being is the only animal that thinks about the future."[1] We are wired to look forward and in looking forward to look for happiness, fulfillment, yes, love. John Piper writes; "The safest place in the universe is with our arms around the neck of God. And the most dangerous place is any path where we flee from his presence".[2]

I AM is the place of beginning and He is the beginning of culmination, of completion, where perfect Absolute Love casts out all fear.

For I AM has declared; "Jer 29:11 For I know the plans I have for you, declares the LORD, plans for welfare and not for evil, to give you a future and a hope."

David F. Wells says; "The Christian confession, as we have seen, is that this future has already arrived, that it has been realized in ways more grand than could have been imagined, that it was divinely ushered in through Christ's death, and that it can be experienced and tasted now, thereby transforming human life. For those in Christ, "the old has passed away, behold, the new has come (II Cor. 5:37). This is not simply a personal statement, that at a certain time their conversion happened. It is even more profound than that. It is Paul's affirmation that those in Christ have already entered the age to come and have been extracted from the world of darkness in which they once were at ease and at home.

Christian hope is not about wishing that things will get better, that somehow emptiness will go away, meaning will return, and life will be stripped of its uncertainties, its psychological aches and anxieties. Nor does it have anything to do with techniques for improving fallen human life, be those therapeutic or even religious.

Hope, instead has to do, biblically speaking, with the knowledge that "the age to come" is already penetrating "this age", that sin, death and meaninglessness of the one is being transformed by the righteousness, life, and meaning of the other, that what has emptied out life, what has scarred and blackened it, is being displaced by what is rejuvenating and transforming it. More than that, hope is hope because it knows it has become part of a realm, a kingdom, which endures, where evil is doomed and will be banished…"[3]

The world planned would not have death, crying or pain. In this world, we live in now there will be pain, heart ache and troubles unending: Joh 16:33 "I have said these things to you, that in me you may have peace. In the world you will have tribulation. But take heart; I have overcome the world." In the world being made new there will be no death: 1Co 15:20-28 "But in fact Christ has been raised from the dead, the first fruits of those who have fallen asleep. For as by a man came death, by a man has come also the resurrection of the dead. For as in Adam all die, so also in Christ shall all be made alive. But each in his own order: Christ the first fruits, then at his coming those who belong to Christ. Then comes the end, when he delivers the kingdom to God the Father after destroying every rule and every authority and power. For he must reign until he has put all his enemies under his feet. The last enemy to be destroyed is death. For "God has put all things in subjection under his feet." But when it says, "all things are put in subjection," it is plain that he is excepted who put all things in subjection under him. When all things are subjected to him, then the Son himself will also be subjected to him who put all things in subjection under him, that God may be all in all."

I AM the three in one is overflowing with love, grace and mercy. His kingdom of love has broken into this world in

Jesus of Nazareth, Yeshua the Messiah, Isa Al-Masih. His sacrificial death has destroyed the power of death, redeeming those who have, do now, and will love Him.

His resurrection from the dead has vindicated the just nature of His mercy and forgiveness, as well as the justice of His anger against those who have, do now and will reject His love. The barrier between I AM and mankind was torn down, his was attested to by many and has been proclaimed throughout the world by faithful followers: Mat 27:51-53 "And behold, the curtain of the temple was torn in two, from top to bottom. And the earth shook, and the rocks were split. The tombs also were opened. And many bodies of the saints who had fallen asleep were raised, and coming out of the tombs after his resurrection they went into the holy city and appeared to many."

So, death is swallowed up in loving sacrifice and what we will be has begun in us in this world: 1Co 15:49-57 "Just as we have borne the image of the man of dust, we shall also bear the image of the man of heaven. I tell you this, brothers: flesh and blood cannot inherit the kingdom of God, nor does the perishable inherit the imperishable. Behold! I tell you a mystery. We shall not all sleep, but we shall all be changed, in a moment, in the twinkling of an eye, at the last trumpet. For the trumpet will sound, and the dead will be raised imperishable, and we shall be changed. For this perishable body must put on the imperishable, and this mortal body must put on immortality. When the perishable puts on the imperishable, and the mortal puts on immortality, then shall come to pass the saying that is written: "Death is swallowed up in victory. "O death, where is your victory? O death, where is your sting?" The sting of death is sin, and the power of sin is the law. But thanks be to God, who gives us the victory through our Lord Jesus Christ."

This present world of fear and danger, then, is not the world planned: Joh 18:36 "Jesus answered, 'My kingdom is not of this world. If my kingdom were of this world, my servants would have been fighting, that I might not be delivered over to the Jews. But my kingdom is not from the world.'"

This world is temporal and fading away, it is not something to cling to I AM is returning and His gracious patience and forgiveness toward us will have an end: 2Pe 3:5-14 "For they deliberately overlook this fact, that the heavens existed long ago, and the earth was formed out of water and through water by the word of God, and that by means of these the world that then existed was deluged with water and perished. But by the same word the heavens and earth that now exist are stored up for fire, being kept until the day of judgment and destruction of the ungodly. But do not overlook this one fact, beloved, that with the Lord one day is as a thousand years, and a thousand years as one day. The Lord is not slow to fulfill his promise as some count slowness, but is patient toward you, not wishing that any should perish, but that all should reach repentance. But the day of the Lord will come like a thief, and then the heavens will pass away with a roar, and the heavenly bodies will be burned up and dissolved, and the earth and the works that are done on it will be exposed. Since all these things are thus to be dissolved, what sort of people ought you to be in lives of holiness and godliness, waiting for and hastening the coming of the day of God, because of which the heavens will be set on fire and dissolved, and the heavenly bodies will melt as they burn! But according to his promise we are waiting for new heavens and a new earth in which righteousness dwells. Therefore, beloved, since you are waiting for these, be diligent to be found by him without spot or blemish, and at peace."

The allure of the world that is to come is not riches, gold or precious metals but the wealth of the absolute love of I AM flooding over us and through us to one another: Rev 21:1-7 "Then I saw a new heaven and a new earth, for the first heaven and the first earth had passed away, and the sea was no more. And I saw the holy city, new Jerusalem, coming down out of heaven from God, prepared as a bride adorned for her husband. And I heard a loud voice from the throne saying, "Behold, the dwelling place of God is with man. He will dwell with them, and they will be his people, and God himself will be with them as their God. He will wipe away every tear from their eyes, and death shall be no more, neither shall there be mourning, nor crying, nor pain anymore, for the former things have passed away." And he who was seated on the throne said, "Behold, I am making all things new." Also he said, "Write this down, for these words are trustworthy and true." And he said to me, "It is done! I am the Alpha and the Omega, the beginning and the end. To the thirsty I will give from the spring of the water of life without payment. The one who conquers will have this heritage, and I will be his God and he will be my son"

. Further we are told: Rev 22:3-5 No longer will there be anything accursed, but the throne of God and of the Lamb will be in it, and his servants will worship him. They will see his face, and his name will be on their foreheads. And night will be no more. They will need no light of lamp or sun, for the Lord God will be their light, and they will reign forever and ever."

In the interim this is all being prepared for those who believe: Joh 14:1-10 "Let not your hearts be troubled. Believe in God; believe also in me. In my Father's house are many rooms. If it were not so, would I have told you that I go to prepare a place for you? And if I go and prepare a place for you, I will come again and will take you to myself, that where I am you may be also. And you know the way to where I am going." Thomas said to him, "Lord, we do not know where you are going. How can we know the way?" Jesus said to him, "I am the way, and the truth, and the life. No one comes to the Father except through me. If you had known me, you would have known my Father also. From now on you do know him and have seen him." Philip said to him, "Lord, show us the Father, and it is enough for us." Jesus said to him, "Have I been with you so long, and you still do not know me, Philip?

Whoever has seen me has seen the Father. How can you say, 'Show us the Father'? Do you not believe that I am in the Father and the Father is in me? The words that I say to you I do not speak on my own authority, but the Father who dwells in me does his works."

These truth's mysteriously have been planned and decided before the foundation of this present world, for I AM is the same yesterday, today and yes forever and He has known and planned for all possible contingencies to the fulfillment of His loving and absolute purpose and His love never fails.

Mat 13:35 "This was to fulfill what was spoken by the prophet: "I will open my mouth in parables; I will utter what has been hidden since the foundation of the world." Mat 25:34 "Then the King will say to those on his right, 'Come, you who are blessed by my Father, inherit the kingdom prepared for you from the foundation of the world."

Luk 11:49-50 "Therefore also the Wisdom of God said, 'I will send them prophets and apostles, some of whom they will kill and persecute,' so that the blood of all the prophets, shed from the foundation of the world, may be charged against this generation." Joh 17:24 "Father, I desire that they also, whom you have given me, may be with me where I am, to see my glory that you have given me because you loved me before the foundation of the world."

Eph 1:3-6 "Blessed be the God and Father of our Lord Jesus Christ, who has blessed us in Christ with every spiritual blessing in the heavenly places, even as he chose us in him before the foundation of the world, that we should be holy and blameless before him. In love he predestined us for adoption as sons through Jesus Christ, according to the purpose of his will, to the praise of his glorious grace, with which he has blessed us in the Beloved."

Heb 4:3 "For we who have believed enter that rest, as he has said, "As I swore in my wrath, 'They shall not enter my rest,'" although his works were finished from the foundation of the world. Heb 9:26-28 for then he would have had to suffer repeatedly since the foundation of the world. But as it is, he has appeared once for all at the end of the ages to put away sin by the sacrifice of himself. And just as it is appointed for man to die once, and after that comes judgment, Heb so Christ, having been offered once to bear the sins of many, will appear a second time, not to deal with sin but to save those who are eagerly waiting for him." 1Pe 1:20-21 "He was foreknown before the foundation of the world but was made manifest in the last times for the sake of you who through him are believers in God, who raised him from the dead and gave him glory, so that your faith and hope are in God."

This world we live in then is neither a mistake nor a surprise.

I AM the three in one in absolute love have planned it and will see it to fruition. Rather than create puppets they have planned to bring about a people who would learn to live loving Him and one another in humility, belief, trust, acceptance, confidence, gratitude, compassion, freedom, stewardship, servant hood, loyalty, purity, justice, rest and determination. These gifts do not belong to us and are not produced by us, they are gifts given to us as by faith we look to Him.

Adrio Koenig writes; … "So it is not at all strange that … self-manifestation, self-revelation and self-communication of God attain their goal when a person comes to faith.

Before the proclamation's goal can be broadly outlined, it is necessary to show that this "addition" of faith is no addition at all, and that because of the nature of faith there is agreement … on the emptiness of faith. This does not mean that faith is unimportant, but rather that its importance-even indispensability- lies in that it is nothing on its own, is not autonomous, is no human contribution, but must receive its content and its meaning from the other side: in fact from God in Christ through the Spirit In faith we confess God as the subject and ourselves as the object of salvation. Salvation means that Christ has fully attained God's goal for us. And when a person believes this, God's goal is attained in that person.

Proclamation has as its goal the bringing of people to this knowledge and trust. How radically this faith involves our whole life is shown by the New Testament's equation of faith with obedience. So it is clear that, because of the nature of faith, no tension can exist between "Christ alone" and the "addition" of faith. Faith lives solely from Christ, and is filled by what he has done. … Christ's attainment of the goal for us (but without us) and his attainment of the goal in us are not concurrent.

Yet it is this very emptiness of faith in itself which leads to its decisive character. Because it is directed solely to Christ and his work for us, faith is necessary-and its lack excludes one from salvation. Without faith, God's goal in us is not reached. Precisely because faith is neither a human accomplishment nor a human contribution, but rather a confession that everything has been done for us by Christ, we have no Christ if we have no faith. This is why Scripture speaks so strongly about the necessity, value, and power of faith. Faith receives value only from its object. And because of faith's necessity, we are bound to speak of the mortal peril of unbelief."[4]

Humility is the characteristic of believing that gives us the ability to admit our needs, weaknesses and limitations so that we can submit to the power of God in our life and receive our strength from Him and through others, it is not powerlessness, it knows where the power comes from. Humility is the beginning of Faith that LOVE works in us as we look outside of ourselves to I AM. Humility involves being able to give to others but also to receive from others as we keep our eyes fixed on I AM and thereby become more like Him in love. The key characteristic of humility is mercifulness. The loss of humility brings about rebelliousness.

Belief flows out of the ability humility provides us to have faith. Belief is an overwhelming sense of hope based on understanding of past actions and in the fulfillment of future promises that gives encouragement so that we can be enthusiastic and self-stretching, in order that we might grow through developing (God given)potential. The key characteristic of belief is hopefulness. The loss of belief brings about despair.

Trust is the characteristic outgrowth of believing that gives us the ability to be open and share who we are and what we have been given so that we can be catalysts in the development of openness and candor in others. The key characteristic of trust is openness. The loss of trust brings about suspiciousness.

Acceptance is the characteristic outgrowth of believing that gives us the ability to forgive ourselves and others so that healing and understanding can take place. The key characteristic of acceptance is forgiveness. The loss of acceptance brings about a judgmental nature.

Confidence is the characteristic outgrowth of believing that gives us assurance of our being accepted and gives us the ability to look past self-promotion to the promotion of others so that their confidence is built up. The key characteristic of confidence is assuredness or certainty. The loss of confidence brings about inconsistency.

Gratitude is the characteristic outgrowth of believing that gives us the ability to look at all good things as gifts from God and causes us give in return so the gifts can be shared by all. The key characteristic of gratitude is thankfulness. The loss of gratitude brings about an expecting nature-ungratefulness.

Compassion is the characteristic outgrowth of believing that gives us the ability to be gracious (giving undeserved favor) and merciful (not demanding retribution) so that we might live in a way that will be most beneficial to ourselves and others and glorifying to God. The key characteristic of compassion is graciousness. The loss of compassion brings about degradation, using of others.

Freedom is the characteristic outgrowth of believing that gives us the ability to set aside personal desires and postpone pleasure, (i.e. physical, emotional gratification), in order that we are liberated to find complete satisfaction in God and be separated from enslaving entanglements. The key characteristic of freedom is purposefulness. The loss of freedom brings about insatiability, inability to be satisfied.

Stewardship is the characteristic of believing that gives us the ability to be inter-connected with each other in a truly loving manner. We do not lose any integral parts of ourselves or disintegrate into another person, yet we value and need each other's gifts and uniqueness for the full use and completion of our own giftedness. The key characteristic of stewardship is carefulness. The loss of stewardship brings about codependence, an inability to be helpful.

Servanthood is the characteristic of believing that gives us the ability to worship in everything that we do by looking to God to fill us and overflow through us into the lives of others for thoughtful attentiveness to God's desires for them. The key characteristic of servanthood is submissiveness or interdependence. The loss of servanthood brings about an uncaring attitude, inattentiveness.

Loyalty is the characteristic outgrowth of believing that gives us the ability to remain true or faithful to IAM, ourselves and others so that we are not pushed or led along by demands other than God's. The key characteristic of loyalty is faithfulness. The loss of loyalty brings about inconsistency.

Purity is the characteristic outgrowth of believing that gives us the ability to be unmixed in our allegiance toward God so that we won't be driven by any other purpose than to love, glorify and enjoy God to the ultimate benefit, enjoyment and fulfillment of ourselves and others. The key characteristic of purity is objectiveness (integrity, congruence). The loss of purity brings about confusion.

Justice is the characteristic outgrowth of believing that gives us the ability to act rightly on behalf of God so that despots (those who want to control, oppress and use others for personal gain) are not allowed to triumph and the defenseless are defended. The key characteristic of justice is righteousness. The loss of justice brings about either apathy or being overbearing (despotism).

Rest is the characteristic of believing that gives us the ability see past obstacles to our own well-being and the well-being of others so that we can peacefully work to overcome those obstacles and overthrow those who are setting them up. The key characteristic of rest is peacefulness. The loss of rest brings about anxiety, panic.

Determination is the characteristic of believing that gives us the ability to persist until that which has been started is completed. The key characteristic of determination is steadfastness, completion. The loss of determination brings about an inability to follow through, indecision.

2Co 13:5 "Examine yourselves, to see whether you are in the faith. Test yourselves. Or do you not realize this about yourselves, that Jesus Christ is in you?--unless indeed you fail to meet the test!"

We are meant for a Kingdom, much better than Camelot or any Kingdom we can imagine on this earth. Anthony Hoekema writes; "The Kingdom of God, therefore, is to be understood as the reign of God dynamically active in human history through Jesus Christ, the purpose of which is the redemption of God's people from sin and from demonic powers, and the final establishment of the new heavens and the new earth. It means the great drama of the history of salvation has been inaugurated, and that the new age has been ushered in. The Kingdom must not be understood as merely the salvation of certain individuals or even as the reign of God in the hearts of his people; it means nothing less than the reign of God over his entire created universe....

It will be evident, therefore, that the kingdom of God, as described in the New Testament, is not a state of affairs brought about by human achievement, nor is it the culmination of strenuous human effort. The kingdom is established by God's sovereign grace, and its blessings are to be received as gifts of that grace. Man's duty is not to bring the kingdom into existence, but to enter into it by faith, and to pray that he may be enabled more and more to submit himself to the beneficent rule of God in every area of his life. The kingdom is not man's upward climb to perfection but God's breaking into human history to establish his reign and to advance his purposes.

It should be added that the kingdom of God includes both positive and a negative aspect. It means redemption for those who accept it and enter into it by faith, but judgment for those who reject it."[5]

Absolute Love never fails, I AM the three in one will bring about a world of love for all who have had faith in Him throughout human history. When all whom He has established as His are complete, we will eternally live in His presence without a wandering heart. Mat 24:13-14 "But the one who endures to the end will be saved. And this gospel of the kingdom will be proclaimed throughout the whole world as a testimony to all nations, and then the end will come."

Enduring to the end and proclaiming the kingdom of God primarily are done through living a life that is connected to I AM: 2Pe 1:2-8 May grace and peace be multiplied to you in the knowledge of God and of Jesus our Lord. His divine power has granted to us all things that pertain to life and godliness, through the knowledge of him who called us to his own glory and excellence, by which he has granted to us his precious and very great promises, so that through them you may become partakers of the divine nature, having escaped from the corruption that is in the world because of sinful desire. For this very reason, make every effort to supplement your faith with virtue, and virtue with knowledge, and knowledge with self-control, and self-control with steadfastness, and steadfastness with godliness, and godliness with brotherly affection, and brotherly affection with love. For if these qualities are yours and are increasing, they keep you from being ineffective or unfruitful in the knowledge of our Lord Jesus Christ". As we rest in determination waiting for the beginning the continual looking away from self to I AM, to Absolute Love will be the way home.

This beginning is finally and fully experienced by most of us through death, the journey begins through humility, but we also wait for completion of the race. Death is the most humbling activity we experience this side of seeing God face to face. Rev 22:17 "The Spirit and the Bride say, "Come." And let the one who hears say, "Come." And let the one who is thirsty come; let the one who desires take the water of life without price."   Rev 22:20 "He who testifies to these things says, "Surely I am coming soon." Amen. Come, Lord Jesus!"

1. Gilbert, Daniel., *STUMBLING ON HAPPINESS,* Vintage Books A Division of Random House, Inc. New York, NY, 2006, page 4
2. Piper, Dr. John., *Future Grace,* Multnomah Books, a part of the Questar publishing family, Sisters, OR.,1995, page 243
3. Wells, David F. ., *ABOVE ALL EARTHLY POW'RS; Christ in a Post Modern World,* Wm. B.

Eerdmans Publishing, Grand Rapids, MI., 2005, page 206

4. Koenig, Adrio., *THE ECLIPSE OF CHRIST IN ESCHATOLOGY; Toward a Christ Centered Approach,* Wm. B. Eerdmans Publishing, Grand Rapids, MI., 1989, pages 158 and 159., MI.,Marshall, Morgan and Scott, London, England, Adapted from Jesus die Laast, Gelowig Nagedink Deel 2, Praetoria, DRC Bookshop, 1980

5. Hoekema, Anthony A.., *THE BIBLE AND THE FUTURE,* Wm. B. Ecrdmans Publishing, Grand Rapids, MI. , 1979, page 45

Summation

Pictorial Outline "Absolute Love: Not the God you are imagining"

O.T. Hesed: Exodus 34:6-7 "ABSOLUTE LOVE N.T. Agape 1 John 4:8-16			
CHARACTER OF GOD(The Sovereign, Personal, Self-Revealing, Self-Existent, Relational God/YHWH-Yeshua, Jesus, Isa			
Applying Truth 1 Cor. 13:7; Gal 5:6			Suppressing Truth 2 Cor. 2:14-16; Heb 10; John 4:18
Motivation-Faith Working Through Love			Motivation-Fear/Shame
Qualities of Faith	Character Qualities	Relational Affect	Antipathy/Fear
Spiritual	Psychological	Sociological/Physiological	Physical/Material
Humility	Mercifulness	Ability to be vulnerable, receive from others	Rebelliousness/Full of Self
Belief	Hopefulness	Ability to be encouraging	Despairing/Lost
Trust	Openness	Ability to share/be transparent	Stinginess/Suspicious
Acceptance	Forgiveness	Ability to absorb pain/facilitate healing	Judgmental/Self-destructive
Confidence	Assuredness	Ability to know and accept self	Uncertainty/Inconsistency
Gratitude	Thankfulness	Ability to see life as a gift/be giving in order to receive something greater	Ungrateful/Expecting
Compassion	Graciousness	Ability to go beyond what is deserved	Using/Degrading
Freedom	Purposefulness	Ability to postpone/forego temporal unfulfilling wants	Insatiable/Controlled by desires
Stewardship	Carefulness	Ability to be beneficial of others	Codependent/Unhelpful
Servanthood	Submissiveness-Interdependence	Ability to attend to the needs of others	Inattentive/Uncaring/Needy
Loyalty	Faithfulness —Being True	Ability to stand consistently beside others	Unreliable/Inconsistent
Purity	Objectiveness	Ability to be certain/unmixed/integral	Incongruent/Confused
Justice	Righteousness	Ability to stand against oppression	Bullying/Overbearing/Apathetic
Determination	Steadfastness	Ability to continue until the end	Indecisive/Cannot follow through
Rest	Peacefulness	Ability to look beyond obstacles to a greater reward beyond not inactivity	Anxiety/Panic
Results in the "Obedience of Faith"		Christ likeness	Results in Lawlessness, Perversion, Apathy / Pathology / Inability
Rom. 1:5,16:26, James 1:25		Ability to be Truly-Loving-Caring/LOVE is active.	Rom. 1:18-32; Rom. 8:7&8, 1 Tim. 1:8-11;
		Counterfeit/Perverted	
		Relativism/humanistic orientation/ or self-righteousness/religious o	
Faith is a supernatural phenomenon developed and experienced through God by the empowerment of the Holy Spirit working through WORD of God to build up the Christ' John 13:34-35, Acts 2:41-47, Eph. 4:4-16, I John 5:2-5 (Proclamation, Worship, Fellowship, Mission)			

There is one absolute GOD, I AM. All people know that that there is a creator God and that He is the beginning and end of all that is created. Even though we all try to suppress the absoluteness of God trying to find our own way. We do not have faith that God has our interest at the heart of His being. We all try to make a God of our own imagining.

God is Absolute Love. He is described in both the Old and New Testaments of the Bible by significant corresponding words. In Hebrew HESED translated Steadfast Love. In Exodus God tells Moses He is overflowing or abounding in this steadfast Love. Likewise in the New Testament He is AGAPE, God is Love. God is Absolute Love.

All people would have a common ground for dialogue and commonality if this was the beginning point. The three major religions all have this common root, for all trace their roots back to the Father of Faith in God, Abraham. Even those who do not believe beginning in the roots of religion can begin at a place of understanding what it is to be loving.

Religions fractured by years of cultural, political and organizational confusion. If Christians, Jews and Muslims could move beyond infighting and anger to begin to understand the Absolute Love of God being poured out to us we could have a starting point.

God's Absolute Love flows out from Him in community. He is one in unity forged into community flowing in, filling up and overflowing to us in entities, Triunity. This community is the basis for Love and the source of all Love.

When we surrender to this Absolute Love it flows freely into us giving us life and causing abundant living. Flowing into us spiritually, renewing us to psychological, sociological and physical health.

The beginning of this is brought about by humble surrender of ourselves. Stephen R Covey says; Humility is the greatest of all virtues because out of it comes all the other virtues. When the God who is Absolute Love pours into us through Humble surrender all is changed.

Love flows into us by producing humility, humility produces belief or faith in the One who is Absolute Love. Belief in Absolute Love produces trust, acceptance, confidence, gratitude, compassion, freedom, stewardship, servanthood, loyalty, purity, justice, rest and determination.

Humility is the characteristic of love that gives us the ability to admit our needs, weaknesses and limitations so that we can submit to the power of God in our life and receive our strength from Him and through others.

Humility is not powerlessness; it is knowing where the power comes from. Humility is the beginning of Faith, that LOVE works in us as we look outside of ourselves to God. Humility involves being able to give to others but also to receive from others as we keep our eyes fixed on God and thereby become more like Him in love.

When Love enters our lives, we do not think less of ourselves. We do not think of ourselves chiefly, our focus remains on the one who Loves us. This focus produces a belief or faith in the other person.

The opposite affect of humility is narcissism leading ultimately to rebellion and anarchy.

Belief is an overwhelming sense of hope based on understanding of past actions and in the fulfillment of future promises that gives encouragement, so that we can be enthusiastic, in order that we might grow through developing, God gifted potential.

Belief then begins to transform all of our life and characteristics, we trust.   The opposite affect of belief or faith in God's Love is a sense of being lost or despairing.

Belief produces hopefulness and the ability to be encouraging.

Trust is the characteristic outgrowth of believing that gives us the ability to be open and share who we are and what we have been given, so that we can be catalysts in the development of openness and candor in others. We can become accepting.

The opposite affect of trust is suspiciousness and stinginess.

Acceptance is the characteristic outgrowth of believing that gives us the ability to forgive ourselves and others so that healing and understanding can take place. We become confident, accepting that we are loved

The opposite affect of acceptance is judgementalism and selfishness.

Confidence is the characteristic outgrowth of believing that gives us assurance of our being accepted, and gives us the ability to look past self-promotion to the promotion of others, so that their confidence is built up. Confidence is not a lack of humility.

The opposite affect of confidence is inconsistency and uncertainty.

Gratitude is the characteristic outgrowth of believing that gives us the ability to look at all good things as gifts from God. Gratitude causes us give in return, so the gifts can be shared by all.

The opposite affect of gratitude is demanding, expecting and ungratefulness.

Compassion is the characteristic outgrowth of believing that gives us the ability to be gracious "giving undeserved favor" and merciful "not demanding retribution" so that we might live in a way that will be most beneficial to ourselves and others, and glorifying to God.

The opposite affect of compassion is being degrading of self and others, to use others.

Freedom is the characteristic outgrowth of believing that gives us the ability to set aside personal desires and postpone pleasure; i.e. physical, emotional gratification, in order that we be liberated to find complete satisfaction in God, freed from enslaving entanglements.

The opposite affect freedom is being controlled by lustful desires to have an insatiable appetite for things because only God's love satisfies our desires.

Stewardship is the characteristic of believing that gives us the ability to be inter-connected with each other in a truly loving manner. We do not lose any integral parts of ourselves or disintegrate into another person, yet we value and need each other's gifts and uniqueness, for the full use and completion of our own giftedness.

The opposite affect of stewardship is being unhelpful, hoarding and codependent.

Servanthood is the characteristic of believing that gives us the ability to worship in everything that we do by looking to God to fill us and overflow through us into the lives of others, for thoughtful attentiveness to God's desires for them.

The opposite affect of servanthood is neediness, being uncaring and inattentive.

Loyalty is the characteristic outgrowth of believing that gives us the ability to remain true or faithful to God, ourselves and others so that we are not pushed or led along by demands other than God's.

The opposite affect of loyalty being unreliable.

Purity is the characteristic outgrowth of believing that gives us the ability to be unmixed in our allegiance toward God, so that we won't be driven by any other purpose than to love, glorify and enjoy God, to the ultimate benefit, enjoyment and fulfillment of ourselves and others.

The opposite affect of purity incongruence and confusion.

Justice is the characteristic outgrowth of believing that gives us the ability to act rightly on behalf of God, so that despots (those who want to control, oppress and use others for personal gain) are not allowed to triumph, and the defenseless are defended.

The opposite affect of justice is bullying, becoming overbearing and apathetic.

Determination is the characteristic of believing that gives us the ability to persist until that which has been started is completed.

The opposite affect of determination is inability to follow through, indecisiveness.

Rest is the characteristic of believing that gives us the ability see past obstacles to our own wellbeing, and the wellbeing of others, so that we can peacefully work to overcome those obstacles.

The opposite affect of rest is anxiety, restlessness leading to panic.

These aforementioned characteristics are not exhaustive of Absolute Love or how God's love transforms our lives, but they are a beginning point. Absolute Love is inexhaustible, God's Love is an unfailing love and a sacrificial love.

Afterword

This book is not intended to be an ending, but a beginning. Genesis starts out, "In the beginning, God" and this is precisely the point of this book. God is knowable yet our knowing of God is inexhaustible. Where God is there is life and growth. God is life, God is love, God is truth and God is light. "In Him there is no darkness. " If this book has given you a desire to learn more about "Absolute Love", I do not know of anyone who has done more to show the connection between our good and the absolute glory of God than John Piper. You can discover more at www.desiringgod.org. Some other very good resources are www.sovereigngraceministries.org and www.enjoyinggodministries.org.

For Muslims who want to find more information on Isa Al-Masih or the Injeel of ISA more information can be found at www.crescentproject.org.

If you are Jewish you can find out more about Yeshua of Nazareth at www.jewsforjesus.org

For scientists who are seeking some reference with other scientists who are not closed to researching and are open to the possibility that the intricate wonders of the world are from an absolute source and not random, refer to places like www.whomadegod.org, www.worldbydesign.org, and www.icr.org.

If you want to help with various types of rescue ministries, to give sacrificial love to help people who are in some type of lie or bondage you could contact some of the following organizations.

www.ijm.org

www.worldvision.org

www.humantrafficking.org

www.amnestyusa.org

www.unicef.org

www.nrlc.org

www.harborhouse.org

www.lifesaverministries.org

www.prisonfellowship.org

www.exodusinternational.org

Addendum

An Unpublished Essay on the Trinity

JONATHAN EDWARDS

IT IS COMMON when speaking of the Divine happiness to say that God is infinitely happy in the enjoyment of Himself, in perfectly beholding and infinitely loving, and rejoicing in, His own essence and perfection, and accordingly it must be supposed that God perpetually and eternally has a most perfect idea of Himself, as it were an exact image and representation of Himself ever before Him and in actual view, and from hence arises a most pure and perfect act or energy in the Godhead, which is the Divine love, complacence and joy. The knowledge or view which God has of Himself must necessarily be conceived to be something distinct from His mere direct existence. There must be something that answers to our reflection. The reflection as we reflect on our own minds carries something of imperfection in it. However, if God beholds Himself so as thence to have delight and joy in Himself He must become his own object. There must be a duplicity. There is God and the idea of God, if it be proper to call a conception of that that is purely spiritual an idea.

If a man could have an absolutely perfect idea of all that passed in his mind, all the series of ideas and exercises in every respect perfect as to order, degree, circumstance and for any particular space of time past, suppose the last hour, he would really to all intents and purpose be over again what he was that last hour. And if it were possible for a man by reflection perfectly to contemplate all that is in his own mind in an hour, as it is and at the same time that it is there in its first and direct existence; if a man, that is, had a perfect reflex or contemplative idea of every thought at the same moment or moments that that thought was and of every exercise at and during the same time that that exercise was, and so through a whole hour, a man would really be two during that time, he would be indeed double, he would be twice at once. The idea he has of himself would be himself again.

Note, by having a reflex or contemplative idea of what passes in our own minds I don't mean consciousness only. There is a great difference between a man's having a view of himself, reflex or contemplative idea of himself so as to delight in his own beauty or excellency, and a mere direct consciousness. Or if we mean by consciousness of what is in our own minds anything besides the mere simple existence in our minds of what is there, it is nothing but a power by reflection to view or contemplate what passes.

Therefore as God with perfect clearness, fullness and strength, understands Himself, views His own essence (in which there is no distinction of substance and act but which is wholly substance and wholly act), that idea which God hath of Himself is absolutely Himself. This representation of the

Divine nature and essence is the Divine nature and essence again: so that by God's thinking of the

Deity must certainly be generated. Hereby there is another person begotten, there is another

Infinite Eternal Almighty and most holy and the same God, the very same Divine nature.

And this Person is the second person in the Trinity, the Only Begotten and dearly Beloved Son of

God; He is the eternal, necessary, perfect, substantial and personal idea which God hath of Himself; and that it is so seems to me to be abundantly confirmed by the Word of God.

Nothing can more agree with the account the Scripture gives us of the Son of God, His being in the form of God and His express and perfect image and representation: (II Cor. 4:4) "Lest the light of the glorious Gospel of Christ Who is the image of God should shine unto them." (Phil. 2:6) "Who being in the form of God." (Col. 1:15) "Who is the image of the invisible God." (Heb. 1:3) "Who being the brightness of His glory and the express image of His person."

Christ is called the face of God (Exod. 33:14): the word [A.V. presence] in the original signifies face, looks, form or appearance. Now what can be so properly and fitly called so with respect to God as

God's own perfect idea of Himself whereby He has every moment a view of His own essence: this idea is that "face of God" which God sees as a man sees his own face in a looking glass. 'Tis of such form or appearance whereby God eternally appears to Himself. The root that the original word comes from signifies to look upon or behold: now what is that which God looks upon or beholds in so eminent a manner as He doth on His own idea or that perfect image of Himself which He has in view. This is what is eminently in God's presence and is therefore called the angel of God's presence or face (Isa. 63:9). But that the Son of God is God's own eternal and perfect idea is a thing we have yet much more expressly revealed in God's Word. First, in that Christ is called "the wisdom of God."

If we are taught in the Scripture that Christ is the same with God's wisdom or knowledge, then it teaches us that He is the same with God's perfect and eternal idea. They are the same as we have already observed and I suppose none will deny. But Christ is said to be the wisdom of God (I Cor.

1:24, Luke 11:49, compare with Matt. 23:34); and how much doth Christ speak in Proverbs under the name of Wisdom especially in the 8th chapter.

The Godhead being thus begotten by God's loving an idea of Himself and shewing forth in a distinct subsistence or person in that idea, there proceeds amost pure act, and an infinitely holy and sacred energy arises between the Father and Son in mutually loving and delighting in each other, for their love and joy is mutual, (Prov. 8:30) "I was daily His delight rejoicing always before Him." This is the eternal and most perfect and essential act of the Divine nature, wherein the Godhead acts to an infinite degree and in the most perfect manner possible. The Deity becomes all act, the Divine essence itself flows out and is as it were breathed forth in love and joy. So that the Godhead therein stands forth in yet another manner of subsistence, and there proceeds the third Person in the

Trinity, the Holy Spirit, viz., the Deity in act, for there is no other act but the act of the will.

We may learn by theWord of God that the Godhead or the Divine nature and essence does subsist in love. (I John 4:8) "He that loveth not knoweth not God; for God is love." In the context of which place I think it is plainly intimated to us that the Holy Spirit is that Love, as in the 12th and 13th verses. "If we love one another, God dwelleth in us, and His love is perfected in us; hereby know we that we dwell in Him ... because He hath given us of His Spirit." 'Tis the same argument in both verses. In the 12th verse the apostle argues that if we have love dwelling in us we have God dwelling in us, and in the 13th verse He clears the force of the argument by this that love is God's

Spirit. Seeing we have God's Spirit dwelling in us, we have God dwelling in [in us], supposing it as a thing granted and allowed that God's Spirit is God. 'Tis evident also by this that God's dwelling in us and His love or the love that He hath exerciseth, being in us, are the same thing. The same is intimated in the same manner in the last verse of the foregoing chapter. The apostle was, in the foregoing verses, speaking of love as a sure sign of sincerity and our acceptance with God, beginning with the 18th verse, and he sums up the argument thus in the last verse, "and hereby do we know that He abideth in us by the Spirit that He hath given us."

The Scripture seems in many places to speak of love in Christians as if it were the same with the

Spirit of God in them, or at least as the prime and most natural breathing and acting of the Spirit in the soul. (Phil. 2:1) "If there be therefore any consolation in Christ, any comfort of love, any fellowship of the Spirit, if any bowels of mercies, fulfil ye my joy that ye be likeminded, having the same love, being of one accord, of one mind." (II Cor. 6:6) "By kindness, by the Holy Ghost, by love unfeigned." (Romans 15:30) "Now I beseech you, brethren, for the Lord Jesus Christ's sake, and for the love of the Spirit." (Col. 1:8) "Who declared unto us your love in the Spirit." (Rom. 5:5) "Having the love of God shed abroad in our hearts by the Holy Ghost which is given to us." (Gal. 5:13-16)

"Use not liberty for an occasion to the flesh, but by love serve one another. For all the law is fulfilled in one word, even in this: Thou shalt love thy neighbour as thyself. But if ye bite and devour one another, take heed that ye be not consumed one of another. This I say then, Walk in the Spirit, and ye shall not fulfill the lusts of the flesh." The Apostle argues that Christian liberty does not make way for fulfilling the lusts of the flesh in biting and devouring one another and the like, because a principle of love which was the fulfilling of the law would prevent it, and in the 16th verse he asserts the same thing in other words: "This I say then walk in the Spirit and ye shall not fulfill the lusts of the flesh."

The third and last office of the Holy Spirit is to comfort and delight the souls of God's people, and thus one of His names is the Comforter, and thus we have the phrase of "joy in the Holy Ghost." (I

Thess. 1:6) "Having received the Word in much affliction with joy of the Holy Ghost." (Rom. 14: 17)

"The kingdom of God is ... righteousness, and peace, and joy in the Holy Ghost." (Acts 9:31) "Walking in the fear of the Lord and in the comfort of the Holy Ghost." But how well doth this agree with the

Holy Ghost being God's joy and delight, (Acts 13:52) "And the disciples were filled with joy and with the Holy Ghost"--meaning as I suppose that they were filled with spiritual joy.

This is confirmed by the symbol of the Holy Ghost, viz., a dove, which is the emblem of love or a lover, and is so used in Scripture, and especially often so in Solomon's Song, (1:15) "Behold thou art fair; my love, behold thou art fair; thou hast dove's eyes:" i.e. "Eyes of love," and again 4:1, the same words; and 5:12, "His eyes are as the eyes of doves," and 5:2, "My love, my dove," and 2:14 and 6:9; and this I believe to be the reason that the dove alone of all birds (except the sparrow in the single case of the leprosy) was appointed to be offered in sacrifice because of its innocence and because it is the emblem of love, love being the most acceptable sacrifice to God. It was under this similitude that the Holy Ghost descended from the Father on Christ at His baptism, signifying the infinite love of the Father to the Son, Who is the true David, or beloved, as we said before.

The same was signified by what was exhibited to the eye in the appearance there was of the Holy

Ghost descending from the Father to the Son in the shape of a dove, as was signified by what was exhibited to the eye in the voice there was at the same time, viz., "This is My well Beloved Son in

Whom I am well pleased."

(That God's love or His loving kindness is the same with the Holy Ghost seems to be plain by Psalm

36:7-9, "How excellent (or how precious as 'tis in the Hebrew) is Thy loving-kindness O God, therefore the children of men put their trust under the shadow of Thy wings, they shall be abundantly satisfied (in the Hebrew "watered") with the fatness of Thy house and Thou shalt make them to drink of the river of Thy pleasures; for with Thee is the fountain of life and in Thy light shall we see light."

Doubtless that precious loving-kindness and that fatness of God's house and river of His pleasures and the water of the fountain of life and God's light here spoken [of] are the same thing; by which we learn that the Holy anointing oil that was kept in the House of God, which was a type of the Holy

Ghost, represented God's love, and that the "River of water of life" spoken of in the 22nd [chapter] of Revelation, which proceeds out of the throne of God and of the Lamb, which is the same with

Ezekiel's vision of Living and life-giving water, which is here [in Ps. 36] called the "Fountain of life and river of God's pleasures," is God's loving-kindness.

But Christ Himself expressly teaches us that by spiritual fountains and rivers of water of life is meant the Holy Ghost. (John 4:14; 7:38,39).That by the river of God's pleasures here is meant the same thing with the pure river of water of life spoken of in Revelation 22:1, will be much confirmed if we compare those verses with Revelation 21:23, 24; 22:1,5. (See the notes on chapters 21, 23, 24)

I think if we compare these places and weigh them we cannot doubt but that it is the same happines2 that is meant in this Psalm which is spoken of there.)

So this well agrees with the similitudes and metaphors that are used about the Holy Ghost in

Scripture, such as water, fire, breath, wind, oil, wine, a spring, a river, a being poured out and shed forth, and a being breathed forth. Can there any spiritual thing be thought, or anything belonging to any spiritual being to which such kind of metaphors so naturally agree, as to the affection of a Spirit.

The affection, love or joy, may be said to flow out as water or to be breathed forth as breath or wind. But it would [not] sound so well to say that an idea or judgment flows out or is breathed forth.

It is no way different to say of the affection that it is warm, or to compare love to fire, but it would not seem natural to say the same of perception or reason. It seems natural enough to say that the soul is poured out in affection or that love or delight are shed abroad: (Rom. 5:5) "The love of God is shed abroad in our hearts," but it suits with nothing else belonging to a spiritual being.

This is that "river of water of life" spoken of in the 22nd [chapter] of Revelation, which proceeds from the throne of the Father and the Son, for the rivers of living water or water of life are the Holy

Ghost, by the same apostle's own interpretation (John 7:38, 39); and the Holy Ghost being the infinite delight and pleasure of God, the river is called the river of God's pleasures (Ps. 36:8), not

God's river of pleasures, which I suppose signifies the same as the fatness of God's House, which they that trust in God shall be watered with, by which fatness of God's House I suppose is signified the same thing which oil typifies.

It is a confirmation that the Holy Ghost is God's love and delight, because the saints communion with God consists in their partaking of the Holy Ghost. The communion of saints is twofold: 'tis their communion with God and communion with one another, (I John 1:3) "That ye also may have fellowship with us, and truly our fellowship is with the Father and with His Son, Jesus Christ."

Communion is a common partaking of good, either of excellency or happiness, so that when it is said the saints have communion or fellowship with the Father and with the Son, the meaning of it is that they partake with the Father and the Son of their good, which is either their excellency and glory (II Peter 1:4), "Ye are made partakers of the Divine nature"; Heb. 12:10, "That we might be partakers of His holiness;" John 17:22, 23, "And the glory which Thou hast given Me I have given

them, that they may be one, even as we are one, I in them and Thou in Me"); or of their joy and happiness: (John 17:13) "That they might have My joy fulfilled in themselves."

But the Holy Ghost being the love and joy of God is His beauty and happiness, and it is in our partaking of the same Holy Spirit that our communion with God consists: (II Cor. 13:14) "The grace of the Lord Jesus Christ, and the love of God, and the communion of the Holy Ghost, be with you all,

Amen." They are not different benefits but the same that the Apostle here wisheth, viz., the Holy

Ghost: in partaking of the Holy Ghost, we possess and enjoy the love and grace of the Father and the

Son, for the Holy Ghost is that love and grace, and therefore I suppose it is that in that forementioned place, (I John 1:3).We are said to have fellowship with the Son and not with the Holy

Ghost, because therein consists our fellowship with the Father and the Son, even in partaking with them of the Holy Ghost.

In this also eminently consists our communion with the Son that we drink into the same Spirit. This is the common excellency and joy and happiness in which they all are united; 'tis the bond of perfectness by which they are one in the Father and the Son as the Father is in the Son.

I can think of no other good account that can be given of the apostle Paul's wishing grace and peace from God the Father and the Lord Jesus Christ in the beginning of his Epistles, without ever mentioning the Holy Ghost, - as we find it thirteen times in his salutations in the beginnings of his

Epistles, - but [i.e., except] that the Holy Ghost is Himself love and grace of God the Father and the

Lord Jesus Christ; and in his blessing at the end of his second Epistle to the Corinthians where all three Persons are mentioned he wishes grace and love from the Son and the Father [except that] in the communion or the partaking of the Holy Ghost, the blessing is from the Father and the Son in the Holy Ghost. But the blessing from the Holy Ghost is Himself, the communication of Himself.

Christ promises that He and the Father will love believers (John 14:21,23), but no mention is made of the Holy Ghost, and the love of Christ and the love of the Father are often distinctly mentioned, but never any mention of the Holy Ghost's love.

(This I suppose to be the reason why we have never any account of the Holy Ghost's loving either the Father or the Son, or of the Son's or the Father's loving the Holy Ghost, or of the Holy Ghost's loving the saints, tho these things are so often predicated of both the other Persons.)

And this I suppose to be that blessed Trinity that we read of in the Holy Scriptures. The Father is the

Deity subsisting in the prime, un-originated and most absolute manner, or the Deity in its direct existence. The Son is the Deity generated by God's understanding, or having an idea of Himself and subsisting in that idea. The Holy Ghost is the Deity subsisting in act, or the Divine essence flowing out and breathed forth in God's Infinite love to and delight in Himself. And I believe the whole

Divine essence does truly and distinctly subsist both in the Divine idea and Divine love, and that each of them are properly distinct Persons.

It is a maxim amongst divines that everything that is in God is God which must be understood of real attributes and not of mere modalities. If a man should tell me that the immutability of God is

God, or that the omnipresence of God and authority of God is God, I should not be able to think of any rational meaning of what he said. It hardly sounds to me proper to say that God's being without change is God, or that God's being everywhere is God, or that God's having a right of government over creatures is God.

But if it be meant that the real attributes of God, viz., His understanding and love are God, then what we have said may in some measure explain how it is so, for Deity subsists in them distinctly; so they are distinct Divine Persons.

One of the principal objections that I can think of against what has been supposed is concerning the

Personality of the Holy Ghost - that this scheme of things does not seem well to consist with [the fact] that a person is that which hath understanding and will. If the three in the Godhead are

Persons they doubtless each of them have understanding, but this makes the understanding one distinct person and love another. How therefore can this love be said to have understanding, (Here I would observe that divines have not been wont to suppose that these three had three distinct understandings, but all one and the same understanding.)

In order to clear up this matter let it be considered that the whole Divine office is supposed truly and properly to subsist in each of these three, viz., God and His understanding and love, and that there is such a wonderful union between them that they are, after an ineffable and inconceivable manner, One in Another, so that One hath Another and they have communion in One Another and are as it were predicable One of Another; as Christ said of Himself and the Father "I am in the Father and the Father in Me," so may it be said concerning all the Persons in the Trinity, the Father is in the

Son and the Son in the Father, the Holy Ghost is in the Father, and the Father in the Holy Ghost, the

Holy Ghost is in the Son, and the Son in the Holy Ghost, and the Father understands because the Son

Who is the Divine understanding is in Him, the Father loves because the Holy Ghost is in Him, so the

Son loves because the Holy Ghost is in Him and proceeds from Him, so the Holy Ghost or the Divine essence subsisting is Divine, but understands because the Son the Divine Idea is in Him.

Understanding may be predicated of this love because it is the love of the understanding both objectively and subjectively. God loves the understanding and that understanding also flows out in love so that the Divine understanding is in the Deity subsisting in love. It is not a blind love. Even in creatures there is consciousness included in the very nature of the will or act of the soul, and tho perhaps not so that it can so properly be said that it is a seeing or undemanding will, yet it may truly and properly be said so in God by reason of God's infinitely more perfect manner of acting so that the whole Divine essence flows out and subsists in this act, and the Son is in the Holy Spirit tho it does not proceed from Him by reason (of the fact) that the understanding must be considered as prior in the order of nature to the will or love or act, both in creatures and in the Creator. The understanding is so in the Spirit that the Spirit may be said to know, as the Spirit of God is truly and perfectly said to know and to search all things, even the deep things of God.

(All the Three are Persons for they all have understanding and will. There is understanding and will in the Father, as the Son and the Holy Ghost are in Him and proceed from Him. There is understanding and will in the Son, as He is understanding and as the Holy Ghost is in Him and proceeds from Him. There is understanding and will in the Holy Ghost as He is the Divine will and as the Son is in Him.

Nor is it to be looked upon as a strange and unreasonable figment that the Persons should be said to have an understanding or love by another person's being in them, for we have Scripture ground to conclude so concerning the Father's having wisdom and understanding or reason that it is by the

Son's being in Him; because we are there informed that He is the wisdom and reason and truth of

God, and hereby God is wise by His own wisdom being in Him. Understanding and wisdom is in the

Father as the Son is in Him and proceeds from Him. Understanding is in the Holy Ghost because the

Son is in Him, not as proceeding from Him but as flowing out in Him.)

But I don't pretend fully to explain how these things are and I am sensible a hundred other objections may be made and puzzling doubts and questions raised that I can't solve. I am far from pretending to explaining the Trinity so as to render it no longer a mystery. I think it to be the highest and deepest of all Divine mysteries still, notwithstanding anything that I have said or conceived about it. I don't intend to explain the Trinity. But Scripture with reason may lead to say something further of it than has been wont to be said, tho there are still left many things pertaining to it incomprehensible.

It seems to me that what I have here supposed concerning the Trinity is exceeding analogous to the

Gospel scheme and agreeable to the tenor of the whole New Testament and abundantly illustrative of Gospel doctrines, as might be particularly shown, would it not exceedingly lengthen out this discourse.

I shall only now briefly observe that many things that have been wont to be said by orthodox divines about the Trinity are hereby illustrated. Hereby we see how the Father is the fountain of the

Godhead, and why when He is spoken of in Scripture He is so often, without any addition or distinction, called God, which has led some to think that He only was truly and properly God.

Hereby we may see why in the economy of the Persons of the Trinity the Father should sustain the dignity of the Deity, that the Father should have it as His office to uphold and maintain the rights of the Godhead and should be God not only by essence, but as it were, by His economical office.

Hereby is illustrated the doctrine of the Holy Ghost. Proceeding [from] both the Father and the Son.

Hereby we see how that it is possible for the Son to be begotten by the Father and the Holy Ghost to proceed from the Father and Son, and yet that all the Persons should be Co-eternal. Hereby we may more clearly understand the equality of the Persons among themselves, and that they are every way equal in the society or family of the three.

They are equal in honor: besides the honor which is common to them all, viz., that they are all God, each has His peculiar honor in the society or family. They are equal not only in essence, but the

Father's honor is that He is, as it were, the Author of perfect and Infinite wisdom. The Son's honor is that He is that perfect and Divine wisdom itself the excellency of which is that from whence arises the honor of being the author or Generator of it. The honor of the Father and the Son is that they are infinitely excellent, or that from them infinite excellency proceeds; but the honor of the Holy Ghost is equal for He is that Divine excellency and beauty itself.

'Tis the honor of the Father and the Son that they are infinitely holy and are the fountain of holiness, but the honor of the Holy Ghost is that holiness itself. The honor of the Father and the Son is [that] they are infinitely happy and are the original and fountain of happiness and the honor of the Holy

Ghost is equal for He is infinite happiness and joy itself.

The honor of the Father is that He is the fountain of the Deity as He from Whom proceed both the Divine wisdom and also excellency and happiness. The honor of the Son is equal for He is Himself the Divine wisdom and is He from Whom proceeds the Divine excellency and happiness, and the honor of the Holy Ghost is equal for He is the beauty and happiness of both the other Persons.

By this also we may fully understand the equality of each Person's concern in the work of redemption, and the equality of the Redeemed's concern with them and dependence upon them, and the equality and honor and praise due to each of them. Glory belongs to the Father and the Son that they so greatly loved the world: to the Father that He so loved that He gave His Only Begotten

Son: to the Son that He so loved the world as to give up Himself.

But there is equal glory due to the Holy Ghost for He is that love of the Father and the Son to the world. Just so much as the two first Persons glorify themselves by showing the astonishing greatness of their love and grace, just so much is that wonderful love and grace glorified Who is the

Holy Ghost. It shows the Infinite dignity and excellency of the Father that the Son so delighted and prized His honor and glory that He stooped infinitely low rather than [that] men's salvation should be to the injury of that honor and glory.

It showed the infinite excellency and worth of the Son that the Father so delighted in Him that for

His sake He was ready to quit His anger and receive into favor those that had [deserved?] infinitely ill at His Hands, and what was done shows how great the excellency and worth of the Holy Ghost

Who is that delight which the Father and the Son have in each other: it shows it to be Infinite. So great as the worth of a thing delighted in is to any one, so great is the worth of that delight and joy itself which he has in it.

Our dependence is equally upon each in this office. The Father appoints and provides the

Redeemer, and Himself accepts the price and grants the thing purchased; the Son is the Redeemer by offering Himself and is the price; and the Holy Ghost immediately communicates to us the thing purchased by communicating Himself, and He is the thing purchased. The sum of all that Christ purchased for men was the Holy Ghost: (Gal. 3:13,14) "He was made a curse for us... that we might receive the promise of the Spirit through faith."

What Christ purchased for us was that we have communion with God [which] is His good, which consists in partaking of the Holy Ghost: as we have shown, all the blessedness of the Redeemed consists in their partaking of Christ's fullness, which consists in partaking of that Spirit which is given not by measure unto him: the oil that is poured on the head of the Church runs down to the members of His body and to the skirts of His garment (Ps. 133:2). Christ purchased for us that we should have the favor of God and might enjoy His love, but this love is the Holy Ghost.

Christ purchased for us true spiritual excellency, grace and holiness, the sum of which is love to

God, which is [nothing] but the indwelling of the Holy Ghost in the heart. Christ purchased for us spiritual joy and comfort, which is in a participation of God's joy and happiness, which joy and happiness is the Holy Ghost as we have shown. The Holy Ghost is the sum of all good things. Good things and the Holy Spirit are synonymous expressions in Scripture: (Matt. 7:11) "How much more shall your Heavenly Father give the

Holy Spirit to them that ask Him." The sum of all spiritual good which the finite have in this world is that spring of living water within them which we read of (John

4:10), and those rivers of living water flowing out of them which we read of (John 7:38,39), which we are there told means the Holy Ghost; and the sum of all happiness in the other world is that river of water of life which proceeds out of the throne of God and the Lamb, which we read of (Rev. 22:1), which is the River of God's pleasures and is the Holy Ghost and therefore the sum of the Gospel invitation to come and take the water of life (verse 17).

The Holy Ghost is the purchased possession and inheritance of the saints, as appears because that little of it which the saints have in this world is said to be the earnest of that purchased inheritance.

(Eph. 1:14) Tis an earnest of that which we are to have a fullness of hereafter. (II Cor. 1:22; 5:5) The

Holy Ghost is the great subject of all Gospel promises and therefore is called the Spirit of promise.

(Eph. 1:13) This is called the promise of the Father (Luke 24:49), and the like in other places. (If the

Holy Ghost be a comprehension of all good things promised in the Gospel, we may easily see the force of the Apostle's arguing (Gal. 3:2), "This only would I know, Received ye the Spirit by the works of the law or by the hearing of faith?") So that it is God of Whom our good is purchased and it is God that purchases it and it is God also that is the thing purchased.

Thus all our good things are of God and through God and in God, as we read in Romans 11:36: "For of Him and through Him and to Him (or in Him as *eis* is rendered, I Cor. 8:6) are all things." "To

Whom be glory forever." All our good is of God the Father, it is all through God the Son, and all is in the Holy Ghost as He is Himself all our good. God is Himself the portion and purchased inheritance of His people. Thus God is the Alpha and the Omega in this affair of redemption.

If we suppose no more than used to be supposed about the Holy Ghost, the concern of the Holy

Ghost in the work of redemption is not equal with the Father's and the Son's, nor is there an equal part of the glory of this work belonging to Him: merely to apply to us or immediately to give or hand to us the blessing purchased, after it was purchased, as subservient to the other two Persons, is but a little thing [compared] to the purchasing of it by the paying an Infinite price, by Christ offering up Himself in sacrifice to procure it, and it is but a little thing to God the Father's giving His infinitely dear Son to be a sacrifice for us and upon His purchase to afford to us all the blessings of

His purchased.

But according to this there is an equality. To be the love of God to the world is as much as for the

Father and the Son to do so much from love to the world, and to be the thing purchased was as much as to be the price. The price and the thing bought with that price are equal. And it is as much as to afford the thing purchased, for the glory that belongs to Him that affords the thing purchased arises from the worth of that thing that He affords and therefore it is the same glory and an equal glory; the glory of the thing itself is its worth and that is also the glory of him that affords it.

There are two more eminent and remarkable images of the Trinity among the creatures. The one is in the spiritual creation, the soul of man. There is the mind, and the understanding or idea, and the spirit of the mind as it is called in Scripture, i.e., the disposition, the will or affection. The other is in the visible creation, viz., the Sun. The father is as the substance of the Sun. (By substance I don't mean in a philosophical sense, but the Sun as to its internal constitution.) The Son is as the brightness and glory of the disk of the Sun or that bright and glorious form under which it appears to our eyes. The Holy Ghost is the action of the Sun which is within the Sun in its intestine heat, and, being diffusive, enlightens, warms, enlivens and comforts the world. The Spirit as it is God's Infinite love to Himself and happiness in Himself, is as the internal heat of the Sun, but as it is that by which

God communicates Himself, it is as the emanation of the sun's action, or the emitted beams of the sun.

The various sorts of rays of the sun and their beautiful colors do well represent the Spirit. They well represent the love and grace of God and were made use of for this purpose in the rainbow after the flood, and I suppose also in that rainbow that was seen round about the throne by Ezekiel (Ezek.

1:28; Rev. 4:3) and round the head of Christ by John (Rev. 10:1), or the amiable excellency of God and the various beautiful graces and virtues of the Spirit. These beautiful colors of the sunbeams we find made use of in Scripture for this purpose, viz., to represent the graces of the Spirit, as (Ps.

68:13) "Though ye have lien among the pots, yet shall be as the wings of a dove covered with silver, and her feathers with yellow gold," i.e., like the light reflected in various beautiful colors from the feathers of a dove, which colors represent the graces of the Heavenly Dove.

The same I suppose is signified by the various beautiful colors reflected from the precious stones of the breastplate, and that these spiritual ornaments of the Church are what are represented by the various colors of the foundation and gates of the new Jerusalem (Rev. 21; Isaiah 54:11, etc.) and the stones of the Temple (I Chron. 29: 2); and I believe the variety there is in the rays of the Sun and their beautiful colors was designed by the Creator for this very purpose, and indeed that the whole visible creation which is but the shadow of being is so made and ordered by God as to typify and represent spiritual things, for which I could give many reasons. (I don't propose this merely as an hypothesis but as a part of Divine truth sufficiently and fully ascertained by the revelation God has made in the Holy Scriptures.)

I am sensible what kind of objections many will be ready to make against what has been said, what difficulties will be immediately found, How can this be? And how can that be!

I am far from affording this as any explication of this mystery, that unfolds and renews the mysteriousness and incomprehensibleness of it, for I am sensible that however by what has been said some difficulties are lessened, others that are new appear, and the number of those things that appear mysterious, wonderful and incomprehensible, is increased by it. I offer it only as a farther manifestation of what of Divine truth the Word of God exhibits to the view of our minds concerning this great mystery.

I think the Word of God teaches us more things concerning it to be believed by us than have been generally believed, and that it exhibits many things concerning it exceeding [i.e., more] glorious and wonderful than have been taken notice of; yea, that it reveals or exhibits many more wonderful mysteries than those which have been taken notice of; which mysteries that have been overvalued are incomprehensible things and yet have been exhibited in the Word of God tho they are an addition to the number of mysteries that are in it. No wonder that the more things we are told concerning that which is so infinitely above our reach, the number of visible mysteries increases.

When we tell a child a little concerning God he has not an hundredth part so many mysteries in view on the nature and attributes of God and His works of creation and Providence as one that is told much concerning God in a Divinity School; and yet he knows much more about God and has a much clearer understanding of things of Divinity and is able more clearly to explicate some things that were dark and very unintelligible to him; I humbly apprehend that the things that have been observed increase the number of visible mysteries in the Godhead in no other manner than as by them we perceive that God has told us much more about it than was before generally observed.

Under the Old Testament the Church of God was not told near so much about the Trinity as they are now. But what the New Testament has revealed, tho it has more opened to our view the nature of

God, yet it has increased the number of visible mysteries and they thus appear to us exceeding wonderful and incomprehensible. And so also it has come to pass in the Church being told [i.e., that the churches are told] more about the incarnation and the satisfaction of Christ and other Gospel doctrines.

It is so not only in Divine things but natural things. He that looks on a plant, or the parts of the bodies of animals, or any other works of nature, at a great distance where he has but an obscure sight-of it, may see something in it wonderful and beyond his comprehension, but he that is near to it and views them narrowly indeed understands more about them, has a clearer and distinct sight of them, and yet the number of things that are wonderful and mysterious in them that appear to him are much more than before, and, if he views them with a microscope, the number of the wonders that he sees will be increased still but yet the microscope gives him more a true knowledge concerning them.

God is never said to love the Holy Ghost nor are any epithets that betoken love anywhere given to

Him, tho so many are ascribed to the Son, as God's Elect, The Beloved, He in Whom God's soul delights, He in Whom He is well pleased, etc. Yea such epithets seem to be ascribed to the Son as tho He were the object of love exclusive of all other persons, as tho there were no person whatsoever to share the love of the Father with the Son. To this purpose evidently He is called God's Only Begotten Son, at the time that it is added, "In Whom He is well pleased." There is nothing in Scripture that speaks of any acceptance of the Holy Ghost or any reward or any mutual friendship between the

Holy Ghost and either of the other Persons, or any command to love the Holy Ghost or to delight in or have any complacence in [the Holy Ghost], tho such commands are so frequent with respect to the other Persons.

That knowledge or understanding in God which we must conceive of as first is His knowledge of everything possible. That love which must be this knowledge is what we must conceive of as belonging to the essence of the Godhead in it's first subsistence. Then comes a reflex act of knowledge and His viewing Himself and knowing Himself and so knowing His own knowledge and so the Son is begotten. There is such a thing in God as knowledge of knowledge, an idea of an idea.

Which can be nothing else than the idea or knowledge repeated. The world was made for the Son of God especially. For God made the world for Himself from love to Himself; but God loves Himself only in a reflex act. He views Himself and so loves Himself, so He makes the world for Himself viewed and reflected on, and that is. The same with Himself repeated or begotten in His own idea, and that is His Son. When God considers of making any thing for Himself He presents Himself before Himself and views Himself as His End, and that viewing Himself is the same as reflecting on

Himself or having an idea of Himself, and to make the world for the Godhead thus viewed and understood is to make the world for the Godhead begotten and that is to make the world for the Son of God. The love of God as it flows forth ad extra is wholly determined and directed by Divine wisdom, so that those only are the objects of it that Divine wisdom chooses, so that the creation of the world is to gratify Divine love as that is exercised by Divine wisdom. But Christ is Divine wisdom so that the world is made to gratify Divine love as exercised by Christ or to gratify the love that is in Christ's heart, or to provide a spouse for Christ. Those creatures which wisdom chooses for the object of Divine love as Christ's elect spouse and especially those elect creatures that wisdom chiefly pitches upon and makes the end of the rest of creatures.